SETON GORDON'S SCOTLAND
AN ANTHOLOGY

Compiled by
Hamish Brown

Whittles Publishing

Published by
Whittles Publishing Limited,
Dunbeath,
Caithness KW6 6EY,
Scotland, UK

www.whittlespublishing.com

Typeset by
Samantha Barden

Copyright © Hamish Brown, 2005
Seton Gordon Literary Estate, 2005 (for the original texts)

Paperback edition 2007; reprinted 2009

ISBN 978-1-904445-73-9

Printed and bound in England
www.printondemand-worldwide.com

CONTENTS

FOREWORD

Seton Gordon (1886-1977) produced his first book when he was twenty one and his last title in his eighties: twenty seven books, besides many uncollected articles and contributions to other books. There are nearly 6000 pages in his major works, about two million words, (they occupy two yards of bookshelf), a prodigious output which has given me many months of reading, reading that turned my house into something of a Seton Gordon study centre. I never met Seton Gordon but before planning to travel to Spitzbergen I wrote to him and his letters from Skye were full of information and the delights of a place he'd visited half a century earlier. Re-reading Seton Gordon has made me realise how important he had been as a source of historical stories and folklore – besides his captivating and intimate interest in wildlife and the wilds which illuminated all he wrote. As Raymond Eagle, and others, have discerned, "The uniqueness of his writing lay in his ability to transport the reader so that they saw the world through his all-discerning eyes".

There will never be anyone quite like him but his influence has been profound: Adam Watson, Desmond Nethersole-Thompson, David Stephen, Tom Weir, Mike Tomkies, Don and Bridget Maccaskill, Jim Crumley, and others were – are – in the great tradition of wildlife observing and writing which runs back to this father figure. He himself had been inspired by the Kearton brothers and as a young man took Richard overnight up Morven to photograph ptarmigan. In 1904, photography entailed lugging about a hefty, half-plate camera. What would he make of today's technological magic? In his last book (1971) he was to recollect an early incident: "I had begun to write articles when I was fourteen or fifteen. When I was seventeen a correspondent wrote that he was anxious to meet me. When he arrived he was at a loss to begin the conversation for, as he said later, he had visualized me as an old gentleman with a white beard!" The outdoors sagacity and youthful vigour were there to the end.

Seton Gordon was extraordinarily dedicated yet self-effacing. We learn little about his family and we only catch glimpses of the people he knew though his friendships ranged from prime ministers to humble crofters. He was indeed a friend of all the worlds he moved in, yet had great strength, both of character and physical ability. He vividly describes some great storms in the hills or at sea but without drawing any notice of *his* long-suffering presence there. His focus was entirely on the scene about him and its inhabitants. His first book in 1907 (aged twenty one remember) is full of observations which could only be the result of frequent and arduous expeditions already undertaken in the Cairngorms. Decades later he would still walk through the Lairig Ghru to Strathspey rather than motor round, or would linger on the high summits to see the sun set and then wander long miles home in the dark. To do all this he must have been *persona grata* to everyone on the ground, from landowner to keeper, yet his stance was unique for the time; he shot fur and feather through a lens.

Many naturalists have come from a sporting background and few can match keepers for their knowledge of our hills and their wildlife. One needs only think of Peter Scott who as a young man was a keen wildfowler yet ended as the greatest champion of wild fowl. It is remarkable that the teenager, living on Deeside with all its opportunities, did not take that path yet gained the respect, help and friendship of those who did. He must have been a charmer, perspicacious and deeply rooted in his Highland environment. I think the dislocations of today would distress him, gentleman that he was. There is not an unkind word in all he wrote and often that peculiarly Scottish sense of the ridiculous breaks through, even when he is the victim of the situation. Even criticisms are gentle. In 1950 he noted, "It is not without humour to read in the press that a cargo of 750 tons of granite chips from Bonawe in Argyll is being shipped to Mombasa for the roads being built for the African groundnuts scheme because I was recently told that the expense of bringing Bonawe granite chips to Skye for the roads was prohibitive".

The charge is sometimes levelled that Seton Gordon was a bit of a snob, fond of name-dropping, but this does not stand up to scrutiny. If he writes about Lord Grey of Falladon for instance it is because of mutual *bird* interests, a passion surpassing politics after all! Any reference like this is directly linked with something to tell, no more and no less so than with anyone else. Nobody sees through social pretensions quicker than keepers, but it was a keeper who walked through the Lairig Ghru to see his old friend after he moved from Dee to Spey. Seton Gordon was simply of his time, making the lifelong friends and taking the social steps one does at university and after.

Largely educated at home and going up to Oxford early in the century friends were, inescapably, from the ranks of the upper class – his included the then Prince of Wales and Prince Youssoupoff (a leader in ridding Russia of Rasputin). An almost exact parallel can be seen in John Buchan who travelled from yet humbler beginnings to Oxford and upwards and suffered the same charge of snobbery. Seton Gordon was liked and welcomed in all worlds. (The

Scots too have this lingering penchant for pulling people down if they show the sin of success.) For the first three decades of the twentieth century Seton Gordon was the only fulltime practising naturalist in Britain.

He grew up on Deeside so came to know the Cairngorms early on. During the first World War he was Admiralty Patrol Officer, based on Mull and other islands, lived for some years in Aviemore and, for the second half of his life, home was in the island of Skye, from which he travelled extensively all over the country – invariably wearing the kilt, on and off the hill.

The practicalities of producing this anthology perhaps should be mentioned. I read through all twenty seven books, a few chapters each night as bedtime reading, and noted the chapters, paragraphs, and photographs that I found most interesting. These were then photocopied and, while in Morocco for some months, I worked through them to make further selections and simply reduce the volume of words, editing, but not changing the characteristic flow of his style. And I still only used a quarter of the original choices. (Without forcing, it worked out that there is something from all his more general titles.)

A fascination in working through his books in chronological order was seeing how he developed as a writer, from enthusiastic beginnings to the assured magic of some of his mature descriptions. Cassell, his main publisher, helped by producing volumes which are a joy to look at with their embossed covers and wealth of illustrations. Some people collect his early books for this reason alone, which doesn't help those who want to *read* Seton Gordon. Hence this 'taster' – which will no doubt hike up the price of first editions even further. Many of his books went through several printings, cheap editions, pocket editions, Book Club editions and half a dozen were reprinted in modern times – his 1927 *Days With The Golden Eagle* by Whittles Publishing in 2003. In 1973 *The Golden Eagle, King of Birds* was translated into Japanese! When Cassells was destroyed by German bombing in 1941 Seton Gordon's 13 books (till then) had sold 29,000 copies.

Seton Gordon began writing in Victorian times and this sometimes shows in his style, his use of phrases and words, which were of the period and in places may be out of fashion today and even (as if it matters) 'politically incorrect'. He talks about island 'natives' for instance which held neither condescension nor racist connotations, he being both friend and supporter – as, for instance, the poignant description of an immigrant ship shows. He was, both in words and pictures, portraying a world which now feels, not just one, but many centuries old and it comes as a shock that some of those immigrants would see men walk on the moon on their television screens and could have travelled on Concorde. Sadly book production was knocked and knocked again by two world wars and the quality of books in general, including his, suffered, yet his wartime and postwar writing has a depth and maturity that makes selecting very difficult; it is all so readable. He simply became better and better.

Such textual editing as I have made has largely been in cutting out paragraphs, phrases, even words, as I fought for space. Some standardisation of format was needed but I have only changed spellings where they'd be unrecognisable to readers today. How do you select from 6000 pages? Selecting the illustrations was no easy task either. He was a pioneer of wildlife photography when photography itself was in its infancy and his early eagle studies are still remarkable. His first wife Audrey Pease who he married in 1915 and who died in 1959, shared his enthusiasms and the practicalities of using hides – two people being essential – from which they could watch in turn and both take photographs as the opportunity allowed. One pair of Skye eagles was studied over seven seasons. As *Days With the Golden Eagle* is readily available I've rationed eagle descriptions to allow a wider representation of other subjects, especially of that vanished world of crofting a century ago – an equally rare and valued record made by Seton Gordon. There are few places he did not write about! Only some of the original illustrations could be found in the National Library of Scotland's Seton Gordon archive and reproduction can't match their first use but this has given the opportunity to add one or two pictures of Seton Gordon himself.

The selected pieces range from evocative long chapters to short, sometimes very short, topical paragraphs. Many of his books made use of previously published articles, bird notes, even letters, so exploratory days in the Hebrides for instance are described in a dozen books, enough to make a book in themselves. Over the years his own interests widened. He noted down local folklore and old traditions. He became heavily involved with piping (playing and judging) and with many specific wildlife commitments. There simply was little time (and I suspect, inclination) to travel abroad after the early Spitzbergen expedition. (Following Oxford University he did study forestry in Russia, France and Germany and later went 'birding' to Norway, Iceland, Holland, the Pyrenees and Switzerland, and he corresponded with naturalists worldwide.) Weeks on end observing in the field, winter lecturing, writing, twice married (Audrey Pease, Betty Badger), bringing up a family, the wonder is that he did so much and did it so well. Who but Seton Gordon could have written as he did in his preface to *Highways and Byways in the West Highlands* "The proofs have been revised by sea, and on moorland and hill. One evening in June (1934) I sat up to midnight correcting proofs beside the summit of Bruach na Frithe ... the glow of the sunset was still so strong that I had no difficulty in reading print". He never lost a moment; in 1945 for instance, despite wartime restrictions, he still made several forays into the Cairngorms and Monadh Liath, and climbed Ben Nevis, Wyvis, Sgurr na Clach Geala, Liathach, Ben A'an, Morven, Meall Fourvounie and Meall na Suireanach – all in his sixtieth year. He was always a field naturalist, spending long days (and nights) on the hill, often sitting for hours watching or spying out wildlife with his treasured telescope.

For weeks my living room floor was covered with the selections being arranged and rearranged and slowly they were thinned down to the manageable number of this anthology. I've tried to reflect the wide range of topics that Seton Gordon wrote about and I have resisted all temptations – and they were many (as readers will find) – to commentate or interpret. The bibliography gives a chronological list of Seton Gordon's major works and a code to titles and dates (given after each selected item) so that the passages can be placed in historical context.

Seton Gordon had to write and lecture constantly to maintain a source of income though payments in those days were relatively far more generous. Some of the scores of publications he contributed to were *The Scotsman, Glasgow Herald, Times, Manchester Guardian, Morning Post, Chamber's Journal, The Field, Country Life, Scots Magazine, Scottish Field, Scotland's Magazine, New English Review, Illustrated London News, Morning Post, Graphic, Daily Mail* and *British Birds*.

I just hope readers, old and new, will enjoy this cull from the works of a remarkable observer, writer, photographer who comes over as a thoroughly likeable man.

Let me finish with just one personal note. In 1966 I found a basement room in Tangier heaped with books – as casually as if they had been coal – neglected, beginning to turn musty, but for sale. (With a train to Marrakech booked I'd limited time to burrow and when I returned weeks later they had all gone, I suspect to the nearest tip.) A title *Irish Stories and Legends* caught my eye and, on opening it, there was a picture bookplate of gannets with the name Seton Gordon. On the facing page I read "Seton Paul Gordon. From his mother. Xmas 1894". He would be eight years old. The drawing is almost certainly his mother's; later his first book was dedicated to her, later, others were dedicated to wives, family, friends and keepers, an ever-widening circle of influence to which we are the happy inheritors.

Hamish Brown
Burntisland

Seton Gordon, about 1950 (courtesy of *Scottish Field*).

ACKNOWLEDGEMENTS

Heartfelt thanks are due to the National Library of Scotland over many visits to study the Seton Gordon archive and especially Sheila Mackenzie who organised the difficult scanning of the pictures. James Macdonald Lockhart, as Seton Gordon's literary executor, gave support throughout. Many friends made suggestions about passages they considered worth including. Permission to use pictures is gratefully acknowledged to *Scottish Field* and *Country Life* and, for text, to *The Scotsman* and Neil Wilson Publishing, Glasgow, whose edition of *Hebridean Memories* is still in print, as is the more recent Whittles Publishing edition of *Days with the Golden Eagle*. And a special thanks to Keith Whittles for taking on the publication of this anthology.

H.M.B.

(Note on spellings: every attempt has been made to retain the original spellings and presentations. Readers will therefore see uncharacteristic, but recognisable, spellings of certain landmarks or places.)

PREFACE

Seton Gordon was an outstanding Scottish writer, photographer, naturalist and hill-walker. Born in 1886, he started to write articles in his late teens, continued having articles published until 1976, and had a letter about whooper swans in *The Field* just days before he died in 1977 shortly before his 91st birthday. His 27 books span 64 years, from *Birds of the Loch and Mountain* in 1907 to *Highland Summer* in 1971. They are thoughtful accounts by a brilliant observer of hills and glens and islands, beautiful views, varied weather, magnificent wildlife, snow-patches, Highland folklore and their old way of life, human history, piping and Gaelic place-names. His papers and photographs are preserved for the nation in a special collection at the National Library of Scotland. The biography *Seton Gordon* was published in 1991, and several of his classic books have been re-published since he died, most recently *Days with the Golden Eagle* in 2003. His other books are now scarce, so this anthology is welcome.

Hamish Brown is well equipped as anthologist. Like Gordon, he has long enjoyed going to the hills on his own as a competent hill-man who feels at home there, and in writing does not exaggerate difficulties on the hill or pander to egotism. He likes writing poetry and prose. Although Gordon seldom wrote verse, his prose has poetic qualities that catch the imagination. It will continue to do so, for his writing is timeless.

Looking at his book *The Cairngorm Hills of Scotland* in 1939 changed my life. Nine years old, I had often seen the Cairngorms from Deeside or Speyside. Now, however, it was as if a light had been switched on in my head, so that I perceived the world very differently. I wanted to be in the Cairngorms as often as possible, and began to do so. In autumn 1939 I sent him a letter and was delighted to receive a reply, with photographs. He encouraged me simply and greatly, and we corresponded for decades. When 13 I cycled to meet him at Crathie, and on a long hill walk he showed me my first eagle eyries.

I relate what happened to me because it showed the power and wonder of his written word. The Preface of his first book starts simply "I have always had a great love for the solitude and calm of the lone Scottish mountains, where a peace and happiness are to be found unknown to the dwellers in the plains. Here one seems to be apart from sorrows and anxieties of the world, and the days I have spent among the Ptarmigan and Golden Plover at a height of considerably more than 3,000 feet above sea level I shall always remember as the happiest of my experience. What can be more lovely than a mid-winter sunset from a dark, lofty mountain, with many a snow wreath lingering on its slopes? As the sun sinks, the wide expanse of hill and valley is lit up in the soft glow, and the snow fields on the sister hills are changed from spotless white to a glorious rosy tinge, while the snow-white Ptarmigan, wheeling across in the setting sun, have their plumage transformed to pink as they catch its rays". He wrote this when 21, and later became a more experienced and versatile writer. That early Preface, however, is still a good example of his ability. He did it so well that the reader easily imagines standing beside him while they look at the scene together.

Adam Watson
Crathes

Seton Gordon fishing in the River Shin in the 1920s.

SETON GORDON BIBLIOGRAPHY

Date	Title	Publisher	Abbrev.
1907	Birds of the Loch and Mountain	Cassell	BLM–07
1912	The Charm of the Hills	Cassell	COH–12
1915	Hill Birds of Scotland	Arnold	HBS–15
1920	Land of the Hills and Glens	Cassell	LHG–20
1921	Wanderings of a Naturalist	Cassell	WON–21
1922	Amid Snowy Wastes	Cassell	(Spitzbergen)
1923	Hebridean Memories	Cassell	HM–23
1925	The Cairngorm Hills of Scotland	Cassell	CHS–25
1926	The Immortal Isles	Williams & Norgate	TIL–26
1927	Days with the Golden Eagle	Williams & Norgate	DGE–27
1929	The Charm of Skye	Cassell	COS–29
1931	In the Highlands	Cassell	ITH–31
1933	Islands of the West	Cassell	IOW–33
1935	Highways & Byways in the West Highlands	Macmillan	H&BW–35
1935	Sea-Gulls in London	Cassell	SIL–35
1936	Thirty Years of Nature Photography	Cassell	30Y–36
1937	Afoot in Wild Places	Cassell	AWP–37
1937	Edward Grey and His Birds	Country Life	EG–37
1938	Wild Birds of Britain	Batsford	WBB–38
1941	In Search of Northern Birds	Eyre & Spottiswoode	ISNB–41
1944	A Highland Year	Eyre & Spottiswoode	HY–44
1948	Highways & Byways in the Central Highlands	Macmillan	H&BC–48
1950	Afoot in the Hebrides	Country Life	AH–50
1951	The Highlands of Scotland	Hale	HOS–51
1955	The Golden Eagle, King of Birds	Collins	GE–55
1963	Highland Days	Cassell	HD–63
1971	Highland Summer	Cassell	HS–71

The Isle of Skye [c1935]. A 30pp well-illustrated booklet, published in Aberdeen, much on history, Flora Macdonald, etc. Scarce!

Seton Gordon also wrote many sections of, or introductions to, guide books/picture books and, of course, articles and papers for many publications.

Biography: Raymond Eagle: *Seton Gordon. The Life & Times of a Highland Gentleman.* Lochar. 1991.

Seton Gordon visited St. Kilda two years
before its evacuation in 1930. The *Dunara
Castle* lies in Village Bay, Dun behind. Life
was never easy, as the burdened women
indicate. Section 10 describes the author's
visit to Hirta, Boreray and Soay.

I

The Cairngorms

Seton Gordon wrote more about the Cairngorms than any other area of Scotland; it was his earliest wildlife haunt – and practical classroom – through sun and storm, at every season. He would return to the Cairngorms throughout his life (the study of the Braeriach snowfields mentioned in the 'Cairngorm Stones' piece became a lifetime study). His first general book, 'The Charm of the Hills' 1912, published in his mid-twenties, has much on the Cairngorms while the classic 'The Cairngorm Hills of Scotland' 1925 is the most sought after of his titles and one hopes may be made available again before too long. All his days, from any Highland summit Seton Gordon would spy to see if he could recognise the distant Cairngorms of his youth.

Braeriach's lingering snowbeds in summer.

OUR FOREST HERITAGE

Nowhere in Scotland is so large an area of old natural-sown pines to be found as in the neighbourhood of the Cairngorm Hills. At one time a great forest covered all Scotland. Even in the Outer Hebrides, where on account of the Atlantic storms trees no longer can grow, the roots of trees are found in peat mosses in different parts, and even below high water mark: where the sand is washed away by the sea, or blown away by the wind, they plainly appear in a kind of black soil or rather moss.

In the forests of the Cairngorms I have seen the weeping fir, a charming tree with pendulous branches, and a very rare variety with golden variegated leaves.

Not long since, passing through Ballochbuie Forest beside Braemar, I chanced upon three old firs, recently felled, lying beside the road. Curiosity prompted me to discover their ages from their annular rings and I found that each veteran had lived a life of over 200 years. Their approximate ages were 220, 214, and 205 years but during recent years their growth had been so slow and their rings were so close together, that accurate counting was not easy.

Doubtless hundreds of fir trees of equal or even greater age still stand in the forests of Ballochbuie and Mar; could they narrate the story of their lives they might tell of birds and beasts that were numerous two hundred years ago but are no longer to be found.

As saplings the old pines saw perhaps the Invercauld men hurry to Braemar for the raising of the standard of 1715, and after the Rising the survivors pass along the forest track to lift, each man, his stone from Carn na Cuimhne.

In those days the cottages of Upper Deeside and Upper Speyside were lighted not by oil but by *candle-fir*. In 1760 we read in the *Records of Invercauld,* "Another destructive practice of the people was their cutting out the Hearts of the finest Trees to serve as Candle-fir, by which the Tree perished, and decayed upon the Foot."

For centuries the fir trees of the Braemar district have been celebrated. Pennant, writing in 1771, records that "here are the finest natural pines in Europe, both in respect to the size of the trees and the quality of the timber:

they were from 80 to 90 feet high, without a lateral branch, and 4½ feet in diameter at the lower end." Elsewhere Pennant writes: "Some of the pines that I measured were 10, 11, and even 12 feet in circumference. These trees are of a great age, having, it is supposed, seen two centuries."

At that time the goshawk nested in the pine forests of the Cairngorms, and Pennant writes: "The goshawk pursues its prey to an end, and dashes through everything in pursuit: but if it misses its quarry, desists from following it after two or three hundred yards flight." He goes on to say, "a shilling is given for a hawk, half a crown for an eagle." Thornton in 1804 writes that there "are some eyries of gosshawks in Glen More and Rothie-murcos forests but this hawk is very rare." For many years now the goshawk has been extinct in Scotland.

Another bird which the old trees must have known in their youth was the kite. It is now sixty years since the kite nested in the pine forests of the Cairngorms but one of the nests remains where it was built, in the fork of an old Scots fir.

A few of the older stalkers in the Braemar district remember the *glead*, as it was called, and one still hears stories of it. A keeper, having occasion to ford the River Dee, left his shoes and stockings on the bank. On his return he found that both his stockings had mysteriously disappeared: they were later discovered in the nest of a kite on the wooded slopes of Creag nan Leathda! The kite was much persecuted on account of its tail feathers. These were used in tying a salmon fly known as the *Gordon*, and so the last surviving gleads were killed for the sake of their plumage. On one occasion a kite lay in a trap, apparently dead. Its tail feathers were cut off and it was thrown carelessly upon the ground. For a few moments it lay there then, miraculously, took flight!

Amongst the old firs pine-martens doubtless played. The marten, too, is extinct in the pine forests of the Cairngorms. Thirty-six years ago the last pair were trapped in the Balloch-buie Forest; they had both reached a great age for the stumps of their teeth alone remained. The marten preyed largely upon rabbits, burying them for future consumption when its hunger was not keen. It was fond of eggs, and on one occasion a marauding pine-marten raised a wild uproar in a heronry when it climbed one of the trees to suck the blue eggs of these patient fishers.

On January 15, 1776, organized warfare was carried on against *vermin*. "which caused a destruction of sheep so great, that it is thought the value of the sheep annually killed was nearly equal to half the rent paid to the proprietors. The scheme continued for 10 years, with so great success, that during that period there were killed 634 foxes, 44 wild cats, 57 polecats, 70 eagles, 2,520 hawks and kites, 1,347 ravens and hooded crows – besides all those which were destroyed by poison, or died of their wounds – and sheep were then in perfect safety to pasture at all times and seasons to the very boundary of where the scheme extended. For the first year the premiums extended only to foxes, eagles, gosacks, and falcons; the second year, wild cats, polecats, and kites, were added; and the third year, ravens and hooded crows were also included."

In the last 150 years a startling number of birds and beasts have disappeared from the country of the Cairngorms. Of the list above mentioned the wild cat, polecat, kite, and raven have vanished.

But while much of the old wild life has gone from the pine forests the golden eagle, fox and falcon remain. The native capercaillie has, like the kite, disappeared from the woods, but from Sweden a number of these fine birds were imported to the Taymouth woods in 1837 and since then they have spread over a large area of Scotland. In the forests of the Cairngorms the capercaillie is thriving and increasing and has already outlived its welcome for it is driving away the blackgame from the woodlands. So bold was a capercaillie cock in Rothiemurchus Forest that it attacked any person venturing into that part of the wood which it frequented. Children lived in terror of it and it attacked with fury a lady with white stockings, pecking at her offending legs as she fled round the trees. But it went a little too far when it flew on to the driver of a dogcart, biting his ear severely. After this misdeed it was caught and banished from the district in disgrace.

Each spring morning the cock capercaillies assemble to display for the benefit of the hens. They spread their tails wide and trail their wings upon the ground. In snow the marks of their feathers are curious.

Each morning and evening, blackcock meet to fight during the months of March, April, and May. It is interesting to lie concealed and watch them at close quarters and hear their low bubbling cries.

Ospreys nested in the forests of the Cairngorms for the last time in 1900. Their home was on the ruined castle of Loch an Eilein and so tame were they that they sometimes perched upon the chimney of a cottage beside the loch. One spring three ospreys arrived at the loch. Two of the birds fought long and fiercely and at last one of them succeeded in holding the other beneath the water until it was drowned. Passing ospreys still cross the Cairngorms from time to time. It is not many years since one of the Balmoral stalkers, while fishing the Dee, saw a great bird fly quickly to the river from its perch on a lofty fir tree, plunge half beneath the water, and fly away bearing in its claws a large trout.

In early summer the pine forests of the Cairngorms are the home of two small summer migrants, the redstart and the tree pipit. The male redstart flirts his beautiful red tail as with his mate he visits the nest in some hollow tree; the tree pipit stands upon the topmost branch of a fir, then suddenly mounts with quickly-moving wings almost vertically into the air and as he sails tree-ward he sings his pleasing song.

Far up some hill burn, near the fringe of the forest, the goosander broods her creamy eggs in the hollow trunk of an old tree. The goosander has greatly increased in numbers during the last few years. It preys upon salmon smolts and trout, and must kill an enormous number of fish in a year. On a certain day in the summer of 1924 the keepers along the whole course of the River Dee made a concerted onslaught upon the goosanders and thinned their numbers.

Winter in the deer forests of the Cairngorms is often a time of much hardship for the birds and deer. Ptarmigan descend below their accustomed haunts and the stags seek the shelter of the woods. Each fir tree in Mar and Rothie-murchus carries a great weight of feathery snow; even beneath the trees the ground is deeply covered. As the sun sinks towards the horizon a couple of hours after midday the snowy hills are suffused with a soft pink glow and by contrast the sky eastward appears hard and cold. The Dee at the Linn is frozen across, and from the rocks here enormous icicles hang. The road to the Derry is blocked with snow; to reach that outlying shooting lodge one must go on foot, or else by sleigh, and pick one's way over the higher parts of the moorland. The grouse are in great packs, restlessly seeking their heather food amid the snowy wastes. Each fallen fir branch has been peeled by rabbits.

Animals feed on strange fare during snow. A cock salmon of about 6 lb. weight had been taken at the spawning beds by an otter. The otter had eaten a piece out of the fish just behind the head and had left the salmon lying on the ice. A stag, hungry and weary from much foraging for food, found the salmon and commenced to eat what must have been very strange fare to him. A stalker friend of mine found the fish, with the footmarks of the stag all round it.

Deer have a taste for flesh, as the two following stories will show. A stalker shot a rabbit. He cleaned the animal and placed the intestines in a fork of a tree about 6 feet from the ground. A few days later they were gone, and all round where they had lain the bark of the tree was rubbed by the horns of a stag. On another occasion the same stalker found a rabbit in one of his traps. It was being eaten by a stoat, and the stalker, hoping to capture the latter animal, baited the trap with the rabbit. The following day he was astonished to see a stag eating his bait. The snare had become twisted round the stag's horns, and each time he raised his head the rabbit was suspended aloft.

When the oldest trees of the forests of the Cairngorms were in their prime Gaelic was the language of upper Deeside and Strath Spey, and of a winter's night, when the storm rushed through the trees, the women in the primitive thatched houses spun by the light of a splinter of candle-fir laid on a small projecting slab within the chimney. How often must the forests have been held in the grip of an intense frost, when Spey and Dee were frozen so firmly that the people could cross them without risk; how often must great drought have parched their roots!

From time to time disastrous fires sweep through the forests of the Cairngorms. In the early summer of 1920 an extensive fire burned in Abernethy and a day or two later a great area of trees were destroyed in Rothiemurchus and Glen More. The origin of these fires is not known but for some time previous to them a strong and dry south-east wind blew day and night uninterruptedly and there was an absence of dew. The young leaves of the blaeberry undergrowth were that year destroyed by caterpillars and so offered no moist barrier to the flames.

At the time of the Rothiemurchus fire my wife and I were camping on the High Cairngorms and one evening saw a wide column of dense smoke drifting across the Spey. For days the fire raged, despite the efforts of every able-bodied man on two estates and even now (1925) acres of blackened trees show the course of that great conflagration. Many birds perished in the flames and hooded crows were found dazed and completely incapable of flight. Families of tits were seen attempting to escape, the old birds leading the young from the danger zone.

A spark was carried on the wind across Loch Morlich and as my wife and I were walking along the road from Glen More Lodge we were astonished to see a new fire break out in front of us. Although we were so near the spot the fire was beyond control before we reached it and stacks of timber left by the Canadian foresters were blazing with a white heat. As we were doing our best to prevent the spread of the flames a body of exhausted men appeared. They had been battling with the main fire on the farther side of the loch when to their dismay they saw the outbreak opposite them, and I shall always feel that our presence there was suspicious to them, and that they imagined we had caused this new outbreak, and, when too late, were attempting to extinguish it! It seemed almost impossible to believe that a spark could have been carried across Loch Morlich.

There has always been the danger of fire in these great forests. About 1693 two men were accused of burning heather in "Abernethie, whereby much fir wood was burned." An assize sat on them. "They are ordained to be taken to the gallows of the moor of Belintomb and their lugs nailed to the said gallows."

The Forest of Mar escaped these fires of 1920, so the old trees remain and are full of life, except where, here and there, a veteran, rotten in the heart-wood, has been uprooted by some wild winter's storm. These aged trees have been burned deep by the sun of many a warm summer, drenched by countless rainstorms, and mantled with innumerable snow-falls. Their long life has been a hard one, for, unlike their sheltered cousins of the close-planted woods, they have relied all their lives upon their own strength to battle with the elements. Each root and each branch has been tested a thousand times, and now the old trees seem to stand with quiet self-confidence, serene and undaunted at the coming of the fiercest gale that sweeps down in furious gusts from the corries of the High Cairngorms.

It is remarkable that each of these ancient firs is the offspring of parents with a like history. And so their ancestors must have flourished on the same ground in the days when Diarmid was killed by a bear on Beinn Ghielleinn and when the wolf and the wild boar and even the elk roamed through the wide Caledonian Forest.

CHS-25

Gleann Einich and Sgoran Dubh.

CAIRNGORM STONES

It was during a recent expedition to the high hills that we came across a rich vein of cairngorms. The corrie in which the stones were found was buried in the most out-of-the-way spot and we discovered the vein in rather a curious way. We set out early one beautiful October morning to obtain a series of photographs of a snow-field which has never, even during the hottest summer, been known to disappear. Our way for some time led through a glen, with a few ancient pines and birches growing near the burn, and on a hill-side near were the remains of what had been a thriving wood, but which had, during a winter storm many years ago, been completely razed to the ground. All the trees had been uprooted from a northerly direction and the trunks were now lying white and bleached in the sunlight.

Rounding the shoulder of the hill, we found a heavy gale sweeping down upon us from the westward; in fact, so furious was it that at times it was almost impossible to make progress, and soon the hill-tops were enveloped in a furious storm of snow. As yet brilliant sunshine prevailed in the pass, and the sun, striking on the driving snow, lit up the flakes as they swirled down before the gale with dazzling whiteness. When the snow was upon us we sought the shelter of a large rock, and awaited, in comparative calm, the passing of the storm. Soon the sun regained the mastery, and with the hill-tops clear and powdered with a thin covering of fresh snow, we pushed on towards the higher grounds. Far up on the hill-side above us the stags were roaring, and every now and again a couple of beasts would fight furiously for a few minutes.

Soon we had for our companions the ptarmigan. All around us these birds kept up a continual croaking. When they took wing we noted that they were rapidly changing from their summer plumage of lichen grey to their winter dress of snowy whiteness. This change of plumage, though a wise provision of Nature, sometimes leaves the ptarmigan in a most awkward position, for in early winter, after the birds have donned their winter dress, a period of mild weather often ensues, leaving the hill-side almost bare of snow. This, of course, renders the ptarmigan an exceptionally easy prey to the fox and the golden eagle and on occasions such as these the birds spend most of their time on any lingering snow-fields.

As we neared the snow-field the weather changed for the better, the hills being clear of mist and the atmosphere much milder than earlier in the day. Close by the drift we found fields of delicate parsley fern—which, by the way, we have almost always found growing in proximity to snow—and the grass, not long freed from its snowy covering, was fresh and green. The snow-field, originally an enormous mass covering the whole of the corrie, had now dwindled until it had split up into four patches.

While measuring the drifts we noticed a vein of quartz running up the rock immediately above the snow, and on examining it were delighted to see embedded in the rocks were the points of some very fine cairngorms. The cairngorm is readily recognised by its hexagonal shape and tip pointed much after the manner of a sharpened lead pencil. The deeper the colour the more valuable the stone and on the present occasion the cairngorms were sherry-coloured and of good quality. The finest stones are very often found embedded in a certain kind of clay, near a quartz vein, but lying quite free of the rock, and as the clay was present in this instance, protruding from under a large rock, we determined to move the stone to see whether any cairngorms were actually beneath it.

Although the boulder seemed in an unstable position, it took a couple of hours' hard work before it was dislodged and sent roaring down into the snow beneath. One of the party was in a precarious position towards the end of the levering operations, and at one time it was feared that he would accompany the rock on its downward journey! Sure enough, in the clay exposed by the departure of the stone numbers of cairngorms were found. They were of various sizes and shapes, but not a few of them were perfectly formed and with scarcely a flaw. A thorough search was made—a search which was somewhat rudely interrupted by a boulder becoming dislodged from the top of the rocks perhaps 300 feet above us—and quite a rich haul of stones was made. The spot was an ideal one, for the rock under which we found the cairngorms is under snow for eleven months out of the twelve, and often remains buried throughout the year.

As we retraced our steps down the corrie the sun was setting in splendour behind the hills to the west. One by one brilliant rays of light shot up into the northern sky, and soon the whole of the pass was lit up by a magnificent display of aurora, by the light of which we made our way to the low country.

COH-12

AT THE SHELTER STONE

Loch A'an (in Gaelic, *Loch Ath-fhinn*) is the greatest loch of the high Cairngorms. It is cradled in the bosom of the hills, two thousand four hundred feet above sea-level and May has arrived before its clear waters are released by the ice. Great hills guard Loch A'an. Northward, Cairngorm rises almost sheer. To the south are the steep rocky slopes of Beinn Mheadhon. West, stands the vast bulk of Ben MacDhui. It is difficult to see Loch A'an, even from the high ground of the Cairngorms and perhaps the best viewpoint is the head of that magnificent Alpine corric which rises to Ben MacDhui from the western shore of the loch.

One July morning of intense heat, when the shaded thermometer at Aviemore was standing at 82 degrees fahrenheit, a companion and I climbed from Rothiemurchus forest by way of Creag an Leth-choin and Lochan Buidhe to the great tableland that extends from Ben MacDhui to Cairngorm. Clouds had hidden the sun ere we reached this plateau, and a warm southerly breeze was bringing refreshing rain to the hills. Red deer are quick to climb to the high ground when there is pasture for them, and a herd of perhaps one hundred and fifty stags were feeding beside Lochan Buidhe. Many of the hinds had their young calves beside them and the soft, high-pitched bleating of the fawns (a sound not unlike the mewing of cats) mingled with the deeper cries of the mothers as they answered.

We walked east over the green carpet of minute Arctic willows, and as we reached the edge of the plateau looked down into dark Loch A'an encircled by black cliffs. We stood at the head of a corrie through which the water known as the Garbh Uisge Beag flows to the loch. Beneath us was a huge snow-field of great depth. Despite the heat, the surface of the snow was icy-hard, for it had been frozen and thawed alternately for many months. At the edge of the snow the grass was brown: a few yards away it was already green and in vigorous growth. Beside the snow a wheatear stood; near it a pair of meadow pipits were flying. Beneath us a heavy thunder-shower formed and grew and drew a veil before Loch A'an. At the passing of the shower the sky was blue, and in the heavens were piled up great thunder-clouds on which the evening sun shone golden. Beneath us Garbh Uisge Beag mingled its waters with those of a sister stream, Garbh Uisge Mór, having its source beneath one of the largest snow-fields of the Cairngorms, a short distance north-east of Ben MacDhui summit. This field of snow was melting so rapidly that Garbh Uisge Mór was a torrent of clear, foaming waters. We followed these waters to the cliff edge and saw them leap to Loch A'an in a series of splendid waterfalls.

By descending a little distance to the north of these falls it is possible to walk down to Loch A'an and its Shelter Stone without difficulty through a great corrie (which, curiously enough, is unnamed on any map) that must surely be the finest in all the Cairngorm range. In this corrie three streams of considerable size meet. They are the Garbh Uisge Mór, the Féith Bhuidhe, and the white foaming burn which drains Coire Domhain of Cairngorm. In the corrie are many Alpine plants: July violets which mingle their flowers of intense blue with those of the butterwort. In the spray of the falls are the pale petals of the starry saxifrage, and here and there are plants of the globe flower and the harebell. At a height of 2700 feet above sea-level I passed a raspberry bush.

It was evening when we reached the foot of the corrie. We looked back in the soft light at a scene of grandeur. Over the rocks at the head of the corrie the Féith Bhuidhe flowed invisible beneath a great snow-field. Below a wide arch of snow the waters emerged then hurried onward in foaming tumult to where Loch A'an serenely awaited their coming and quietened their youthful eagerness. From a precipice south of the loch great rocks in a past age have been hurled and lie in confusion beneath the parent cliff. One enormous boulder rests upon several others in such a manner that a recess or hollow capable of sheltering and concealing a number of persons has been formed. This is the celebrated Clach Dìon or *Shelter Stone* which for centuries has been used as a sleeping-place by hunters and, more recently, by lovers of the high and solitary places of the Cairngorms. As we reached the Shelter Stone the air was warm and still and perfumed by the young shoots of the crowberry plants.

The Shelter Stone stands 2500 feet above sea-level and the Alpine vegetation surrounding it is unusually luxuriant. It was curious to find the blaeberry plants here taller than those of the same species in Rothiemurchus Forest. The berries in the sun-heated forest were already ripe; here they were small and green. Mingled with them were plants of the great blaeberry, distinguished by their glaucous leaves and more woody stems. This plant rarely flowers or fruits in the Cairngorms, but the unusually warm summer had encouraged the production of a few blossoms and berries as yet far from ripe. Around the great boulder was a carpet of cloudberries with many fruits, already large and red, upon them. It is a peculiarity of the cloudberry that the fruits when imperfectly ripe are red, but when ripe become almost yellow.

Close to the Shelter Stone lay Loch A'an, opal-tinted in the soft evening light. Many small trout were rising on its windless waters; their rings crossed and re-crossed one another. That night at ten o'clock we sat beside the sandy bay where the hill torrent entered the loch and in the crystal-clear water saw many trout cruise around and every few seconds rise to the surface to suck down some small fly or midge. One very dark trout in his wanderings apparently entered the territory of his neighbour, for a light-coloured trout drove the trespasser away with vigour. At half-past ten, as twilight was deepening, a goosander flew up quietly and alighted with a splash in the sandy estuary of the stream. She had failed to observe us and after preening her feathers awhile began to fish. With stealthy movements, throwing her head forward at each stroke of her webbed feet, she cruised around, and the trout, seeing her, hurried into deeper water. Once she made a sudden rush but it was too dark to see whether she caught a fish. A little later, when she was close to us, a trout unsuspectingly swam near her and we were sure that she would capture it but it easily escaped her and then she rose from the loch and was quickly lost to sight in the dusk.

Beside the Shelter Stone was the small earth of a fox, and a cock grouse, rising from the dew-drenched heather, broke the silence with his cheery becking. The interior of the Shelter Stone on so fine and warm a night was dark and depressing. We therefore chose for our couch a narrow, heathery shelf out in the open, protected from dew and rain by an overhanging corner of the great stone. On this shelf we lay during the short hours between sunset and sunrise with the noise of falling waters in our ears and the peace and silence of the great hills all about us.

Many persons have passed a night beneath the Shelter Stone. The Prime Minister, Mr. Ramsay MacDonald, who is a great walker and hill lover, gave me an interesting account of his experience there. Readers may recall the tragedy of the New Year of 1933 when two climbers incautiously passed a midwinter night below that great stone. On their return over Cairngorm to Aviemore they were overtaken by a winter blizzard of great severity and both died in the snow beside the burn of Coire Cas with the worst of their journey behind them and not far from the shelter of the pines of Glen More.

At midnight the sky was clear and a star burned in the depths of Loch A'an. At one o'clock thin mists began to form on the slopes of Beinn Mheadhon. These mists grew stealthily and by sunrise Loch A'an was hemmed in by a billowy cloud. An hour later this cloud had reached us. We were shut in by a grey, motionless vapour that deadened the murmur of the waterfalls above us. There was no chill in the air and we remained on our hard couch in the hopes that the clouds would lift before midday. We were not disappointed. Shortly after eleven o'clock the sharp summit of the great cliff known as the Sticil, which rises almost sheer from the Shelter Stone, loomed grandly through the cloud and gradually the whole precipice, dark and grim even on this summer morning, stood revealed. A narrow gully in the cliff was still filled with snow and high up on the precipice was a curious circular hollow. It gave the impression that a stream at times issued from the hollow which called to mind Ossian's Cave in Glencoe.

The air everywhere was clearing. In soft woolly balls the clouds hung on the sides of the great snowy corrie of the Garbh Uisge, then gradually dissolved. Shortly before noon we left the Shelter Stone. A pair of meadow pipits were courting beside the stone, and the sun was now faintly seen above the upper clouds. The Garbh Uisge had shrunk in size—for during the night hours the snows melt more slowly—and we crossed without difficulty. The air was sultry as we climbed the steep corrie and reached the snow.

While we were climbing the corrie the mists had collected into a dense cloud above Loch A'an and now, floating up into the corrie, they pressed in upon us so that we walked through dense vapours. We followed Garbh Uisge Beag until we had reached a height by aneroid of 3500 feet above the sea, then turned north towards Feith Bhuidhe. Soon a wall of snow towered almost vertically above us, its top invisible in cloud. Along the foot of this great snow wall we groped our way hearing as we walked the crying of many hinds and their calves, near us but hidden in the mist. By compass and aneroid we steered for Cam Lochan (the western outpost of Cairngorm, just under 4000 feet) and as we reached it we emerged above the mist. We looked across a sea of cloud to where the dark cone of Lochnagar and the rocks of Ben A'an rose above the mist. West, the mist-ocean flowed in upon Brae Riach. All the low country was hidden. We looked over the precipice. In clear weather we should have seen the Spey valley and the houses of Aviemore beneath us, but we looked instead upon a vast ocean of mist gently stirring in places as a light eddy of air played upon it.

Late that day, as we crossed Creag an Leth-choin and looked into the misty depths of Lairig Ghru, a mutter of thunder came from a black cloud high above us to the east. It was strange to walk across this lonely country with black thunder-clouds high in the heavens and dun-coloured clouds far beneath us. A swift was hawking for insects above the sea of mist and although rain was falling the still air was very warm. Into the mist we made our way and found in the Lairig twilight gloom and an air temperature at least ten degrees lower than on the high tops. The mist had dropped so low that even the forest of pines was hidden in it, and that evening, as we shivered before a fire in the Spey valley, we pictured the hinds and their calves grazing above the clouds in summer warmth on the lonely plateau of Ben MacDhui, four thousand feet above the sea.

IOW-33

AT THE POOLS OF DEE

On a dark, thundery day I was traversing the Cairngorms, the air heather-perfumed on the lower slopes. At the Pools of Dee I reached a favourite haunt of the ptarmigan and first one, then several of these white-winged birds, rose snorting from the grey rocks. The ptarmigan I had expected to see; the small flight of teal which rose from one of the Pools and winged their way fast southward were unexpected. I had never before seen any bird save a dipper on the Pools of Dee. They lie nearly 3,000 feet above sea level, and there is no vegetation growing in their ice-cold waters. The teal (it was late August) were probably on migration, like the swallows which I saw shortly after sunrise one morning in late summer here.

I had walked across from Aviemore to Braemar to assist in the judging of the piping at the Braemar Gathering and as I was expected to do the same thing at the Kingussie Gathering the next day it was necessary for me to return through the Lairig Ghru very early the next morning in order to reach Kingussie in time. It was a perfect morning. I saw the sun rise on Braeriach and Cairntoul and shortly after its rising reached the Pools of Dee. There, in the faery light of that glowing sun, I wondered for an instant if my eyes were not playing me a trick, for I saw what at first glance appeared to be small animals travelling snakelike at tremendous speed along the rock-strewn pass. Then I realised that these were no terrestrial creatures but a flight of swallows, winging their way toward the south a foot or more off the ground. So low did they fly that I could look down on them and admire the lovely dark-blue plumage of their backs.

Like the teal, they were on migration and had perhaps passed the night somewhere along the valley of the Spey and before sunrise had set off on their journey through the hills. How different was the weather that early morning in late summer to the conditions which had forced down the robin that in spring I had found lying lifeless on deep snow here!

HY-44

THE TAILORS' STONES

As we passed the Tailors' Stone, *Clach nan Taillear*, grouse were all round us, crowing cheerily. Clach nan Taillear is a large flat-topped boulder standing beside the Lairig at the base of Carn a' Mhaim opposite Coire Odhar. Certain tailors, to the number of three or more, one winter long ago wagered that within twenty-four hours they would dance at the "three dells,"—Abernethy, the Dell of Rothiemurchus, and Dalmore near Braemar. They danced at Abernethy and Rothiemurchus, but a blizzard of snow overtook them in the Lairig, and they died in the shelter of the stone that now bears their name.

There is a Tailor's Stone on Cairngorm too, but the story of this stone is a cheerful one. A certain tailor was also a keen stalker. At the season when the Mar stags were in the habit of crossing to Glen More Forest to seek the hinds, this tailor, taking his cloth and his gun to the hill, used to sit at his work upon this stone, all the time keeping a sharp look out for any stag that should come within shot.

Near Clach nan Taillear a deep scar has been torn down the face of Carn a' Mhaim. It is the work of the great cloudburst of 1893. Old Charles Robertson was watcher at the Corrour bothy at the time, and he told me that one July afternoon the water from a black thunder-cloud struck the hill-top with the noise of thunder. Simultaneously another great volume of water struck the Devil's Point behind him, and in the resulting torrent of water his bothy narrowly escaped destruction.

CHS-25

BY THE LAIRIG GHRU

There is a very old right of way by Lairig Ghru from Rothiemurchus to Braemar. Sheep and cattle were driven over it, and in former times there was much crossing of the Lairig by the people of Mar and upper Strath Spey. Young girls of Rothiemurchus used to cross the Lairig in threes and fours to Braemar. Each carried a basket of eggs upon her head to sell in that Upper Deeside village. I believe that an old man who lived in Rothiemurchus was in the habit of taking the long walk merely to have a *céilidh* or talk with the stalker in Glen Derry, and, his talk ended, thought nothing of the sixteen-mile tramp back across the hills.

CHS-25

THE LAIRIG AN LAOIGH TRAGEDY

At the end of December of the year 1804 seven soldiers left Edinburgh on leave, intending to walk the whole distance to their homes on Strath Spey. They reached Braemar and rested there a night. The Cairngorms were deep in snow and a storm was threatening. The travellers were urged to wait, but were anxious to get home and started north on the morning of old Christmas Day. They reached the valley of the Avon in snow and drift, and from here had to fight every foot of the way against the drifting snow. Gradually they weakened, and five out of the seven men fell into their last sleep on the snowy slopes. Two brothers, named Forsyth, kept together and when one of them fell exhausted in the snow his brother took him an his shoulders and struggled bravely on. The rest revived him, and when his brother set him down he was able to make his way alone. He escaped, but soon his brother, exhausted by his great effort, sank forward and died.

CHS-25

Seton Gordon on one of his annual studies of the Braeriach snowbeds (early 1900s).

Seton Gordon and the piper John Macintosh at Corrour bothy.

2

The Length of the Land

There were few areas of Scotland (the Borders?) which Seton Gordon had not frequently visited and described, authoritatively, because he used his feet, and interestingly, because he searched out the background lore and history. This selection is, proportionately, the least represented because of this abundance. The two 'Highways and Byways' books could have been used in their entirety and remain invaluable companions for the curious traveller. His diary for 1945, given later, shows how far he ranged throughout his long life.

In Glen Canisp.

Looking to Suilven and Canisp.

FARTHEST NORTH IN BRITAIN

The voyager from Aberdeen or Leith to the Shetland Islands perhaps notices, while yet that island group is invisible, that a strange bird joins the seagulls following the steamer. The newcomer is a large, dark brown bird, with an area of white on either wing, and its flight is undistinguished, and apparently aimless, until a seagull swoops down and picks up a scrap of meat which has been dropped overboard by the cook. The great skua—for this is the name of the dark brown bird—which has been idly following the ship then shoots forward, like a racing car suddenly accelerated by its driver, overtakes the gull, and very soon forces it to drop or disgorge its prize.

There is something remarkable in the sudden speeding-up of the great skua's flight and the impression is given of most formidable power in reserve. The great skua, or bonxie, as it is almost universally named in Shetland, is so powerful that even the greater black-backed gull is afraid of it. A light-keeper of the Out Skerries light told me that he watched one day a bonxie deliberately murdering a greater black back on the rocks below the lighthouse, and I heard of a great skua which, on seeing a greater black-backed gull snatch a herring from the deck of a drifter in Lerwick Sound, swooped down, killed the great gull with a single blow, swallowed the herring, then flew unperturbed away, as though slaying greater black backs was an everyday affair.

On the water below the great cliffs of Noss I saw another bird tragedy. East of Lerwick, chief port of Shetland, is Bressay Isle, and east of Bressay is the grassy isle of Noss, inhabited only by a shepherd. On its east face Noss is a sheer precipice, and the cliffs, 600 feet high, appear even higher when viewed from the sea immediately below them.

It was on a July morning that my friend and I left Lerwick in a small open motor boat. In Lerwick harbour hundreds of herring drifters were moored to the quays and to one another. Boats from Yarmouth and Lowestoft rubbed shoulders with Scottish craft from Peterhead, Fraserburgh and ports of the Moray Firth. Out in the Sound were anchored fishing craft from Holland and Norway, and there were fish-carriers from Germany and the Balkan States.

We steered north through the entrance to the Sound, where many fulmars were resting on the deep blue water or flying gracefully above the sea, and felt the lift of the north-easterly swell which broke white against Beosetter Holm and Score Head. Soon we had left Bressay astern and were sailing along the north coast of Noss. As we approached the great cliffs on the east side of that island we saw many birds ahead of us and it was here that I realized first the reprehensible habits of the bonxie.

On the sea beneath the great precipice of Noss a bonxie was deliberately murdering a kittiwake. Like a winged stoat, the great skua had attached itself to the victim's back and was eating away the flesh at the back of the neck while the kittiwake flapped its wings despairingly, and attempted to rise from the water and throw off the deadly grip of its implacable enemy. We rescued the kittiwake, but too late to save its life.

In most parts of Britain the gannet has no enemy, and fishes in peace. But we soon realized that the gannet's life on Noss is not one of peace or ease. During the hour that we were in sight of the cliffs of Noss, a former haunt of the sea eagle, we saw gannets often chased and attacked and sometimes forced to disgorge their fish. Kittiwakes, fragile and delightful birds, are the bonxie's easy victims, but the gannet is made of sterner stuff. Yet a gannet singled out for attack by a great skua fled in peril of its life, and its outraged, astonished expression was comical. The bonxies, wheeling high above the cliffs, seemed to know, after a short pursuit, whether the gannet was 'travelling light', or whether it was bringing back fish to its young on the cliffs. If the pursued bird was thought to have fish it was relentlessly pursued and chivvied until it disgorged its herring, which the bonxie skilfully caught and swallowed in mid-air. On one occasion a great skua actually alighted on the back of a gannet in full flight and maintained its footing, like a skilled equestrian, until the gannet in despair dropped to the water. On another occasion a bonxie seized a gannet's tail, and tugged so hard that the gannet shrieked in terror. It may be that this gannet-baiting is a recent habit of the bonxie, and that its increasing numbers have given it greater boldness—at all events the gannet does not at first appear to realize the skua's intentions, and when, too late, it discovers that it is to be the victim of an assault it wheels and swerves, but to no purpose, for the hooligan will not be denied.

The bonxies of Hermaness were much better behaved. It was as though I had gone suddenly from Whitechapel to Mayfair. For several days I watched the bonxies of Hermaness and I rarely saw a gannet or indeed any bird molested by them. As I sat quietly on the hillside watching a pair of great skuas which had young near me I became impressed by the behaviour of the pair when a third bonxie flew over them, as it did many times. When the flying bonxie was immediately above them, the pair on the ground raised their wings in greeting with a quick, simultaneous motion, and held them with the tips pointing skyward as they gave their friend the Fascist salute. The sudden glint of white on the upraised wings of the saluting birds was striking, and the precision with which they gave this greeting was remarkable. Sometimes, when in full flight, a great skua would raise its wings and soar a little way with wings held almost vertically, like a butterfly.

The herring gull, another bird which upon occasion attacks the human intruder near its nest or young, swoops at him from the rear but the great skua attacks from either front or rear. There is something grand in the way this great bird flies rapidly towards the object of its attack, and as it lowers itself with wings held motionless and slightly upraised for the final rush its deep 'keel' and firmly held wings recall a flying-boat gliding to the water. Sometimes during the attack the skua utters a short raven-like croak, or a cry somewhat resembling that of a greater black-backed gull.

Close to the Hermaness nesting ground of the great skuas is a small loch where a pair of red-throated divers have in recent years nested. The watcher told me that the diver is the only bird the skua fears. Before the divers took up their nesting station on the loch the great skuas were in the habit of bathing here but the divers lost no time in driving them away. If any great skua still has the temerity to bathe the diver submerges, swims below water to it, then with its strong, sharp bill seizes and pulls out a mouthful of feathers and sends the aerial buccaneer into the air in a panic. The Hermaness skuas now go for their bathing parade to Loch of Cliff, about three miles away.

Here they have their bathing place at a special part of the loch, near the centre. At the north end is the kittiwakes' bathing place, and midway between the kittiwakes and the great skuas the Arctic skuas bathe themselves. I watched for some time the bathing of the great skuas, and never have I seen birds so greatly revelling in their dip. They threw the water over themselves; they saturated their wings by flapping them violently in the water, then actually lay on their backs, their feet sticking straight into the air, as though they were dead birds. I have seen no other bird deliberately lie on its back while bathing although the black-throated diver when preening its feathers sometimes approaches that position. After bathing, the great skuas flew to a heathery slope above the loch, where they dried their feathers, standing in the breeze until the moisture had evaporated from their plumage.

During the summer when I visited the skua colony upon Hermaness two tame skuas were often near the watcher's hut. One of these birds, an Arctic skua, was tamed by an earlier watcher as long ago as 1911, and at the time of my visit was 26 years old. This skua flies to the door of the hut for any scraps the watcher may give him. His nesting-place is near the hut, and when he returns to his nesting territory his mate at once flies up to him, to share the food he has brought from what to her is a danger zone.

The other tame bird is a great skua, but its visits to the hut are discouraged because the Arctic skua hates and fears the bonxie and he is the greater pet of the two. One evening when I was in the watcher's hut the great skua arrived outside the door and was evidently rather doubtful of its reception. The watcher threw it some scraps from his dinner and the skua stood, with bill open, and with a worried look, before picking up the food. A few evenings later I was eating a sandwich on the grass outside the hut when I saw the tame Arctic skua standing near me. I threw a crust of bread towards him. At once the bird took wing, and after hovering over the crust and inspecting it carefully, swooped down, snatched it in his bill, and flew away. His mate then flew up to inspect the booty and perhaps the family were fed on it, but my view-point was too low for me to see this. I then threw down another crust, and the Arctic skua was about to carry it off when he uttered a shrill chirping cry of rage and flew at speed almost vertically into the air. Looking up, I saw that the object of his wrath was a passing great skua.

But this Arctic skua was only partially tame where I was concerned for he knew very well that I was not his friend the watcher, who fed him each year during his nesting. Perhaps patrolling the seas off the African coast in winter, he gave a thought to that human friend on his northern mist-hidden isle.

It was on a Sunday afternoon that I embarked at Lerwick on the small ship *Earl of Zetland* as she raised steam for her passage to the North Isles. Her deck was crowded with isles folk, dressed in their Sunday best. The tourists and hikers who in summer form a large proportion of the passengers on the Isle of Skye mail boat were absent for the long and often stormy passage from the mainland of Scotland to Lerwick must be a deterrent to all but the most enthusiastic travellers.

My friend and I were voyaging to Unst, a rock-girt isle lying almost 150 miles to the north-east of Duncansby Head in Caithness. Unst, the most northerly island of the Shetland group, is indeed remote but is not isolated in the sense that Fair Isle or Foula are isolated.

It is 12 miles long and 6 broad. Its main port is Baltasound, where there was at one time a whaling station, and where formerly great quantities of herrings were landed. But now whales are scarce, the herrings are landed at Lerwick, and ruinous sheds are all that remain to tell of these earlier industries. Unst was a Norse island for centuries after Norway ceded the Hebrides to Scotland, and indeed it lies nearer to Norway than to the mainland of Scotland. Most of the old island names are Norse.

Our first call was off the island of Whalsay, from which a ferry boat put out to meet us; then we very slowly made our way toward the north, entering Balta Sound late in the evening. The illusion of having at last reached a foreign land was heightened by the Swedish and Norwegian mackerel craft which lay at the pier and by the Swedish fish-curing schooner anchored in the voe. Shortly after our arrival a Swedish gunboat entered the sound, and at once the foreign fishing fleet hoisted their ensigns, so that the port was gay with bunting.

Unst is a wind-swept island and in appearance is even more storm-swept than the Outer Hebrides. The only trees I saw were in Dr. Saxby's garden. These trees, after a life of over 100 years, remain stunted by the almost continuous winds but give shelter to the garden where, the doctor told me, fulmars sometimes alight and have to be helped into the air again by human hand. For many years Dr. Saxby has been weather observer at the meteorological station of Baltasound and each morning at nine o'clock by Greenwich Time he makes a record of wind, rainfall and temperature. The instruments are in the garden, and he told me (this was in 1937) that he reckoned he had walked 3000 miles in making these island observations. He told me that the glass ball of the sunshine recorder had originally been in use at the summit observatory on Ben Nevis (4400 feet above the sea) and had thus the unique record of use at the highest, and also at the most northerly, British station.

At the entrance to Balta Sound is Balta Island, a pleasant, grassy island that ends in a cliff on the ocean side. On a quiet, sunless day we rowed across during an expedition after sea trout (sea trout are caught here in the sea as well as in the fresh-water lochs) and landed beside a derelict pier where fulmars were sitting tamely on the low rocks. On a spit of sand and shingle a colony of Arctic terns were nesting: they now rose and flew overhead, calling angrily. We climbed the grassy slope and looked over the cliff, where fulmars were brooding their young chicks. The sea was calm, but suddenly at one place the water's surface was agitated by countless tiny waves and there was a loud sighing, as though a phantom wind-squall off the rocks had suddenly stirred the sleeping sea. The mackerel shoal—for it was this which had broken the ocean's calm—moved forward quickly on the top of the water, then disappeared towards the depths. Farther out to sea the dorsal fins of two basking sharks broke the surface, and from the highest part of the island a raven flew furtively away.

The traveller who alights from the steamer on the pier at Baltasound and walks up to the small village sees fulmars wheel and glide over the land as they do but rarely on the Scottish mainland. Above the village road they swoop, circle round the houses, and sometimes alight on some wall or ruined house, where they chatter excitedly in fulmar language. In a few years I am convinced that the fulmar will be found breeding inland on Unst. My memories of Spitsbergen, where the fulmar is seen far from the salt water, were revived one misty evening when my friend and I were crossing one of the inland hills of Unst. Near this hilltop is an old disused quarry, and a pair of fulmar petrels were soaring in play here, gliding in and out of our vision on that mist-filled hilltop. Sometimes a great skua would emerge from the mist, banking and gliding not unlike a great shearwater.

On Unst crofts are small; in some of the houses Shetland tweed is woven and Shetland shawls are made. To one arriving from the Hebrides it was surprising to be told that there was no lobster fishing off the island shores. The hills of Unst are wide and rolling and resemble the Border Country. The heather and hill grass are grazed very closely by Shetland sheep and Shetland ponies.

The most northerly promontory of Unst is Hermaness. According to tradition Hermaness received its name from a giant called Herma. He and another giant, Saxa, both lost their hearts to a beautiful mermaid. Saxa's home was on the hill of Saxavord on the east side of the Burra Firth, and the mermaid said that she would give her love to the giant who should follow her to the North Pole without touching land. As she dived gracefully beneath the waves Herma and Saxa plunged with a great turmoil after her. Thus the three set out on their long, cold swim, and were never again heard of.

To bird lovers, Hermaness is of special interest since the great skua nests on the promontory. In 1861 Saxby found only five or six pairs of great skuas here, and believed that the extermination of the race was near. Richard Kearton in one of his books mentions that when he visited Hermaness about the year 1897 there were thirteen pairs; when my friend and I saw the colony in 1937 it consisted of no less than ninety pairs. That the great skua was not exterminated on Hermaness is due to the family of Edmondston of Buness, who owned the land. They built a hut and appointed a man to keep watch on the colony and prevent egg collectors and 'men with guns' visiting it. The pioneer work of this Unst family has since been carried on by the Royal Society for the Protection of Birds.

To the hilltop above Hermaness a footpath leads from the end of the road, and along this track a lighthouse-keeper in times of peace daily climbed to signal to the lighthouse on Muckle Flugga, an outlying stack washed by the Atlantic swell. Near the hilltop is the birdwatcher's hut, where the guardian of the colony had his home during spring and summer, surrounded by skuas.

Below Hermaness, on its landward side, is a long and narrow fresh-water loch named Loch of Cliff. On this loch is to be seen a great flock of kittiwakes fluttering on white, black-tipped wings above the water or bathing happily. A continuous stream of these graceful birds is seen, hour after hour, arriving at or leaving the loch; as they return seaward to their nesting cliffs they pause for an instant in full flight to shake out their feathers. Thousands upon thousands of kittiwakes must bathe in the fresh water daily.

The shores of the Burra Firth are bright sands and green links where ringed plovers call but as one climbs to Hermaness one enters a country of hill vegetation where, among the peat hags, small golden flowers of the tormentil grow close to the ground and in the sunlit air is the scent of crowberry.

During the whole of the two miles' walk from Burra Firth to Hermaness the climber is in skua country. The lower slopes are tenanted mainly by Arctic skuas, of which there were more than a hundred pairs present. In July, when the young are hatched and are hiding in the heather, the parent skuas on the approach of their enemy, man, stand in prominent positions with open beaks, fluttering their wings as though injured. This trick is played in the hopes of distracting attention from the defenceless young.

We walked past successive pairs of acting Arctic skuas until we reached, near a small tarn, the great skua colony and were attacked fiercely by one after another of these large birds which at times call to mind the buzzard in their easy flight and graceful soaring. But the buzzard's wing primaries when soaring are sometimes open; those of the great skua are always tightly closed. It is hard to avoid ducking one's head at the swoop of a great skua: the bird with a rush of wings approaches relentlessly at the height of one's head and at the speed of an express train.

As we watched the skuas on the most northerly cape of Britain a cloud approached from the Atlantic and Hermaness for a brief space was shrouded in thin mist; but when the cloud passed the day became even clearer than before. Surrounding us was an immense sea horizon. Only to the south was land visible, and here the Shetland Isles lay beneath the summer sun. Beyond the island of Yell was what is called the mainland of Shetland. The isle of Bressay, near Lerwick and almost 50 miles distant, was plainly seen. Beneath us were Muckle Flugga and the neighbouring Vesta Skerry, snow-white in the sun. This whiteness was from the great gannet colony which nests here. The birds are comparatively recent comers, for they first arrived here in 1920, and each year since then have increased.

We descended the seaward grassy slopes of Hermaness, with Bruce the bird-watcher as our guide, and found ourselves at the edge of a formidable cliff, down which led a narrow sheep track. Considerable care was necessary to descend this track, and as we crept warily from ledge to ledge, with the waves sparkling in the sun far beneath us, rows and groups of puffins standing beside their burrows eyed us with curiosity. Fulmars sailed past so near that they almost touched us and on the rocks below grey Atlantic seals slept. The climber when he has descended with relief to the cliff foot finds himself in a country as grand and majestic as any to be found in Britain. Not even in the Hebrides or on St. Kilda have I found cliff scenery to equal that of Hermaness.

On St. Kilda the cliffs are on too vast a scale to be appreciated. On Hermaness they are small in comparison, yet have more character. We had reached the foot of the cliff opposite a magnificent stack named Burra Stack. Through a natural arch in this great stack the Atlantic swell flowed snow-white; the whole scene was instinct with life and motion. To the north of Burra Stack with its numerous kittiwake population rose Humbla Stack and its spur Humbla Houll where clustered gannets made loud, harsh music. We ventured out on to Humbla Stack, past crowded guillemot ledges, and stood beside the gannets on their nests. Some of the solans took flight, but others remained to guard their white, downy young. As we looked back, the narrow path by which we had descended now appeared more formidable; nor were we cheered by the watcher's tales of climbers who, half-way down that track, had turned back, or crofters who, when the time had come to gather the sheep which had strayed to the cliff foot lacked the nerve to follow them. It was with a feeling of relief after a testing return climb we found ourselves at last safe on the grassy slopes above the cliff. Here we rested in glorious evening sunshine with many puffins as our close companions. Along the face of the cliff flight after flight of kittiwakes passed; as they flew they seemed like a long, white pennant slowly shaken by the breeze. Below them gannets fished, plunging meteor-like into the blue sea, and a great skua made half-hearted dives at a passing raven.

That evening at a quarter-past nine the sun was still hot. Great skuas soared majestically high overhead, tier upon tier, the low sun shining on the white markings on their wings. The blue of the sea became more intense. The spirit of ocean was at rest, and for a brief space Hermaness forgot the rain-laden tempests which even in spring and summer often vex her, and her wild beauty increased as the sun at last dipped towards the sea horizon and long hours of sunset and afterglow replaced the heat of the day.

ISNB-41

THE GREAT GLEN;
THE CANAL AND THE MONSTER

No history of Inverness would be complete without a short account of the construction of the Caledonian Canal — that great water-way which links the Atlantic with the North Sea. Mr. Telford, the celebrated engineer, estimated that the undertaking would cost £350,000 and would take seven years. Actually the work lasted considerably longer, and cost the huge sum of £1,300,000. Mr. Telford proposed that the canal should be large enough to admit the largest class of British and American traders or a 32-gun frigate, fully equipped.

The length of the Caledonian Canal is sixty miles, of which forty are the lochs of Ness, Oich and Lochy; the summit level (at Loch Oich) is 100 feet above the sea. In the construction of the canal it was found necessary to raise the level of Loch Lochy 9 feet, and to cut a new passage for the River Lochy in the solid rock, where the famed Mucomer salmon-pool now is. The dredging of Loch Oich proved both difficult and costly, because a great number of oak trees, which during the ages had been carried down the River Garry in times of flood, had to be removed, and some of these old trees were as much as 12 feet in diameter. The first passage from sea to sea was when, in October 1822, a steamship reached Fort William from Inverness in thirteen hours, but the Caledonian Canal was by no means completed; not until 1843 was the work finished.

The latest change has been the construction of the great highway between Inverness and Fort William, called the Glen Albyn road, from which the Loch Ness monster has often been seen.

During many centuries the River Ness has flowed unchanged yet ever-changing through the town. This river, so short in its course, is nevertheless in times of flood one of the most mighty in the Highlands. Its waters never freeze, even at the margins, and on a morning of hard frost it is interesting to see the majestic Ness flowing seaward, with waters steaming like those of a hot spring in Iceland. Here in winter many water ouzels fly backwards and forwards. In December, January and February eager salmon, fat and silver-sided, from the deeps of the Atlantic enter the Ness and pass swiftly through to Loch

Ness to the clear foaming waters of the Garry, where they are sometimes caught with the fly on days of January so cold that the angler's line freezes to the rings of his rod.

The original name of Fort Augustus was Cill Chuimein (named after Cummein, abbot of Iona). The fort was built by General Wade, and the name Augustus is said to have been given it to honour the Duke of Cumberland. In the early part of 1746 the fort was captured by the Jacobites. When Johnson and Boswell made their tour they stayed a night at Fort Augustus where, writes the learned doctor, "Mr. Trapaud, the governor, treated us with that courtesy which is so closely connected with the military character". He continued: "In the morning we viewed the fort, which is much less than that of Ft. George. It was not long ago taken by the Highlanders. But its situation seems well chosen for pleasure, if not for strength; it stands at the head of the lake, and, by a sloop of sixty tuns, is supplied from Inverness with great convenience."

Fort Augustus as a military station has disappeared. Where the fort stood is now a well-endowed Benedictine abbey. Lord Lovat bought from the Government the fort and the farm attached to it, and the present monastery was completed and opened in 1878. The old fortress has now become part of the abbey, and the room where Lord Lovat was confined as a prisoner can be seen. The old tree planted in memory of the battle of Culloden is still alive. Jacobite prisoners were shot on what is now the cricket field of the abbey.

The [Inverness] road passes above the grand old ruin of Urquhart Castle, a ruin now in the care of the Government department of Ancient Monuments. Little is known with certainty concerning the early history of this great castle, stately in its ruins. Pennant writes that it was "the seat of the once powerful Cummins, and was destroyed by Edward I."

Pennant, writing of the Urquhart and Glen Moriston district, has an observant natural history note on the capercaillie. He writes: "Above is Glen Moriston, and East of that Straith Glas, the Chisolm's country; in both of which are forests of pines, where that rare bird the Cock of the Wood is still to be met with. Formerly it was common throughout the Highlands, and was called Capercalze."

Not so many years after Pennant visited the Highlands the old race of the capercaillie did become extinct and the breed which inhabits the Highland pine forests at the present day was introduced into Scotland from Sweden.

From the neighbourhood of Urquhart Castle of recent years the strange but now well-attested creature, the Loch Ness monster, has on a number of occasions been seen. There is in my mind no doubt that such a creature— there may be more than one—does exist in Loch Ness. Among a number of reliable witnesses who told me that they saw the monster was the late Captain

Grant, of the MacBrayne paddle steamer *Pioneer*, which regularly plies on Loch Ness during the summer months. From Captain Grant's observations — and from the observations of other reputable witnesses — it would seem that the strange creature is timid and that the sound, or vibration, of a steamer causes it to submerge while the ship is yet a considerable distance off. Mr. Goodbody of Invergarry House and his daughter watched the creature for forty minutes through a stalking-glass. The Loch Ness monster is indeed no recent find, although at the present day it is known to a much larger number of people than ever before. The chief reason, I believe, why many more people now see it is that the new high-road along the north shore of Loch Ness gives a much better view of the loch. But there is another reason. Before the monster became, so to speak, public property, those who saw the unchancy creature decided that the less said about it the better. They realised that they would be laughed at, or pitied, or would be set down as addicted to a dram. So long as half a century ago, to my own knowledge, children were told by their nurses that if they persisted in naughtiness the loch monster would take them. I heard of a well-known resident on Loch Ness-side who one day, after rowing down the loch in his small boat, appeared at a friend's house white and shaken, and asked for brandy. His friend for some time vainly endeavoured to ascertain the cause of his distress, to receive as answer, "It is no use my telling you, for even if I did you would not believe me." But in the end, when prevailed upon to unburden himself of his secret, he said to his friend, "As I was rowing down the loch some creature came to the surface beside me — and all I can say is that I hope I may never see the like again."

May it not be that in the monster of Loch Ness we have a survival of an ancient race which, living for the most part under water and being of a timid disposition, has existed in comparative obscurity during successive centuries?

Hills rise steeply from Loch Ness throughout the length of its northern shore, the most prominent graceful Mealfourvonie (2,264 feet). Geikie describes this hill as "one of the most elevated masses of Old Red Sandstone in the country", and points out that its position shows how old the valley of the Great Glen must be. Professor Watson gives the Gaelic name of the hill as Meall Fuarmhonaidh, *Hill of Cold Moor*.

Looking up Loch Ness, it can be realised how straight is the depression of the Great Glen, a depression which Geikie considered to coincide with a line of fracture of great geological antiquity and one which has been subjected again and again to disturbance and displacement. Even at the present day, earthquake tremors are more frequent here than elsewhere in the Highlands.

H&BC-48

31

LOCHIEL'S COUNTRY

Lochiel's Country is perhaps the most romantic district in all the Western Highlands. Many of the great highland families have had to part with their lands, which are now in the possession of strangers, but Lochiel, Captain of Clan Cameron, and its twenty-fifth chief, still lives where his people have lived from time immemorial, and it will be a bad day for the Western Highlands when there is no longer a Lochiel at Achnacarry.

In Lochiel's Country the past and the present join hands. In the castle at Achnacarry are priceless relics of the '45, and of still earlier times. The most interesting of the '45 relics is perhaps a silver flask given to the Gentle Lochiel by Prince Charles Edward with the following inscription on it: "Snuff Box or Dram Cup, while skulking in ye Highlands, given by him to Lochiel A.D. 1747, at Paris." On the castle wall hangs the clan banner, which escaped the hands of the English after Culloden. MacLachlan of Coruanan, hereditary standard-bearer to the Lochiel of the day, wrapped the standard next his skin that evening of disaster, and carried it safe to Lochaber—and in the family of the Coruanan MacLachlans it remained until recent years, when it was given to Lochiel. On the castle wall near the standard are a claymore (two-handed sword) used at the Battle of Harlaw, an old targe (pierced thrice by deadly thrusts which must have caused grievous wounds to him who carried it) on which is written in bold lettering, "Fear God, Honour the King," and the gun with which Sir Ewen of Lochiel, perhaps the most renowned of a long line of outstanding chiefs, killed the last wolf in the highlands.

At Achnacarry, beside the friendly Arkaig river, which sings a soft lullaby, or an eager song of triumph, according to the season and the weather, it is easy to visualise the days of the '45. The old castle was burned to the ground by Cumberland's troopers. Not a trace of it remains. But the beech avenue stands high and green and stately and if one looks at it closely one notices that the trees are planted in a curious manner. At the beginning of the avenue they are carefully spaced; farther on they grow so closely together that the stems press one upon another. The explanation is that when Lochiel in 1745 crossed the hills to meet Prince Charlie he hoped to dissuade the Prince from his reckless enterprise and thought soon to return to his planting of the beech avenue which he had planned. But dark days came to Lochiel. His lands were confiscated, Lochiel died in France, and the beeches were left to grow as they had been temporarily set into the ground.

Near this avenue are older trees and on them are still to be seen the hollows which supported the beams on which were hung the kettles of Cumberland's troopers. On the wooded hill-side above the castle stood the hut to which Lochiel retreated when in hiding. Today the last traces of that hut have gone. The site of it was marked by willows, and when the woods were felled during the Great War, these guiding trees were cut down also. Not far from where the hut stood is a cave where the fugitive Prince is said to have rested.

When the dipper sings his autumn song beside the hurrying waters of the Arkaig he sings quietly. He and his clan have lived here for many generations but the osprey, who for so long had her eyrie on Loch Arkaig, has gone never, it is to be feared, to return. Despite watchers and barbed wire entanglements the osprey's nest was frequently robbed and on their journeys to and from their winter quarters in the south the birds themselves fell victims to unscrupulous gunners.

For its size the Arkaig must be one of the shortest rivers in Scotland. It is little more than a mile in length and flows from Loch Arkaig to Loch Lochy. Loch Arkaig, a long narrow loch more than twelve miles in length, is sheltered by high hills. On a still autumn evening, when the last of the sun-fire lingers on Fraoch Bheinn and the moon rises golden in the east, salmon leap and play in the still waters of Loch Arkaig and the clan of the bats flit delicately and uncertainly above the old oak woods and the dark pines of the Caledonian Forest.

On the north shore of the loch the road to Glen Dessary winds through oak woods. The tree is still standing behind which Cameron of Clunes awaited his special enemy, an English officer of the army of occupation. The story may be told in a few words. During the troublous times that followed the '45 one of Cumberland's officers made himself so disliked by his brutal and overbearing behaviour that Cameron of Clunes determined to take his life. The officer was the owner of a handsome white horse, which made him easy to recognise. He heard of this plot against his life, and arranged that on the day in question a brother officer, Major Monroe of Culcharn, should ride his horse. This highland officer, who was serving in the Hanoverian army, unsuspectingly did so, and as he rode at nightfall along the side of Loch Arkaig he was shot dead by Clunes, who in the failing light recognised the horse but failed to recognise the rider.

On Loch Arkaig is a wooded isle which was, according to one tradition, the burying-place of the MacPhees. It was probably on this island that the renowned Sir Ewen of Lochiel confined three English colonels and Colonel Duncan Campbell. He had surprised and captured these officers near Inveraray, and took them "to Locharkike to ane isle there." Loch Arkaig never freezes. "Its water is admirably light and delicat, being well stored with salmond and other fishes," says an old account, which goes on to describe how Sir Ewen, who in time came to have a great regard for his prisoners, organised a deer drive for them. Some hundreds of his clansmen, skilled hunters all made a long line across the hills, and enclosed a great number of deer. They drove these deer to an appointed place and prevented them from breaking out while the prisoners killed them with their broadswords. The old pines of Glen Mallie beside Loch Arkaig must have been striplings on the day of that memorable deer drive.

When a part of this pine forest was felled some twenty years ago a number of the oldest trees were spared. They are believed to be almost 300 years old. Even the splendid pine forests of the Cairngorms have, I believe, no trees to compare with them in age. One of the old Glen Mallie firs is known as the Three Sisters because of its three stems. On a dark day when mist covered the hills I first saw this tree and as I looked upon it the sun for a few minutes pierced the clouds, and shone full upon the Three Sisters so that the tree stood out from the dark hillside in radiant beauty.

That old tree during its long life must have seen many things. It must already have been well grown when Prince Charles Edward, a fugitive with shattered dreams, journeyed, disconsolate, westwards along Loch Arkaig. Cumberland's troops may have camped in its shade. During many years it must have seen the osprey sail across to its island nest, carrying in his talons fish for the hungry brood. It has watched the *each uisge,* or water horse, playing upon the surface of the loch, before it was banished by the thoughts of a materialistic age. Lord Malmesbury in his Memoirs writes (1857): "My stalker, John Stuart at Achnacarry, has seen it twice, and both times at sunrise in summer, when there was not a ripple on the water. The creature was basking on the surface; he saw only the head and hind-quarters, proving that its back was hollow, which is not the shape of any fish, or of a seal. Its head resembled that of a horse. The highlanders are very superstitious about this creature. They believe that there is never more than one in existence at the same time."

As one walks along the Mile Dorcha (*the Dark Mile*) at sunset the water horse, and other mysterious beings, seem more real than many a creature of the material world. Invisible stags roar hoarse and menacing challenges from the depths of the forest. A wild cat ambles across the track with long, easy strides that appear deceptively slow. A heron shrieks: overhead a flight of mallard pass. The last of the sunset burns pale upon the snows of Ben Nevis—so long as snow lies on the Ben all is well with Lochiel and his house—and night lays her hand lightly upon Lochiel's Country.

Between Lochiel's Country and the Glengarry lands of Knoydart great hills tower to the clouds. The eagle, the raven, the hill fox, and the red deer, have their home here, and traces of human handiwork are seen in General Wade's old track which leads from Glen Dessary, beside Loch Arkaig, westwards to the Atlantic tides of Loch Nevis. The hill pass at the head of Glen Dessary is named Mam na Cloiche Airde, *the Pass of the High Rock*, and the name is singularly apt. At the head of Loch Arkaig two glens lead away west. One is Glen Pean, in Gaelic Gleann Peathann, the other is Glen Dessary, in Gaelic Gleann Deiseirgh, *the Glen with a Southern Exposure*. Glen Pean crosses to Loch Morar. Prince Charlie traversed it at least once during his "skulking in ye Highlands," and Cameron of Glen Pean and MacDonald of Glen Alladale met the Prince subsequently at Ranachan in the Loch Ailort country, and discussed future plans with him there. Glen Pean is a narrow glen, and does not rise to any great height above the sea. Near its head-waters is Loch Leum an t-Sagairt, *the Loch of the Priest's Leap.*

The story is that a priest was in hiding, and was surrounded by soldiers. On every side his escape was hindered. Only by jumping across the loch, which is several hundred yards wide, could the hunted man win free. But leap it the saintly man did, aided by supernatural powers, and made good his escape. Since that day the Loch of the Priest's Leap has been the name of this lonely tarn. Glen Dessary was the old home of the Camerons of Glen Dessary, a cadet branch of the Lochiel family. It was Miss Jenny Cameron of Glen Dessary who rode at the head of the men from Kinloch Arkaig to meet the Prince at Glen Finnan. She was mounted on a white horse and wore a green jacket. Scarcely a trace remains of the old house of Glen Dessary and the barracks, where Cumberland's troops were quartered, are not easily recognised today, although the firmly built walls are still standing beside the road at the mouth of the glen. Perhaps two miles up Glen Dessary from the site of the old barracks, on the far side of the river near the only house that stands hereabouts, is a small knoll known as Cnoc Dhuic, *the Duke's Knoll*, where Cumberland's soldiers had their camp on one occasion.

It was a dark day in autumn when a friend and I made our way up Glen Dessary by General Wade's old track. Beside Loch Arkaig the leaves on the rowans were dark red, an ample crop of scarlet berries on which fieldfares from Norway were feeding eagerly. A pair of swans swam on the dark waters of the loch. On Guilven and Streap across the glen the mist rose and fell, and

Sgùrr na h-Aide for a moment showed his graceful peak. The hill grasses in the glen were yellow and gold beneath the dark sky, through which a haloed sun for a short time shone palely. Near the foot of Glen Dessary General Wade's track unaccountably disappears for a short distance. One theory is that two parties of soldiers, one from Loch Nevis, the other from Loch Lochy, worked to meet one another, but made an indifferent joining. Perhaps an urgent summons was received by them to proceed elsewhere. This track—it cannot be called a road—of the General's is not one of his best, even making allowances for the hand of time. In a number of places the path almost disappears and it is rough, wet and stony throughout its course.

Ahead of us as we walked, Sgùrr na Cìche rose steeply, gloomy and mist-capped. From its precipitous sides many burns were falling in grey spray. At 1,000 feet above sea level we reached the watershed and Mam na Cloiche Airde. Here three cairns stand beside the track. They mark the bounds of three old territories—Lochiel, Lovat and Glengarry. Of the three Lochiel is the only property remaining in the hands of the old family.

On the pass rather more than a mile west of the watershed are two small lochs, on the shores of which scattered rowan trees grow. On the shore of the second loch a collection of mussel shells lay. Perhaps the shellfish were used as bait for trout but it is more likely that they made a light meal for some wanderer travelling to the east who had gathered them on the shore of Loch Nevis at low tide and had carried them up to the lochan. We were discussing the origin of the shells when we saw travellers approaching. Two pleasant-faced lads were driving before them a stirk and a young bull; a couple of sagacious and friendly collie dogs completed the party. They were crossing from Loch Nevis to Loch Arkaig on their way to Fort William for the sales and were moving slowly for the beasts were ill at ease in their unaccustomed surroundings. Few cattle now use the pass but at one time many drovers must have crossed. Ruined shealings are still visible beside the track and they were apparently built before General Wade made his path through the hills for the bridle track deviates in order to pass near them. We conversed with the drovers and, cheered by their highland courtesy, watched them pass slowly out of sight.

We had now entered a country of high rocks, gloomy gorges, and mist-covered peaks. The scene was stern and grand. Somewhere above us a stag roared. A pair of golden eagles circled overhead, and were mobbed by a pair of grey crows: the eagles, as is their custom, treated the furious attacks of the hoodies with contempt. We continued on our westward journey perhaps a couple of miles beyond the watershed, then (since the surrounding rocks and knolls still hid the view westward) we climbed a little way up Sgùrr na Cìche and soon were in sight of the white-capped waves of Loch Nevis far below us. The tide was low and a long line of golden sea wrack was visible along the shore. On the far western horizon Eigg showed faintly and the dim outline of Rhum appeared like some distant cloud. A small yacht steered towards the mouth of Loch Nevis. Beside the shore scattered houses could be seen; through the narrows the tide flowed like a river in flood. We had intended to descend to Loch Nevis by the path, continue along the shore of Loch Nevis to Tarbet and then cross the narrow neck of land to Loch Morar but a heavy storm was approaching us and we decided to return to Achnacarry. Far up the hill-side above us a stag with strong broad antlers was wandering restlessly in search of hinds. In a grassy sheltered hollow near us a hind and her calf were lying. Although winter was near, the milkwort, the lousewort, and a *ranunculus* still held their flowers towards the dark sky and beside wee burns the yellow saxifrage's leaves were dark green and full of vitality.

The air grew heavy; still more sombre became the heavens. A rain-storm hid Eigg and approached the green slopes of Mallaig Bheag. We finished our spying, turned east, and with the wind at our backs set out for Loch Arkaig, invisible beyond the hills. Soon the rain reached us. It fell upon us in sheets, as only a West Highland rain can fall. The hills ran water. Sgùrr na Cìche was the birthplace of innumerable milky torrents. Majestically the rain-filled mists swept across the rocky slopes where the eagles, unperturbed, faced the squalls. Darkness came early to Glen Dessary. In the gathering dusk we splashed our way down the glen and reached Loch Arkaig in the blackness of a moonless night.

H&BW-35

WHERE EDAL AND GAVIN MAXWELL LIVED

Although I never met Gavin Maxwell, author of the world-famous book *Ring of Bright Water,* I have a warm corner in my heart for him because of the following rather strange reason. He light-heartedly spread the rumour, which for a time was seriously believed, that it was necessary for me to have a bowl of porridge in my lap to ensure concentration and enjoyment when I was judging the classical piping at a Highland Gathering. I have no idea how this rumour originated; at any rate it dies hard. It caused serious interest among those who had no sense of humour.

His many readers and admirers knew that Gavin Maxwell wrote his *Ring of Bright Water* (over a million copies of this work have been sold) at a place he disguised as Camusfeama, *Bay of the Alder Trees.* This is on the Atlantic shore, mid-way between Glen Elg, of MacCrimmon piping fame, and Arnisdale on Loch Hourn, where Commander Glen-Kitson's celebrated yacht *Golden Hind* used to anchor before the second world war and incidentally transported the Queen Mother and her husband "Over the Sea to Skye" (when Duke and Duchess of York) on their memorable official visit to Skye. I knew the bay before Gavin Maxwell gave it world fame.

At that time, as seen from the road to Arnisdale, which passed above it at a distance of two miles, a shepherd's house with thatched roof was the only human dwelling in sight and the name of the shore, as given on the map, was Sandaig, which may be translated as *the Sandy Place.* The area is now completely changed in appearance by acres of young forest, and a new tar-macadam road to Arnisdale.

There is now a rough track which follows a stream through plantations of larch and spruce to the small clearing, near the shore, where Gavin Maxwell and Edal the Otter had their retreat. On my recent visit the larch and spruce were healthy, (the aroma from larch needles scented the air) but the young firs were brown as the result of the unusual ferocity of the south west and west gales being thus salt-impregnated from the Atlantic ocean. At the sides of the track wild hyacinth, birdsfoot trefoil, and milkwort flowered, delicately coloured. Banks of gorse, like the firs had their sharp needles brown and dead from the salty gales yet their golden flowers were undamaged and added brightness and warmth to a sombre scene.

At the end of half an hour's walk the track descends more steeply and the walker has the first sight of his destination, a small sandy bay and beside it a comparatively small level treeless clearing where an atmosphere of sorrow seemed to brood.

The shepherd's house which formerly could be seen had disappeared without trace. It may be remembered that it was destroyed in the fire in which Edal the Otter lost her life and that Gavin Maxwell had given instructions that all trace of the dwelling should be removed. Perhaps fifty yards from where the house stood, to the east of its site, is a large stone on which is cut, in clear and graceful lettering, a quotation on the merits of his otter friend, taken from one of Gavin Maxwell's books.

The darkness and the stillness of a sunless day added to the solemnity of the scene, described in his book so vividly by a master of descriptive prose. Across a leaden sea rose the coast of Skye where, through dark, wind-driven clouds of a gathering storm the vast bulk of Blaven rose to a height of 3,000 feet above the Atlantic, and I recalled the exceedingly clear day when I could see the abbey church of Iona, sixty four miles distant, from that hill of Skye. More distant were the hills of the Isle of Rum, where the Golden Eagles have become infertile through eating Shearwaters, themselves impregnated by the widespread curse of pesticides.

A pair of Oystercatchers called from the tide on the low shore where I stood, and I remembered the Gaelic tradition in the Outer Hebrides that this bird, which they named, and perhaps still name as Gille Bhride, *Servant of Saint Bride,* was of special merit because it saved Christ by covering him with seaweed when enemies were close on his track. It was said to be a bird of sorrow and its presence in this solemn scene was therefore fitting.

Gavin Maxwell has departed, but his books will long be read and the site of his house, and of Edal's burial place, will long remain a place of pilgrimage for those who appreciated the charm and beauty of his writing.

(Typescript NLS)

BLACK WOOD AND BLACK DEEDS
AT RANNOCH

The traveller as he crosses the watershed by Wade's road and descends to the valley of the Tummel and the lands of Rannoch realises that the valley of Rannoch is broader by far than the glen of the Lyon, and is of a quite different character. If he travels west along the Rannoch road he passes near Dùn Alasdair, the ancestral home of the Struan Robertsons. The first of the Struan family was, according to the tradition of the country, Donnchadh Reamhar, *Duncan the Stout*: he was an ardent supporter and follower of Robert the Bruce, and was given land in the district in the fourteenth century. It is from their ancestor that the Robertsons receive their name, Clann Donnchaidh, *Children of Duncan*.

At Kinloch Rannoch[1] — it is here that the road reaches Loch Rannoch — Dugald Buchanan, religious poet of the Gael, lived and laboured in the eighteenth century, and his memorial is seen in the village of Kinloch Rannoch. The name Kinloch Rannoch is strangely applied to this village. The prefix Kinloch, which is found in many Highland names, means "Head of the Loch," yet Kinloch Rannoch is at the foot of the loch of that name.

One branch of the road here crosses the Tummel (where it leaves the waters of Loch Rannoch) by an old bridge, on which is the following quaint inscription:

ERECTED AT THE SOLE EXPENSE OF HIS MAJESTY

OUT OF THE ANNEXED ESTATES 1764

The feeling of admiration at King George III's generosity which the passer-by experiences is abruptly qualified on reading the second line, and he feels that things could have been put just a little less bluntly!

It was on a grey misty morning of late September that I visited Rannoch. A thin cap of mist clothed the summit of Schiehallion and as the mist rose and fell it showed at times a faint golden gleam as the sun lit up the fringes of the cloud. It was 1938, a time of the most tense international crisis, and the air was heavy with forebodings which called to mind the early days of the great war.

That day the *Queen Elizabeth* was to be launched and, in Rannoch, for from the sea the thoughts of men for a brief space turned to the launch of that great ship which they could follow on their wireless sets, but the shadow of war apparently approaching inexorably fell upon even that memorable event. A police car was distributing gas masks: the constables talked quietly one to another as though they could scarcely credit this menace of imminent war. Yet as I crossed the River Tummel, travelled along the road that leads by the south bank of Loch Rannoch, and entered the celebrated Black Wood of Rannoch, I forgot for a time the evil days through which Europe was passing in the strength and beauty of the old pines which form the Black Wood. One of the pines at the edge of the loch had been sawn off near the base and out of curiosity. I counted the rings of that great tree. Each ring of a tree denotes one year of its growth and this tree showed by its rings that it had lived 214 years.

There is a sense of security in the Black Wood. These great trees, centuries old, seem to tell of wisdom and peace. The wood is a relic of the old Caledonian Forest, and none of the trees have been planted by human hands. Some of them were well-grown when the Fiery Cross was sent round the district in 1745 and the men of the country rose to support Prince Charles Edward in his great adventure. In these natural-grown pine forests the trees do not grow so densely as to destroy the lesser vegetation, and the heather, this day of late September, was purple beneath the old pines. A wandering tramp, having made a careful and (as he hoped) furtive inspection of my two companions and me, now picked a sprig of heather and, appearing in our full view, offered it ingratiatingly for sale. The little comedy was well played, with the assurance which a tramp in the course of a hard life necessarily acquires.

After a time the road leaves the Black Wood and retreats a little from the edge of the loch. Between the loch and the road is the small burial-ground of St. Michael's and, at the west side of its entrance, a large stone may be seen. This is Clach nan Ceann, the Stone of the Heads, and Alexander Cameron in his valuable book, *A Highland Parish,* thus tells the tragic story of the stone.

A Duncan woman of great beauty was wooed by a Cameron of Camghouran and a MacIntosh of Moy. Cameron, the successful suitor, took her to his home in Camghouran. There they lived happily and had a fine family of boys. But MacIntosh did not forget his unsuccessful suit, and an accident which occurred at Perth rekindled his wrath against Cameron. One Saint Michael's Day, while attending a market at Perth, MacIntosh went into a shop and bargained for a bunch of arrows. He did not take the arrows with him, but said that he would call for them before returning home. Cameron was at the same market, and went into the same shop in quest of arrows. The bunch bought by MacIntosh was the finest in the shop, and when Cameron saw them he wanted to buy them. He was told that they had already been bought by MacIntosh, but in the end he overcame the shopkeeper's scruples and prevailed on him to hand over the arrows. When MacIntosh returned and learned that Cameron had carried off his arrows his slumbering resentment against Cameron was roused to fever-heat. In characteristic fashion he swore, kissed his dirk, and vowed that he would have his revenge. He gathered his men who were at the market and made straight for Camghouran. On arrival there he told Cameron's wife that she would have to leave her husband and go with him, but she refused. "If you don't," said MacIntosh, "I will brain every one of your sons." "And if you dared," she replied, "I should not shed a tear." (For she believed all the while that he would not dare.)

But the infuriated MacIntosh took the boys one by one and dashed their heads against a large stone till the mother broke down and begged him to desist. According to some accounts he had already killed three, according to others, six boys. He consented to spare the other boy or boys on condition that the mother would go with him. But ere he could carry her away Cameron arrived, and a fight between MacIntoshes and Camerons ensued. In the end every MacIntosh was slain save one, who escaped by swimming across the loch: when he reached the opposite shore he was cut down by a MacGregor.

The road continues west up the south side of Loch Rannoch to a small post-office (the postmistress was "listening in" to the launch of the *Queen Elizabeth* when I called there), then crosses the river to meet the road on the north side of the loch. Here the traveller looks west and sees the high tops of the Blackmount Forest and of Glen Coe, and if he should continue his journey westward for a few miles he reaches the railway station of Rannoch, on the West Highland Railway from Glasgow to Fort William and Mallaig.

H&BC-48

3

The Outer Hebrides

No part of Scotland would change so much in the course of Seton Gordon's life so he was fortunate to wander the Outer Isles early on and record a lost lifestyle and wildlife of a richness scarcely known today. His long interest in the Hebrides is seen in this selection coming from the titles spanning forty years.

The Callanish standing stones, Lewis.

The tidal crossing from Colonsay to Oronsay.

LIGHT

There is a peculiar quality of light in the Hebrides. So soft is that light, there are times when, as you stand at the edge of the sand at ebb-tide and look out over the sea, you have difficulty in marking where the sand ends and the sea begins and where the sea ends and the sky begins.

At all times of the year these days of beauty occur. When they come around the longest day the charm of the daylight hours continues with added power during the hours of night. Indeed, the word 'night' is a misnomer, for throughout June and during the first fortnight of July night is banished from the Isles. They do not, it is true, see the midnight sun as the north of Norway sees it, a low red orb, or as far Spitsbergen sees it, a midnight sun with warm rays that shine on the saxifrages and Arctic poppies. The sun is indeed hidden from the Isles, but it swims northward so close to the horizon that land and sea are bathed in its subdued light. Seen from the Inner Hebrides, the northern sky is even more beautiful than from the Outer Islands, for dark against the afterglow rise South and North Uist, Harris and Lewis, sharply silhouetted against a rosy horizon. To be high on the hills during a summer night of this sort; to see the sun, quivering with life and power, slowly move northward, touching the Island hills, disappearing for a minute behind a hill-top, then reappearing through the dip beyond it; to see it finally disappear—that is an experience good to recall in the dark days of winter, in the dark days of the spirit.

AH-50

SEA MUSIC

Mar chirein nan stuagh uaine ta mo ghaol.
(*As the crests of the green waves is my beloved*)
Old Gaelic Love Song.

As I write the south wind has been blowing strongly and steadily for four days. It has rushed across the Hebridean island of North Uist, lifting the water in spindrift from the peaty lochs and rocking the corn-stacks in its path. But—an unusual thing for the Outer Hebrides—the gale has brought with it no rain, no clouds, and the sun has shone continuously from a sky hazy with the salt spray of the disturbed Atlantic.

From the distant North Irish coast the south wind, with irresistible strength, wanders eagerly to the Western Isles of Scotland. On its path are the great cliffs of Barra Head and Mingulay. Across them the gale sweeps, then hurries onward to Barra Island and Eriskay (where in 1745 Prince Charles Edward first landed on British soil), and finds Hecla and Beinn Mhor of South Uist fair in its track. How the tempest screams over the narrow ridge of Beinn Mhor, two thousand feet above the heaving Atlantic! Even a grown man is not safe here; he may be snatched from his scanty foothold and tossed far over the precipice that forms the northern face of Beinn Mhor.

Past the lochs of Houghmore sweeps the wind, and now it is lashing the waters that surround Benbecula. From that isle the storm quickly arrives at North Uist, and as I pen these lines is making mournful music around the lodge. From here I look out upon Houghary a mile seaward, and watch the great waves roll in one after the other, while the wind whips their crests from them and carries the spray far to leeward.

Northward of Houghary is a lonely bay where firm white sands rise from the edge of the tide to the bent grasses that grow thickly here. Even in fine summer weather the long ocean swell breaks on this wild shore in gleaming spray. But as I write, in a time of winter storm, all the waters of the bay are churned into foam by the enormous waves which roll in on the flood-tide in a magnificent, unending army.

The waves are reaching their journey's end.

With majestic, unhurried rhythm the green quivering walls advance shoreward hour after hour. They near the sands and feel the shoal water. Like living things they rise quickly, and grow to a height of fully fifteen feet before they curl over and break with the deep roar of thunder.

How sublime is this Ceol Mara, this sea music! It seems to come to us from the approaches to Tir nan Og, on which the sun casts a flood of amber light when he dips behind the cliffs of distant Hirt, on the rim of ocean.

How wonderfully beautiful is the actual breaking of each wave! Slowly the high wall of green water curls over, hangs for an instant in space, then crashes down, imprisoning as it does a layer of air between crest and base. And as each wave breaks in spray, a transient rainbow is lighted above its crest, and (since the whole of the long wave does not break at the same moment) this spray-bow seems to dart magically from one end of the roller to the other. As suddenly as they appeared the colours vanish and the wave is no longer afire.

Whence come these immense waves? How far into the Atlantic is their birthplace?

Far west of Rockall—that lonely mountain-peak that just tops the waters one hundred and eighty miles west of Saint Kilda—the long Atlantic swell has its birth. The waves that break on the white shores of Uist may the previous day have spouted high against Rockall, striking impotently against its dark rocks.

Of Rockall a curious story was told me recently by an officer of His Majesty's navy. During the Great War his ship was employed on convoy duty, and one dark night was steaming eastward towards her Scottish base, having escorted a west-bound convoy out beyond the submarine zone. Suddenly ahead of her loomed up a dim, dark shape, apparently a vessel without lights. The strange vessel seemed to be approaching, tossing the spray from her bows. From my friend's ship the recognition signal was shown, and since it was ignored, action quarters was sounded and all was excitement, when suddenly it was seen that the supposed enemy vessel was Rockall! At once the helm was put hard over, only just in time to avoid shipwreck.

On their lonely course to the eastern shores of Uist the waves have passed Saint Kilda with its sheer twelve-hundred-feet cliffs and, later, have rushed eagerly through Haskeir's mighty arches, where *ron mor*, the Atlantic seal, has his home.

How curious is the periodic lull that comes after a succession of great waves! The sea has almost freed itself from frothy foam, the thunder and rush of the surf are momentarily stilled, when a high wall of green water is seen approaching the shore. With unhurried speed it moves forward, momentarily becoming steeper and more menacing, until, breaking with terrible might, it rushes impetuously upon the strand.

As I listened to the sublime deep-toned music of the sea, a small company of bird-visitors passed unexpectedly across the stormy Atlantic. Flying in the teeth of the gale, five barnacle geese steered south. At times they sped like shearwaters close above the water's surface, their background some great wave, green and white crested, against which their handsome black and white plumage was seen to perfection. Although two green cormorants, steering the same course, had been brought momentarily to a standstill by the wind, the geese forced their way southward against the gale at an astonishing rate. I am doubtful whether the eagle himself could have travelled so fast as they.

Whence had come the geese on this testing flight? From Shillay or Harris, perhaps, or from spray-drenched Gaisgeir, or mayhap even from far northern lands already in the grip of snow and frost.

Abroad upon the wild and foam-flecked waters were other birds. On back-bent wings a solan skimmed southward in the shelter of seas that towered but did not break; in a turmoil of waters a cormorant fished, heedless of the surf that momentarily threatened to engulf it. Along the shore, wherever the rocks gave them shelter from the gale, bright-plumaged redwings fed, and from his bed among the bents a snipe sprang high into the air, and was instantly blown like a leaf at the mercy of the storm.

In the path of the oncoming seas one great rock stood sturdily. Through a narrow opening in it each wave rushed with a loud, hissing sound. Quickly the wave passed, and the rock, streaming white with frothy rivulets, emerged from the foamy maelstrom.

It is not only during southerly and southwesterly gales that the Atlantic waves sweep magnificently in upon the shores of the Isles. West winds bring mountainous breakers, and on some of the northerly Isles the north-west seas are heaviest of all.

It is curious that on the veering of the wind from west to north-west the ocean haze should vanish, and a steel-green heaven, set with vast *cumulus* or *nimbus* clouds of pale grey, stretch away and away to the heaving horizon. On the breath of these north-west storms thunder travels—for in the Isles thunder is a thing of winter rather than of summer, and comes almost always on a gale of west or north-west wind. With uncanny speed the storms of thunder and lightning sweep in towards the low spray-drenched shores. They strike the land, and a squall of hail sweeps the sodden fields with such violence that neither man nor beast can stand against it. The lightning is vivid, but the roll of the thunder can scarce be heard above the roar of the wind and the hiss of the hailstones. But quickly the storm passes away to leeward, and the winter sun once more sheds his pale beams over the land.

And what of *Gaoth Tuadh,* the north wind, and his three sons that were named White Wings, White Feet, and White Hands?

White Feet wanders swiftly down upon the Isles from the blue ice-masses which lie always upon the breast of the Greenland ocean. It is the tread of White Feet upon Hebrid seas that churns the Atlantic into short-crested seas so that the westerly swell is broken up and rushes no more on Haskeir nan Ron.

In the Isles the north wind is a fine-weather wind, and brings with it sharp invigorating air, so that even the most distant rocks and isles stand out clearly. In the blue sky white clouds sail southwards. The ocean, and each peaty loch, reflect the blue of heaven. The surf upon outpost reefs gleams white, and even in autumn larks mount into the country of the air with joyous song. By the people of the Isles the north wind, provided it be not too boisterous, is greeted with pleasure. By none is it more appreciated than the crew of the small mail-boat, for in the Minch the northerly seas are seldom heavy.

But of late years the north wind in winter has rarely held for more than a day or two at a time. Towards evening on the second, if not indeed of the first, day of its life, the black wind (as the north wind is sometimes called) drops to the lightest of airs. The Isles are bathed in a soft rosy glow; the peat smoke rises in thin blue columns into the serene sky, where, one by one, the planets and the fixed stars light their lamps. At nightfall a band of pale light burns on the northern horizon and sends out ghostly streamers towards the zenith. These are the Northern Lights or the Merry Dancers, and there is a legend in the west that when the fallen angels were cast out of heaven, one company became the Fairies, a second the Blue Men that of a moonlight night play shinty on the waters of the Minch, and the third the Northern Lights.

The Merry Dancers almost always herald a change of weather, and before dawn the crisp air and the clear skies are gone, and our old friend the south wind is sweeping with momentarily increasing speed across the misty shores of the Isles.

T11-26

ON BEINN MHOR OF SOUTH UIST

As one reached the higher slopes of Beinn Mhor the heather gradually became more stunted and weather-beaten. Not even the hardy club moss, *Lycopodium selago,* existed above 1,500 feet on Beinn Mhor, yet from that height up to 2,000 feet many violets showed their blue flowers amongst the green of the hill grass. July violets are rare. To find them one must climb to the highest and most wind-swept grounds. Yet on this fifth day of July the violets of Beinn Mhor were scarcely yet in full blossom. Their flower shoots are very short at such an elevation, for they are dependent upon the shelter of the scanty grass in their fight for life in this region of storms.

To the very top of the hill the blaeberry, *Vaccinium myrtillus,* extended but nowhere did one see a single flower bud or blossom and each leaf was deeply pigmented with reddish brown—perhaps as a protection against the strong and cold winds which so often blow here.

The last few hundred feet of the hill—short, springy turf with a few stones scattered across it—seemed ideal ground for ptarmigan, but this bird does not nest upon any hill of South Uist, although stragglers, perhaps from Skye, occasionally are seen in autumn and winter.

There are three tops to Beinn Mhor. From the west top a very narrow, rocky ridge leads to the main top, Buail a' Ghoil, and from that again to the south top, a full mile distant, overlooking the Minch. Of a windless summer day the way along the ridge is narrow enough. During the gusts of a winter storm it must be quite impassable.

The summit of the Beinn, when seen on a summer's day, is remarkable for its alpine flowers. No cushion pink *(Silene acaulis)* brightens the hill-top, but its place is taken by an unlooked-for plant, the sea thrift *(Armeria maritima).* During the climb one had noticed it at 1,000 feet, but sparingly. Now, upon the summit it was everywhere. In niches of the barren and wind-swept rocks, growing upon even the most exposed knolls, and in the more sheltered situations covering the ground, these flowers of varying shades of pink and red were a delight to the eye.

The sea thrift, it is true, is generally associated with the shores, yet it is found upon many of the Scottish hills, and even far inland upon the tops of the Cairngorms.

The alpine willow, *Salix herbacea,* which grows so plentifully upon the high hills of the Scottish mainland and extends towards the North Pole as far as Bear Island, grows but sparingly upon Beinn Mhor, and the soil formation is unsuited for the mountain azalea. On the slopes of the hill *Saxifraga stellaris* had been passed in flower beside the wells and small hill burns; here upon the summit it clustered about the dark rocks, its flowers weather beaten and stunted, or long-stemmed and flourishing, according as to whether they had received shelter or not.

The habitat of the plant and the appearance of its flowers on the hilltop were very different from those of this saxifrage at the lower levels, and it was not easy to recognize them as belonging to the same species. There is one characteristic, however, which unfailingly identifies the starry saxifrage: the two small spots of yellow at the base of each petal.

From the top of the hill a great buttress dropped sheer, grim even on this perfect summer day. Yet its stern aspect was softened by the flowers that clung precariously, so it seemed, to each minute ledge. Besides many plants of the sea thrift and starry saxifrage, the rose root, *Rhodiola rosea,* bloomed here in profusion, its golden flowers contrasting with the crimson blossoms of the sea thrift and the white fragile petals of the saxifrage, so that the great cliff formed a natural rock garden of surprising beauty. Beneath this cliff, where the peregrine nests and where many years ago the eagle had his home, a narrow, grassy ledge crosses the hill diagonally. Only one man, so tradition has it, has ever crossed this dangerous pass, and he was Gillespie Dubh, fleeing from his enemies in close pursuit. Thus the rocky and narrow ledge is known to this day as the Bealach of Gillespie Dubh. Another pass—an accessible one, this—across the shoulder of Beinn Mhor is named after one Donald Gorm.

At one's feet, so it seemed, lay the Minch, altogether still. Great masses of cumulus clouds—for a thunder plump was forming out to sea—were reflected in the water, so that the sea assumed unlooked-for colours, such as would have enchanted the eye of an artist. Softest greys and blues imperceptibly mingled, while away to the south the sea showed a curious and very beautiful lilac tint—such a tint as the snowy spires of distant Spitsbergen assume when seen from the cold waters of the Greenland Ocean.

HM-23

BARRA

The most southerly of the Outer Hebrides is Barra or, more correctly, the Barra group. Barra, and her lesser neighbours Vatersay and Sandray, Mingulay and Berneray, end in the high headland known as Barra Head. The journey from the mainland to Barra may be made either from Oban, by way of Mull and Tiree, or from Mallaig, by way of Eigg, Rum, Canna and Lochboisdale. I chose the latter approach and at midnight on a clear July day found myself off the Sound of Barra, with the island of Eriskay, where Prince Charlie first landed on Scottish soil, rising dark against the last of the sunset. As we approached Castlebay fog descended and it needed skilled seamanship to bring the steamer into this, the only port on Barra, guarded by the old ruins of Kiessimul Castle, rising dark from its tiny island.

Barra is generally supposed to be named after St Barr or Findbarr. His church, Cill Barr, was in olden times the principal church on the island, and in Martin Martin's day there was an image of the saint here. Barra has a population of 2,500, of whom all but 150 are Catholics. The MacNeils, of old named the 'Clan Neill Barray', make up most of the population (the Barra Head lighthouse relief boat and the lifeboat are manned entirely by MacNeils), their chief being MacNeil of Barra, who in earlier times owned, in addition to Barra, the islands of Vatersay, Sandray, Pabbay, Mingulay and Berneray. It is recorded that in the year 1427 Alexander, third Lord of the Isles, granted Barra to Gillean MacNeil, but the family seem to have been established here even before that time. Although so powerful a chief in his own country, MacNeil, as Martin records, in the year 1700 held his lands in vassalage of Sir Donald MacDonald of Sleat, 'to whom he pays £40 per annum and a Hawk if required, and is oblig'd to furnish him a certain Number of Men upon extraordinary Occasions'. The hawk was probably taken from Muldaonich, a high, rocky island standing near the entrance to Castlebay and, in Martin's day, a deer forest holding seventy to eighty deer.

Kiessimul Castle, MacNeil's island stronghold, probably dates from the fifteenth century and stands a quarter of a mile from the shore, off the port of Castlebay. Built on a small, rocky island, the castle embraces the whole of that island. It is surrounded with a wall, as Martin says, 'two stories high', and within the wall are the ruins of a tower, entered by a stair rising along the north wall, a hall, and other buildings. When MacNeil and his lady were absent, a constable was in charge of the castle, and Martin tells us that he was refused admittance to it, being thought the representative of a foreign power. The approach to Kiessimul Castle at high water is remarkable; one lands actually on the castle steps and walks through the sea gate in the high wall. The keep is in a fair state of preservation and before the war MacNeil of Barra, who is an American citizen, had thoughts of restoring it. In the smallness of its island it is probably unique among Hebridean castles. Castlebay is, next to Stornoway, the chief herring-fishing centre in the Outer Hebrides. The herring taken here in summer are of unusual quality and Castlebay kippers are celebrated for their succulence.

The eastern side of Barra is rocky; from it rises Heaval, 1,260 feet, giving a magnificent view on a clear day. The shore of Barra on its west side is of white sand, and green, fertile machair. When my friend and I walked round it on a July day of sun and shade, the Atlantic waves were breaking white on these sands and on the machair and the fields adjacent to it many flowers scented the air. On the low promontory named Borve Point are the ruins of St Brendan's chapel; below the chapel it can be seen that the rock has been hewn out to form a harbour which, Father John MacMillan tells me, was much used in the days before Castlebay became a port. He said that in those days the west side of the island was more important than the east as a fishing centre, and that the people fishing from Borve Point used to cast lots for their fishing-ground on February I (old style), and that no one would think of fishing beyond the ground they had been given by lot. Alexander Carmichael mentions this custom in his *Carmina Gadelica*. Cod and ling were the fish generally taken; Martin says that smacks used to come from Orkney for the fish. A short distance north of this promontory the Amhuinn Mhór, *Great River*, enters the sea. Although called the Great River it is easy to leap across it; in Martin's day salmon used to be caught here with the net. This stream enters the Atlantic at a particularly beautiful sandy shore, Traigh Thammara; as the tide ebbs the stream cuts a deep and narrow channel through it, with vertical sides as though cut with a knife. The countless grains of sand which are constantly being carried seaward on the current give the stream here a milky appearance not unlike that of a glacier river.

The coast road, after passing close to Traigh Thammara and crossing the machair, soon turns east, leaves the coast, and crosses a stretch of rough moorland country. At North Bay it again reaches the sea, and here a road strikes off northward to Traigh Mhór, *the Great Strand*. At the south end of Traigh Mhór, Barra is nearly divided into two by the Atlantic. In the words of a seventeenth-century account, 'the Main seas doth come from the West, and the other sea from the east, and almost the said two seas doth forgadder and meet with other'.

Traigh Mhór is important to Barra, since it is the landing-ground of the aeroplane which twice daily flies in over the strand. In the morning the plane arrives from Renfrew then continues northward to Benbecula, calling again in the afternoon at Traigh Mhór on its return journey to Renfrew. The sea at spring tides recedes a whole mile eastward from Traigh Mhór, leaving exposed a broad stretch of firm white sand—an ideal natural landing-ground for aircraft. Many Barra people have travelled by air but not by railway!.

Since time immemorial Traigh Mhór has been noted for the abundance of its cockles. The people of Barra were formerly accustomed to bring their horses with them, and load them with cockles 'and cold (could) come, they should have als many as there horses were able to carrie everie day'.

The narrow strip of machair which rises between the east and west seas is much broken up into little mounds of grass-grown sand. This was the site of the small chapel of Cill Mhuire, *St Mary's*, of which only a small part of one wall remains. The earth within this chapel had miraculous properties. If those at sea should be in peril, the possessor of the sacred soil, 'if the wind or stormie strong weather were cruell and vehement, if he wold caste a litle of this earth into the sea, it wold pacifie the wind and the sea wold grow calme immediatelie efter the casting.'

To the north of Traigh Mhór is Cill Barr, *the Church of St Barry*. In Martin's time a wooden image of the saint, covered with a linen cloth, was exposed on the altar. There are several Irish saints of the name Find-barr and it is not certain which of them the chapel of Cill Barr commemorates. The inhabitants celebrated the anniversary of St Barr on September 27, and on one occasion, so Martin Martin tells us, a foreign priest landed on the island on the very day and hour of the ceremony. According to ancient custom, he was asked to preach a commemoration sermon on St Barr. He replied that he would gladly preach on St Peter or St Paul, but of St Barr he had never heard, so was unable to extol him. The inhabitants thereupon told the stranger that he could be no true priest if he had not heard of St Barr and they parted much dissatisfied with one another.

Within the church of St Barr, now a ruin, is the burial-place of the MacNeils of Barra and there are ancient recumbent stones recalling the sculptured stones of Iona. The only rune-inscribed stone known in the Hebrides was formerly in the churchyard of Cill Barr; it is now in the National Museum of Antiquities. The stone bears on one face a cross of Celtic type; on the other an inscription in runes, which have not been satisfactorily deciphered.

The ruins of two smaller chapels stand near the church. In fine weather a wide and inspiring view may be had from the little hill, Beinn Eoligarry, which rises behind Cill Barr.

There is beauty on the sea and on the land; the sea shows many shades of colour, from cobalt far out in the deep water to green above the sand, the green becoming very pale where the water is shallow. Across the Sound of Barra rises the long ridge of Beinn Mhór of South Uist; north-east and east are the Cuillin of Skye and the Cuillin of Rum; on the far eastern horizon, on the Scottish mainland, the peaks of Knoydart are seen faintly, among them being the sharp, unmistakable summit of Sgurr na h-Aide, *Peak of the Hat*. Coll and Tiree are on the south-east horizon, with the hills of Mull behind them. St Kilda may be visible in very clear weather, but could not be seen on the day when I was on Beinn Eoligarry. Fulmar petrels rarely fly overland yet on this summer day these ocean birds were gliding backwards and forwards like gigantic swallows low over the machair, backwards and forwards without rest, although there were no nesting cliffs in the neighbourhood. It may be that the nearness of the sea, east and west, gives them confidence; they added a great charm to the machair on that July day.

The chain of islands running southward from Barra and ending with Berneray (on which stands the well-known lighthouse on Barra Head) is high and rocky, with sandy bays which shine snow-white in summer sun. Mingulay, with cliffs over 800 feet high, is the highest of these isles. Some fifty years ago its entire population of 180 persons migrated to the island of Vatersay, near the main island of Barra. Vatersay is the only Hebridean island with a population entirely Catholic. On Bagh an Iair, its west bay, on September 28, 1853, the *Annie Jane,* carrying emigrants, was wrecked and some 350 men, women and children were drowned. The cliffs of Mingulay are the home of great seabird colonies, and the inhabitants of the island were accustomed to take these birds and salt them for winter use.

Separated from Mingulay by the wild Sound of Pabbay is the island of Pabbay, now deserted and a grazing place for sheep and cattle. There is an old graveyard here; unusual, in that it is on an artificial mound, the graves being near, or on, the summit of the mound. Through the action of water some of the bones were exposed of a man of exceptional stature. My informant was born on Pabbay. His father was a man of six feet four inches in height, and the jaw-bone which became exposed was so large that it 'fitted over his jaw, and scarcely touched his whiskers'. In a stone coffin was found a skeleton with a clam shell over the face. Clam shells were used as drinking cups, and it has been suggested that this man had been buried with his favourite drinking shell.

Berneray, on Barra Head, the most southerly of the Outer Hebrides, has a lighthouse at its highest point where, 683 feet above the sea, a light is exhibited from a white stone tower sixty feet in height. The tower is built on Sron an Dùin, at the western side of the island, one of the highest and most stormy lighthouse sites in the British Isles. On the summer day when I visited it the north wind was blowing with great power past the lighthouse buildings, and was sending dark flurries over the sea at the cliff foot. Puffins nested at the top of the cliff, and on the ledges beneath sat guillemots in close ranks, razorbills, a few fulmars, and, farther down, colonies of kittiwakes. Occasionally the sun lighted up the green grassy slopes of Mingulay (the precipices are on the west and north-west sides) and the white sands of Village Bay, where the school and church still stand. Waves were rolling through the sound of Mingulay, and were breaking tumultuously at the foot of the cliffs. There is some truth in what a native of Barra once said to me: 'Barra is nothing but a breakwater.'

I have mentioned that Barra enjoys the benefits of an air service, which now brings the first-class mail of the islanders. Yet the communications between Barra and Skye show no improvement with the years. Take my own journey back to my home in northern Skye. My friend, who was returning to London, left Traigh Mhór by air and was home for supper in his own house. I left at approximately the same time, yet twenty-nine hours elapsed before I reached home. Taking the steamer from Castlebay to Lochboisdale, I joined the midnight mail-boat for Mallaig. At Mallaig I caught the morning boat to Kyle of Lochalsh, there awaited the afternoon steamer to Portree, completing my journey to northern Skye by bus, nearly twenty-four hours after my friend had eaten his supper in London.

AH-50

THE NARRATIVE OF DOMHNALL MÓR

In the storm of May 1 in the year 1897 the entire able-bodied population of a Hebridean island was lost at sea. The isle which suffered this tragic and sudden loss is Pabbay. The meaning of Pabbay is *Priest's Island* and there are several islands bearing this name. This is the Pabbay which rises near Barra Head, most southerly of the Outer Hebrides. The narrator of the Saga was Domhnall Mór Eileanach, *Big Donald of the Island*. He bore the title 'Islesman' because he was born on Mingulay (the island next to Barra Head) and when Mingulay was depopulated moved to the neighbouring island of Vatersay. From Vatersay he later lived on Barra where, at the small township of Brevaig, I heard his narrative, and was thrilled by the intensity and beauty of his language as he recalled, half in English and half in Gaelic, the exciting hours of that memorable tempest of long ago.

Domhnall Mór, whose name officially was Donald MacPhee, was of distinguished lineage. He was a MacPhee of Colonsay. The earlier form of the family name was MacDuffie, and in *The Annals of Ulster* can be read a record of the founder of the family, MacDubh Shithe, a name which may be translated *Son of the* Black Man of Peace, and was head of the school on Iona in the year 1164. The MacPhees later incurred the wrath of the Lord of the Isles who killed the head of the family but the ancestor of Domhnall Mór, Coinneach Mór, *Big Kenneth*, escaped in his boat to the island of Eigg. When, at a later period, the MacLeods of Dunvegan ("Maybe," said Domhnall Mór to me fiercely, "Maybe you'll be a MacLeod?") massacred the population of Eigg by suffocating them by smoke as they hid in a cave, Coinneach Mór was one of the few survivors. He escaped in his boat together with two old men (who died at sea) and a boy. They sailed towards the north-west and reached Barra where Coinneach Mór placed himself under the protection of MacNeil of Barra.

It so happened that no news had come to Barra for some time from the precipitous outlying island of Mingulay and MacNeil, taking Coinneach Mór with him, sailed in his galley to Mingulay, sending Coinneach Mór ashore to investigate. He found no living person on the isle: the entire population had died of the plague. When Coinneach Mór returned to the shore and reported this grim news to MacNeil he was forbidden to embark or indeed to leave the island lest he should have caught the infection. He was provided with a glowing peat with which to kindle a fire and a supply of food and was left alone on Mingulay for a year. The hill on which he was accustomed to watch for the coming of the relief boat is to this day spoken of as MacPhee's Hill and the ledge of the rock on which he rested is MacPhee's Bed. At the end of the year MacNeil arrived at Mingulay. He brought with him a wife whom he had chosen for the lonely man, but he forbad him to return to Barra for another year. The loneliness of Coinneach Mór was now lessened and his direct descendant was Donald Mór Eileanach, this tall, erect man, with flashing eyes and distinguished bearing. He was over eighty years of age when he narrated his story.

As he described the loss of the Pabbay boat, in which was the entire able-bodied population of the island, he lived again those intense, momentous hours of May 1897 when his own boat, from the neighbouring island of Mingulay, was often on the verge of destruction. In those days the men of Pabbay and Mingulay were accustomed to set long lines ('the great lines' as they are called) for cod and ling during the months of April, May and June. At this season of the year good, steady weather is to be expected over the Atlantic, and on the morning of this early May day Big Donald's boat was lifting the great lines on the fishing bank known as Cuan a' Bhocain, *the Fishing Bank of the Monster*, when a hard breeze sprang up from south by east, increasing rapidly to gale force.

A wild sea rose and with the sail made as small as they could reef it and the bottom of the boat filled with great fish, they set out on their hazardous six-mile passage to Mingulay, the waves breaking in every direction and threatening to engulf their small undecked craft. The Pabbay boat at this time was farther out to sea and neither they, nor any other human eye, saw it again. By skilled use of the helm, the greatest of the breaking waves were avoided and gradually they reached the neighbourhood of Barra Head.

Here, said Big Donald, was the abode of two great and terrible giants who lived in the air currents which a severe gale imprisoned in two high and narrow passages named Slochd na Beiste, *Hollow of the Beast*, and Slochd Dubh an Dùin, *Black Hollow of the fort*. Both these ravines are on the west side of Barra Head (more correctly Bernera) near the lighthouse. The wind held prisoner in the hollows periodically burst from them in squalls of extraordinary violence. Exulting in their might they contended with extreme ferocity above the turbulent tide-swept sound between Barra Head and Mingulay. The giants as they fought and wrestled rose high in the air then descended, forming whirlpools and eddies which penetrated a score of feet beneath the surface of the ocean. The giants were accompanied by the grey, frenzied Marcaichean Sìne, *Riders of the Tempest*, the poetic Gaelic name for spindrift that was evidently held in high esteem by Donald Mór. The Riders of the Tempest on this day rose almost to the ceiling of low cloud which raced across the sky.

The appearance of the terrible whirlpool and spindrift was watched for closely and with anxiety for they might well engulf a small open boat. As a Rider of the Tempest bore down upon them the close-reefed sail was instantly lowered and the crew stood on the sail to prevent it being torn or carried away; when the spindrift had passed the sail was again hoisted. The intensity of feeling in the narrator's voice brought that stern and tremendous scene vividly before my mind.

The wind had now veered to south-south-west, bringing in the full forces of the Atlantic waves and swell. It was with profound thankfulness that the crew sailed beyond the reach of the giants, and it can be imagined with what thankfulness the people of Mingulay saw their approach and safe return.

Since the shift of wind would have made it still more difficult for the Pabbay boat to reach that island their only hope, as Donald Mór emphasized during his vivid narrative, was to have sailed across the Minch to Dunvegan Head in Skye but he believed that the boat filled and sank while attempting, close-hauled, to reach Pabbay. He said that some of the bodies were washed ashore on the north coast of Ireland, almost one hundred miles to the south.

Although that storm occurred more than half a century before the early spring day when Donald Mór narrated his story, his tale was told with such a wealth of detail that the tragedy might well have occurred only a few weeks before. When describing the battle of the giants he rose from his chair and stood erect with arms held high above his head, while his voice rose and shook with emotion. The past became the present, and in that small room one could sense the coming of the huge, breaking waves and the tense moment when the skill of the steersman was pitted against them. It was evident that they had sailed very close to death and did not expect to reach land.

I realized that I was present at one of the closing scenes of an era when I listened to the narrative of Domhnall Mór Eileanach, which lasted for the best part of two hours—two hours of dramatic fervour, with never a dull moment. The sun shone through the small window, lighting up the bowed figure, at times lost in thought and sunk on the chair, at times with erect bearing and voice vibrating with feeling and passion. He was an islesman of the old type, a grand man.

HD-63

Gannet and young on the Bass Rock.

4

Ways That Are Gone

People were never absent from Seton Gordon's world and he had a great facility for making friends wherever he went among the islands. All too aware of the irreversible changes, he records this world with a tenderness born of first-hand involvement. How many children today – or their parents – would even know what a haystack is?

Croft house in Barra, 1921.

Islanders gathering sand for spreading on the earth floors of their houses.

FELLOW-PASSENGERS

The sky is grey and leaden. Mist streams across the low hills. The machair and the fields run water. In the friendly shelter of a house are standing a small group of people who are ready to leave this mist-drenched isle for the wide world beyond. In the harbour, sheltered by encircling skerries, small fishing-boats ride at anchor. A skiff rowed against the strong wind slowly approaches one of them and its occupants, clambering aboard, endeavour to coax the engine of this motor-boat to life. The moisture-laden wind has dulled the magneto. It obstinately refuses to supply the vital spark. The men tirelessly swing the starting-handle. The small gathering of would-be wayfarers behind the house optimistically watch their efforts. Four sheep, tied in pairs and also destined for the mainland, absorb the general attention. A sagacious but nervous collie shepherds the sheep anxiously. They slide over seaweed-covered rocks and are finally halted at the water's edge where they nibble listlessly at the *fucus* seaweed. In a neighbouring field a cow with pig-like actions ploughs up the sandy soil with her nose in her search for discarded potatoes.

At last the men desist in their efforts to bring the refractory motor to life. They now board another fishing-boat but its engine is equally sullen. The small assembly on the shore remains hopeful. The people talk in Gaelic animatedly among themselves. They watch a lobster-fisher's craft which approaches the harbour with swaying sails, moving swiftly through the sounding seas. Slowly the tide creeps in along the streaming shore. On the sandy beach stranded seaware lies thickly. Here birds from the Arctic feed actively among the seaweed that will soon be spread upon the fields to nourish the grass. In summer, these far-travelled birds nest beside eternal snows; in winter, they rarely see snow but are often lashed by hail squalls that scour the Atlantic when the south wind veers to west.

At length the engine of the motor-boat unwillingly awakens. The anchor is weighed and the boat is brought alongside the slippery seaweed-covered rocks. With difficulty passengers, sheep, and luggage are taken on board. A chorus of farewells is heard. "Beannachd leth agus turus math" (*Blessings and a good journey*) are wished. A dog whose master is on the boat leaps on board at the last moment. He is caught and thrown protesting ashore where he falls half in the water and laboriously climbs the wet rocks. Undaunted he is preparing to spring on board a second time when he is caught by a restraining hand. Wild-eyed he turns his head and seems about to bite the hand when he is pulled back relentlessly and falls with a splash into the sea. In curious contrast to this animated picture is an old bearded fisherman who sits impassive and silent on the wet rocks and at intervals hoists one—and sometimes two—small saithe into the air. He drops them into his tin, rebaits his hooks, and casts them upon the troubled waters.

We are an interesting company in the boat. One man has passed most of his life in China and other distant lands. It is he who is in charge of the sheep. A young fellow is journeying to Greenock to join a thousand-ton yacht for a Mediterranean cruise and is looking forward to the calm sea and bright sunshine of Monte Carlo where he has found the climate in winter finer than the weather in the Isles in summer. He remarks that there are five Gaelic-speaking men on the yacht and that the skipper, "a fine man, has the Gaelic and plenty of it." The speaker knows the Mediterranean well. He has even tempted the goddess of chance in a mild way at the tables at Monte Carlo.

We steer out into the crowded and confused waves. Our craft is small but sturdy. She is ballasted with granite blocks, laid side by side with skill so that they form an even floor. One hears short disjointed conversation. The spray from the short, eager waves is blown by the gale over the craft. Daylight ebbs. Dusk falls on land and sullen sea. A handsome long-tailed drake flies across our bows. With him is his sober-plumaged duck. Black guillemots ride the seas. Ahead of us is the churn of the flood-tide as it sweeps in a mighty stream eastward. A smother of white waves marks a submerged sand-bank, treacherous in thick weather. We are now almost across the Sound and approach a seaweed-covered shore where stands a lonely house. The boat is skilfully brought in close to the rocks and a light-footed member of the crew leaps ashore and by means of ropes draws the boat nearer. A narrow board is laid between the shore and the boat and, like Captain Hook's victims, we walk the plank one at a time. In the cottage the woman of the house welcomes us. She does not speak English but her Gaelic is clear and musical. The kettle is boiled and with true island hospitality she entertains the visitors to tea. The woman is anxious for her son who has put out to sea alone in his small boat after saithe. All agree that the evening is too wild for fishing and as dusk deepens the coast is searched through binoculars for the boat.

At length comes the welcome news that he has been sighted, rowing strongly homeward against wind and tide. Soon her son enters the house and, dripping with rain and sea water, displays his catch. He is tall and strong, a player on the *piob mhor* and with much war service. He entertains the company with piping while search is made for the owner of a motor-car.

He is found gathering in the cattle for the night and, after an interval, a wee boy enters the room with a lantern and announces in a deep voice that the car is ready. We seat ourselves in an ancient Ford and are borne across a country of rushing wind, driving rain, and hurrying mists to the mail-boat's port of call on the far side of the Hebridean island. We remain here until five o'clock on the following morning. Pitch darkness hides land and sea at that hour. The mail-steamer, moored at the pier, sways gently. By her lights small waves can be seen to crowd in upon her from the darkness. Here and there on the quay phantom-like figures dart, coaxing unwilling cattle down the steamer's gangway by the light of a flickering lantern. The captain, a dark figure in oilskins and sou'wester, takes his place on the bridge and rings down to the engineer. The engines throb. We leave the pier and glide out across the sea loch to the open Minch beyond. One of the officers holds a small bird which he has found lying on the deck. It is a storm petrel, dazed by the strong electric lights which have attracted it unwillingly to the ship. It lies quietly in the hand—a small, delicate, black bird, no larger than a swallow. It is uninjured, and when thrown into the air rises with graceful flight on the breath of the storm and in a second is lost to view in the darkness. Mother Carey's Chicken, as seamen name the storm petrel, is a nocturnal bird that is rarely seen. It is oceanic in its habits and when it seeks the shelter of sea lochs the weather in the Atlantic is unusually stormy.

Soon we are on the open sea, and are rolling heavily. An inhospitable lee shore slowly becomes visible as dawn strengthens. Dark skerries and low rocky islands against which the surf breaks in clouds rise to the dreary dawn. The travellers of yesterday again meet on the swaying decks and are joined by one who was not with us last night—a keen politician who is voyaging to support his candidate on a neighbouring island. Conversation is difficult. The wind snatches at our words and hurries them away. Angry seas, roaring menacingly, follow and pass us. We roll giddily. As daylight strengthens we see many birds around the ship. Fulmar petrels urge themselves into the gale, flying gracefully and powerfully and making the flight of the kittiwakes seem untrained and feeble. A fine great northern diver a bird as large as goose passes us and, like the fulmars and kittiwakes, he also is heading into the wind. A great northern diver flies so rarely that many fishermen believe he is unable to rise into the air. A rare bird appears: a fork-tailed petrel, a bird very slightly larger than a storm petrel. With erratic, curious flight it keeps station ahead of us. Now, like St. Peter (after whom it is named) it drops lightly to the sea and seems to walk upon the heaving waves. Now, like a leaf tossed by the storm, it drifts far over the waters, only to return with careless ease and again dip to pick up some minute object invisible to the human eye. Gannets, strong-winged and determined, pass us, flying into the wind and flocks of duck move fast and high beneath the stormy heavens. Thus throughout the morning we pitch and roll. When the weather forecast is brought from the wireless room to the bridge it gives no comfort but a further gale warning to all ships.

But the Isles are not always storm-beset. Comes at length a winter day when the air is clear, the sky is blue, and hill and island rise in beauty. The people of the Isles may seek their fortunes in the four corners of the earth, but in their hearts the love for their island remains and burns more brightly during prolonged absence. They think often of that island home. In their minds they hear the roar of Atlantic waves; in foreign lands they smell the fragrant peat smoke that rises above the small thatched houses. Thus they return home happily to tell of strange sights and customs and to be refreshed by the peace and quiet of the Hebrides.

IOW-33

The *Earl of Zetland*.

A DAY AT THE PEATS

A May morning in Trotternish of Skye, a grey sky, thin showers over the Minch, a light air from the west blowing across the land. From the wee houses people are appearing. They meet on the road and a procession is formed to the moor—to the peat moss where there is to be much hard work before the day is done.

When the peat moss is reached there is great activity. Some of the people combine to help a neighbour less fortunate than themselves at his or her peat-cutting, others work in little family parties.

It is a peculiarity of Trotternish that peats are dug with an ordinary spade, although in most parts of Skye the old-fashioned wooden spade, or *toirsgian,* is still used.

In digging peats the topmost layer of vegetation must first be pared off then, working along a straight and narrow strip, the peat-cutter slices off the peats with his spade while his wife, or perhaps one of his children, picks them up and lays them flat on the moor to dry. They rest there, soft and spongy, altogether unlike the peats that one sees when, fully dried, they burn brightly on the crofter's fires.

Noon comes. The air is warmer. Larks mount into the sky with joyous song. The *cannach,* or bog cotton, waves its feathery heads. Here and there upon the heather peat fires are lighted for the midday meal. Blue smoke rises into the air. It curls slowly upward. White table-cloths are spread upon the moor. Tea is brewed. The people sit round the fire, tired but contented. But the rest is a short one, for there are many peats still to cut and the weather may change.

Work is renewed. Skilfully the brown peats are sliced off. They are thrown across the moor to dry in the sun, and fall with a thud. From time to time branches of hazel trees are dug up; occasionally even the nuts are exposed. Far down in the peat the blades of a wiry grass have been so wonderfully preserved that they are apparently as fresh and strong as on that distant day when they were over-grown by the *sphagnum* moss. Perhaps Norse galleys sailed the Minch in the summers when these grasses grew and these hazel twigs were clothed with leaves, and Biornal, the Norwegian princess who has her grave beside Quirang, dwelled in Dun Daibhidh.

So the peat-cutters, working without pause, bring vividly to the imagination the old forgotten times. Now and again a remark in Gaelic is passed round, a joke is enjoyed. The dogs doze contentedly. At the margin of the peat-moss cattle pasture the grass. Flowers of the milkwort, some of them deep blue, others of delicately tinted pink, are growing on the boggy ground. The draw moss, beloved of sheep and deer, is in blossom, and the red lousewort also.

Evening approaches. Everywhere upon the heather wet peats lie. They represent the labour of the day. On the ground they will remain until they are drier. Then they will be set up on end, in threes.

The best peats are black when dry. They are as hard as coal, and burn as brightly and as well. Such peats are of great value, but are not commonly found. Often they are so far from the nearest road that the labour of bringing them in is too great.

Tea-time comes. Fresh peats are thrown upon the moorland fires. Again columns of thick blue smoke rise in the quiet air. Kettles are boiled. The tea is infused. The people discuss the day's work, then wander slowly homeward across the moor, past Martin's Well, past the ruins of Martin's House. This Martin's end was tragic. Though he was of a well-known Skye family his house was humble and thatched. He married a grand lady. Martin one stormy day lay ill in bed with pneumonia. The house was leaking. His wife said to him, "My father's hen-house is better than this." Martin rose from his bed. Ill as he was, he went out into the rain and wind. He repaired the leak in the roof. The next day he was dead.

The Martins are said to have come to Skye from Ireland originally as part of the dowry of Nighean Chathain. In those days men were of more value than money, and so the lady brought with her twenty young men from three Irish clans. We are told that the Martins and the MacQueens were two of these clans.

That early classic, *The Western Isles,* published in 1703, was the work of Martin Martin, a man of immense strength. On the hill near Duntulm is a great stone, known as Ultach Mhartin a' Bhealaich (*the Armful of Martin of the Pass*), and it is said that Martin Martin placed it in the position in which it now lies and whence none now living can so much as move it.

For centuries the MacQueens held the farm of Garafad, near Staffin, rent free, on condition that they supplied yearly a certain number of salmon to the proprietor. They are said to have lost their farm through their inability to supply MacDonald of the Isles with the requisite number of these fish.

At evening the clouds are dispersing; the air is very clear. Northward, sea and sky are pearly grey. It is hard to see where the two meet for the sleeping ocean seems as cloud. Rudha Reidh of Gairloch creeps, tapering, out into the Minch. The low coast of Lewis, beyond the blue Shiant Isles, lies on the horizon. Behind the black ruins of Duntulm thin shafts of sunlight move slowly southwards across the Minch. They resemble the pale fingers of the Merry Dancers, or the rays of a searchlight.

Pools of light lie upon the Minch. There is no breeze stirring here. Beinn Rodil of Harris seems near; Eaval, most graceful of Outer Hebridean hills, towers from North Uist. Upon Clisham of Harris a wandering cloud rests. At first no larger than a man's hand, it grows fast. It encircles the hill, but above it the shapely cone emerges free.

Here, on the slopes of Trotternish, a lamb bleats. The waves murmur drowsily upon Scour Bay. Sea-gulls call. From a hillside of stunted birch a wandering cuckoo chimes her bells. A heather linnet mounts into the air in song. On the fields beside the shore the young grass is emerald. Upon the brown soil the oats are faintly green. Dust lies thick upon the road, for no rain has fallen for weeks.

The sun sets. Twilight deepens. The people are back at their homes, tired and contented after their day's work. The cows are milked. The evening's labours before the Sabbath rest are completed. Suddenly the Scalpay light across the Minch flashes—once, twice, thrice. The black smoke of a passing steamer lies on the horizon. At midnight the afterglow creeps northward beyond the hills of Harris.

Another day at the peats has come and gone.

COS-29

The day at the peats.

SHEARING THE ISLAND SHEEP

The Minch lay grey, silent, and windless, beneath a dappled sky. On the shore beneath the old castle of Duntuilm a number of men were launching a large black boat from a hollow in the rocks. The heavy boat was dragged to the water's edge and floated on the flood-tide, a cargo of sheep was taken on board and with two men at each long oar we steered out into the Minch, our destination Fladday Chuain. Here, island sheep were to be sheared and the fattest of them taken from the islands where they had fed during the past year on the rich grass that is nourishing even in midwinter. Our crew consisted of strong Gaelic-speaking crofters, deeply bronzed by the ocean winds and summer sun. They bent to the heavy oars with a will, and as they drove the old boat through the quiet water they told stories of past days. We heard the narrative of the Aberdeen trawler which ran upon the rocks of Fladday Chuain during a winter storm. Her crew were on that inhospitable isle, six miles from Skye, for the best part of a week before their signals of distress were observed. The rescue party when they arrived at Fladday found that the crew of the trawler had built a raft on which they were preparing to venture across the stormy Minch had no help reached them.

As we crossed the sea puffins stared at us in mild surprise then dived precipitately when we were almost on them. Gannets passed low above the quiet waters, flying to and from distant fishing ground. Across the Minch the hills of Lewis and Harris, cloud-capped and deep blue, rose to the quiet sky.

In rather more than an hour's time we approached the island group. Bòrd Cruinn, *the Round Table*, Guala Mhor, *the Big Shoulder*, Gearran, *the Gelding*, were left astern and now we crossed the narrow sound separating that group from Fladday Chuain. Along the low shore of Fladday we sailed then landed from a small creek which monks long ago named Port an Teampuill, *the Harbour of the Temple* or *Church*. In this creek we anchored and, with difficulty because of the lowness of the tide, the sheep were lifted from the boat and skilfully passed on to the dry rocks by one of the crew who stood on a slippery seaweed-covered skerry beside the boat. The sea-thrift was almost over, and the grass was long and green. Above the tide-mark lay the long lines of some lobster fishermen who had trustingly left their gear on Fladday until they should return. When the last of the young sheep had been put on shore our crew took a few peats from the boat, lighted a fire, and made tea. The blue aromatic smoke curled into the air as the piper of the party by his music tempted the seals to swim close inshore.

When tea had been taken the resident sheep population of the island was rounded up and driven into a hollow in the rocks. Men stood at the entrance to this natural sheep pen and held pieces of sacking between them, giving the sheep the illusion that a firm barrier surrounded them and they made no attempt to break out. One after another the rams and ewes were skilfully and quickly shorn and then allowed their liberty, all but three or four which were to be taken back to Skye. The mail-boat with many passengers passed outward bound for Harris as we sailed from Fladday Chuain and crossed to Guala Mhor. In mid-channel a sunken rock rises: Bogha Mór, and it is fair in the way of any vessel foolhardy enough to venture through this narrow tide-swept channel. One winter night an unknown steamer had a wonderful escape. The lobster fishers from their bothy on Fladday heard her pass at full speed through this channel. How she escaped the sunken rocks they could not tell but in a very few minutes (such was her speed) she had reached the open sea all unaware of her recent deadly peril.

On Guala Mhor we landed to clip the sheep which were pastured there. Puffins in rows watched our arrival with dignified surprise. Razorbills flew backwards and forwards or guarded their large eggs and small grey-headed chicks. Kittiwakes called and guillemots grunted, groaned and squeaked. The bills and feet of many puffins were strewn about this island. Their murderers were perhaps the greater black-backed gulls which flew over our heads with hoarse cries. A party of razorbills hurried past, silvery fry dangling from their strong bills. The isle was full of sound and activity; even the midges were active.

It was late in the day when we landed on Bòrd Cruinn and its flat summit was none too easy to reach, since there is but one narrow defile up which it is possible to venture. Many storm petrels had been killed on this island; their wings lay about on the green grass. Here also the greater black-backs may have been the culprits.

Late that night we embarked for the return passage to Skye. Fog hid the hills of Uist, but on the horizon north-east the peaks of distant Sutherland rose up in soft sunlight. There was no wind to fill the sail and again a heavy row had to be faced. The ebb-tide had spent itself and as we approached Skye the flood, surging in from the west, threatened to bear us off our course. Steamships passed us, the grey smoke from their funnels rising straight into the air and the last of the gannets flew low on their graceful wings towards the distant fishing grounds to the east as the grey hand of dusk approached the Minch.

IOW-33

SUMMER SHIELINGS

In bygone days the summer shieling was an integral part of the life of the Highlands and islands of Scotland. But like many others of the old customs it has disappeared entirely from the mainland and almost entirely from the Isles.

To see summer shielings occupied, and to see shieling life, one must go to Lewis, the most northerly of the Outer Hebrides, for only on this island does the old custom survive.

Here the common grazing in some communities is not sufficiently fertile or extensive to feed the cattle during the whole year. It is arranged therefore to close the grazing for a certain period each summer and during that period the cows are taken to the moorlands to be pastured there, and the people tending their stock live in small primitive dwellings reached by means of a rough moorland track and often far from the nearest village.

Summer shielings are occupied only so long as the common grazing is closed. Some communities close their grazing for five, some for six, others for eight weeks. By the end of July the shieling season is over and the people return to their homes.

There is romance in shieling life. How delightful must it be to set out for the moorlands on a fine June morning with one's dog and one's cattle and live the simple life during the two finest months of the year! Long may the old custom continue.

It was late one evening when a friend and I reached the country of the shielings. The air was still, and here and there across the moor the blue peat smoke from the shielings rose into the air. My friend knew the inmates of one of the shielings, and as he conversed with them in Gaelic it was evident that we were expected to pass the night with our hosts, who insisted on giving up their dwelling to us and removing to the shieling of a neighbour.

The sun set, and the cows were herded in and were tethered around the wee house. On the horizon could be seen cattle being driven home to neighbouring shielings; here and there boys and girls were talking together, and perhaps discussing the arrival of the strangers. The peat fire was fanned into flame, and we sat down to a wonderful meal of eggs and bacon, scones, newly churned butter, and sweet cheese of which the Gaelic name is *gruth*. After supper there was much piping and dancing on the rough moorland outside, and as the moon rose golden in the east there was the singing of old Gaelic songs, such as Crodh Chailein and Fhir a' Bhata.

The peat fire flickered brightly, the two stools were as comfortable as many an armchair in more pretentious surroundings. Girlish voices singing the old songs with a lilt in them in the gloaming seemed to carry one back to things of a past age—to the days when Tearlach Og, Prince Charles Edward, sought sanctuary in the Long Island after his defeat. Only that afternoon we had visited a house upon the island of Scalpay on which the following inscription was written above the door [translated]: On this foundation was the house in which Prince Charles as a wanderer passed some days as a fugitive in his rightful kingdom.

Summer-time finds no favour in the Isles, and it was after midnight when the *ceilidh* came to an end and we were left alone in the shieling.

Through the hole in the roof the blue smoke curled upward; outside could be seen the dim forms of the cattle as they lay upon the heather. The shieling was larger than most and instead of the usual heather couch possessed an excellent bed. Above the bed was another hole in the roof, which gave ventilation and which could be closed in wet weather. The walls were thick: the roof of turf rested upon a wooden framework. Each year the shielings are roofed anew, for the thatch is not built to stand the winter storms.

Every summer shieling has two entrances. They are not doors in the usual sense of the word, but are openings in the walls of the house. Let us imagine the wind is blowing from the east. Then the east entrance is closed with turf and wood and the western door is opened; if during the day the wind shifts, then the doors are changed. But at any time of the day or night one entrance is always open, for there are no windows to light those small summer houses.

Early next morning the sun, shining through the open doorway, flooded the shieling with golden light. It was impossible to lie long abed under such conditions, and for an hour before breakfast the "songs" (as they say in the west) of the pipes carried far across the moor. More peats were carried in, the fire (which is not allowed to die out during the night) was soon burning brightly, and we were not long in sitting down to a breakfast which we shall always remember.

During the night the wind had shifted, and so the alternate entrance was opened before breakfast and had the effect of changing the whole appearance of the shieling. The breath of heather entered the room with the wind; the moorland grasses waved and nodded, and there were wavelets upon the stream with deep peaty pools that flowed near. Upon the hills of Harris southward the clouds rose and fell, and on the western horizon were the hazy Atlantic plains, where ceaselessly the swell broke upon the outlying isles in a smother of misty spray.

That very evening shieling life would end for the year and the people would return to their homes—glad, perhaps, to see their friends again, but sorry to leave the heather-scented moorland and the lochs on which the moonbeams play during the hours of the short summer night.

T11-26

Shearing on Fladda–chuain.

THE MAKING OF TWEED

The derivation of the word 'tweed' may be of interest. It is not a Highland but a Lowland Scots word and in its original form was 'tweel'. The word 'tweel' was used to describe a simple weave in which the longitudinal threads, called the warp, are woven over and under the transverse threads, called the weft. In the year 1826 a clerk intended to write the word 'tweel' on an invoice. Whether his handwriting was indistinct, or whether unconsciously he wrote a 'd' for an 'l', the fact remains that the word was read as 'tweed'. Thus the name 'tweed' is a 'ghost-name', and has nothing to do with the river Tweed.

The most tedious process in tweed-making is the carding of the sheep's wool, – teasing the wool into its individual strands. It is then dyed, usually with vegetable dyes, heather, bog myrtle, tormentil and other plants being used in the dyeing process. During the dyeing the wool is placed in a three-legged iron pot, together with water and the dyeing medium. In the open air a peat fire is lighted below the pot, which is allowed to simmer for hours while the wool is becoming thoroughly impregnated with the dye.

The wool is spun on a spinning-wheel and is then ready for the hand loom which is often of a great age, worn and polished by the work of one generation after another. The peat smoke impregnates the wool which is in contact with the smoke of the peat fire during the carding, spinning and weaving and it is this that gives Harris tweed its distinctive aroma. I was told recently by a Border weaver that a special scent of peat can now be purchased in bottles in order that spurious Harris tweed may be made with the distinctive smell.

The final act in the making of the Hebridean tweed is the shrinking or, as it is called, waulking. I do not know the derivation of the word waulking for it has nothing to do with the Gaelic word which is *luadh*. The waulking or fulling of the tweed is a community action and is a time of good cheer and singing. Young women are usually the waulkers. They sit at a long table, which may be in the living-room of the house, or in a barn or outbuilding. At one end of the table the tweed lies soaking in a wooden tub of urine. Yard by yard it is taken out of the liquid and circulated time after time round the table. As it passes each waulker in turn she pounds and squeezes it vigorously with her hands. The waulking is accompanied always by singing of a distinctive type, in which the rhythm is very pronounced, each person pounding the tweed at the appropriate measure of the song. The best singer, or several singers, sing a verse, then the whole assembly join in the chorus. Some of the waulking songs have a primitive and haunting melody; often the leading singer extemporises as she sings, with sly digs at local personalities figuring in the latest scandal or gossip. These sallies evoke shouts of laughter and the pounding of the cloth is continued with redoubled energy. The waulking causes the tweed to shrink. The final act of the waulking is the rolling up of the finished tweed by two of the assembly: as they roll up the moist cloth they sing a song of good wishes to the future wearer.

The making of hand-carded, hand-spun, hand-woven and vegetable-dyed Harris tweed is rapidly dying out. Much of the Harris tweed on the market at the present time is carded and spun by modern machinery and dyed with commercial dyes. It is woven, it is true, in the crofters' own homes but mostly on automatic man-power looms and often sent to Lowland mills to be finished. It has thus entirely lost its distinctive character.

AH-50

Hougharry children, North Uist.

THE GUGAS OF SÙLA SGEIR

Up to the eighteenth century, and probably later, it was the custom to raid the gannet colonies off the British coasts each year, to kill the young for food. In Scottish waters the Bass Rock, Ailsa Craig, St. Kilda, all yielded their quota of young birds for the neighbouring population. Since none of these nesting stations is now molested the gannet is on the increase in Scotland. New colonies in recent years have been founded in the Shetland Islands. To see the rocks of Muckle Flugga white as snow from the droppings of the great colony is a memorable experience and it is difficult for the bird lover to believe that this colony has been established within the last 20 years. This holds good also with the other Shetland colonies—on Noss and Hermaness.

In the Hebrides the young gannet is known as a *guga*, and there is at the present time but one gannet colony on which the gugas are taken for food—Sùla Sgeir.

The killing of the nestling gannets on that rock is so old a custom that its origin is lost in the mists of tradition. At one time three boats from the north of Lewis used to make the annual expedition to Sùula Sgeir, but that number has decreased to one. Indeed, at the outbreak of the present world-war, its crew were on Sùla Sgeir and did not hear until their return to Skigersta in Lewis of the gravity of the situation. At least one of the crew, a naval reservist, had to hurry straight to Stornoway to report for duty.

Sùla Sgeir is a lonely Atlantic rock standing between 40 and 50 miles north-east of the Butt of Lewis. It is a long sail in an open skiff. Here is the record of a typical passage, made in September, 1937.

The 19-foot skiff and her crew left the small fishing township of Skigersta at 9 p.m. on an evening of early September, landing on Sùla Sgeir at 5 p.m. the following day. For 19 of the 20 hours occupied in that long passage the skipper, Murdo MacKay steered the skiff. For hours the skiff was beyond the sight of any land and the wind carried them far off their course. Skilled navigation must therefore have been necessary to have brought them safely to the inhospitable shore of Sùla Sgeir but the skipper and what may be termed his mate are hardened seafarers. In the last great war Norman MacLean, second in command of the Sùla Sgeir expedition, served in an armed trawler, first off the coast of Iceland then out on the Atlantic 200 miles west of Scotland where mighty waves sweep milky white over the dark cone of Rockall; he has also had 30 years service in the R.N.R.

It was Norman who gave me the account of the Sùla Sgeir expedition. He said that a landing on the rock is possible only from two hours before to two hours after high water. The landing-place is a ledge of rock. Before landing each man removes his boots (this practice was always adhered to by the men of St. Kilda, who were famed as rock climbers), and the most agile of the crew leaps first on to the slippery rock as the boat rises on the crest of a wave. In turn six of the nine members of the crew then jump, leaving three in the skiff to hand out what the men call the 'luggage'. This consists of three to four tons of peat (for fuel), water and provisions sufficient for a month's enforced stay on the rock. Before rest or food can be thought of it is necessary to drag up the skiff to the only ledge safe for a boat on the rock. The labour necessary to accomplish this task must be great for the ledge is at least 60 feet above high tide and 200 feet from the water's edge.

This done the men retire to a stone bothy to cook their first meal and to sleep. The bothy they use was built by their ancestors a century and more ago and is constructed of rock slabs, even the roof being of stone. Fork-tailed petrels nest in crannies of the bothy walls and the men are lulled to sleep by their purring song during the night hours. Murdo MacKay the skipper here interposed to say that the trip to Sùla Sgeir in 1937 was uneventful, but he remembered passages far different when he and his crew *for eight weary days and nights* were sheltering in their skiff in the lee of Rona (an uninhabited island 10 miles from Sùla Sgeir) in sea and weather conditions so severe that no landing on Rona, let alone Sùla Sgeir, could be effected.

After a night's rest the men, if the day be dry, set about killing the young gannets. The weapon is a wooden mallet made specially for the purpose and the bird is killed instantaneously by a blow on the head. Those young birds near the edge of the cliff are first caught by a snare at the end of a bamboo rod for if the fowler himself approached too near the cliff edge he would alarm the birds and drive them over the rock. No adult gannet is killed, nor are small young taken. Despite the raids the gannet colony on Sùla Sgeir flourishes. Norman MacLean reckoned that 4000 young birds were left undisturbed on Sùla Sgeir in 1937, not counting several hundred which saved themselves by flight. Murdo MacKay the skipper said that 45 years ago it was necessary to take all the young birds possible, and the men were lowered by ropes to the difficult ledges. Now there are sufficient young birds on the top of the rock, and the ledges are not disturbed; indeed the men take no rope with them. Murdo believes that the breeding stock has increased by more than 100 per cent during that time.

At the end of each day, the gugas killed are taken to a hut specially built for their reception. Here they are carefully plucked and the next day, if the weather is dry, the birds are cleaned, the heads cut off and the bodies split open and salted. It was possible, the men told me, to clean and salt 500 gugas in a day. The birds are then laid on the rock and covered with a tarpaulin. The skiff is not able to carry more than around 2000 gugas home to Lewis across the 50 miles of stormy sea, and as there is only one expedition in the year it is evident that the colony of gannets can hold its own at the present day. Murdo MacKay reckoned the weight of the young gannets they carried as six tons: with a cargo of this weight it is necessary to await settled weather and a fair wind. In 1938 the men were fortunate in their weather but in 1937 they were obliged to remain a fortnight on the rock.

When the harbour of Skigersta is reached the gugas find a ready market at two shillings each; indeed the demand is so great that each person may be limited to a ration of one brace. In 1938 the cargo brought in £200. It has been suggested by some bird protectionists that the slaying of the gugas is wilful destruction, but nothing could be farther from the truth, for each bird killed is eaten. Let it be remembered that 1000 brace of pheasants or grouse are shot, and no protest is made. But there is this great difference—pheasants and grouse are shot mainly for sport, without discomfort or hardship, and gugas are taken at the risk of the lives of those who venture 50 miles into the Atlantic in an open boat.

Martin Martin, in his *Voyage to St. Kilda* made about 250 years ago, mentioned that 'on Stac Lii the natives counted on gathering five, six or even seven thousand Solan geese in a year, provided the wind did not disappoint them of their harvest'. On Stac an Armine, another nesting stack of the gannet on the St. Kilda group of islands, there were, according to Martin, 'stone pyramids' in which the fowlers preserved the gannets for a whole year. The men had no salt with which to preserve the birds, which were slit down the back and then stored on an uninhabited islet for a year, at the end of which time an epicure would have scarcely found them palatable. Martin himself visited Stac an Armine, and describes his return to the mainland with a harvest of 800 dried gannets of the previous year's taking. The birds were shared out, each gannet having on its foot a mark (made at the time of its capture) which showed who the owner was. During his visit on St. Kilda in 1696 Martin made careful inquiries as to the number of gannets consumed by each family, and found that during the previous year 22,600 had been eaten on the island.

In William Abercrummie's *Description of Carrick in 1696* it is mentioned that there were on Ailsa Craig 'store of solan geese in so great plenty, that the very poorest of the people eat of them in their season at easie rates'. Sir

William Brereton, who visited the mainland opposite Ailsa Craig in 1635, writes that 'in this isle of Ellsey (Ailsa) there breed abundance of Solemne Geese, which are longer-necked and bodied than ours, and so extreme fat are the young that when they eat them they are placed in the middle of the room, so as all may have access about it: their arms are stripped up and linen cloaths placed before their cloaths, to secure them from being defiled from the fat thereof, which doth besprinkle and besmear all that come near unto it'.

This harvest of young gannets was gathered annually on Ailsa Craig until the year 1870 or rather later.

On the Bass Rock gannets were used as food since time immemorial. There are three records of this bird having been purchased for the king's household in 1511—on September 11, 14, and 15.

In the year 1526 Hector Boece, Canon of Aberdeen, writes of the gannets of the Bass in his *Cosmographe and Discription of Albion:*

> The keparis of the castell forsaid (the Bass) takis the young geis fra them (the old birds) with litill impediment; this cumis gret proffet yeirlie to the lord of the said castell. Within the bowellis of the geis is ane fatness of singulaire medicine; for it helis mony imfirmeties, speciallie sik as cumis be gut (such as come by gout) and cater (catarrh).

Pennant in his *Tour in Scotland* (1771) sailed out to the Bass, but the waves ran too high to permit of a landing. He writes:

> Various sorts of water fowl repair annually to this rock to breed; but-none in greater numbers than the Gannets, or Solan geese, multitudes of which were then sitting on their nests near the sloping part of the isle and others flying over our boat. It is not permitted to shoot at them, the place being farmed principally on account of the profit arising from the sale of the young of these birds, and of the Kittiwake, a species of gull, so called from its cry. The first are sold at Edinburgh for twenty-pence apiece and served up roasted a little before dinner.

As a footnote to Pennant's interesting account is printed an advertisement taken from the *Edinburgh Advertiser* of August 5, 1768, reading as follows:

SOLAN GOOSE

There is to be sold, by John Watson, jun., at his Stand at the Poultry, Edinburgh, all lawful days in the week, wind and weather serving, good and fresh Solan Geese. Any who have occasion for the same may have them at reasonable rates.

In the books of John, Duke of Lauderdale, a precise account is given of the number of young gannets gathered from the Bass. In the year 1674, 1118 young birds were taken; in 1675 the number was 1060, and in 1676 1150. In 1677 the number dropped to 985. Coming to more recent times, John Wolley mentions that in the year 1850, 1700 young gannets were taken on the Bass, but by the summer of 1876 the number had fallen to 800. In the year 1885 the lessee of the rock told Mr. Evans that he had taken 2000 eggs but no young that year. Although Sir Robert Sibbald was of opinion that 'the art of cookery cannot form a dish of such delicate flavour, and combining the tastes of fish and flesh, as a roasted solan goose', so powerful was the cooking aroma from these young birds that on occasion they were cooked in the open air.

Human interest was gradually transferred from young birds to gannets' eggs as an article of food. In or about the year 1856 gannets' eggs were sold at Canty Bay, North Berwick, for as much as 6s. a dozen: they were admitted to be indistinguishable in taste from plovers' eggs, and were apparently appreciated at the Royal table. But many young were still taken, and J. H. Gurney in his exhaustive monograph on the gannet mentions that in 1876 the tenant of the Bass employed five or six women to pluck the young birds killed for food.

It might have been thought that the killing of so many young in the past must have been a severe strain on the nesting colonies, yet the species never became scarce. The gannet is one of the most fortunate birds, for it has no enemy but man, except the great skua, which molests it only at the Shetland colonies.

ISNB-41

CUSTOMS OF THE FLANNAN ISLES

When, in the seventeenth century, the natives of Lewis visited the Flannan Isles in summer for sea-birds and their eggs, and for the down of the eider duck, they observed certain ceremonies with the greatest care—for the voyage in their small boats was a hazardous one. They would sail for the isles—about thirty miles distant—only if a breeze from the east was blowing. Should the wind change into the west before they had reached the Flannans, they would at once put about and steer for home.

Should the wind remain steady and the passage be completed in safety, the voyagers on arriving at their destination at once uncovered their heads, making a turn sun-ways and returning thanks that they had been preserved.

Sun-ways in Gaelic is *deiseil,* from *deas,* which signifies both right and south. For, as one faces the rising sun in the east, the fitting way to turn is toward the south (that is, toward one's right).

This turning sun-ways is still observed—for what piper would turn against the sun in his playing, and how important it is to pass the after-dinner port sun-ways also!

The Flannan Islands were always sacred to the people of the Lewis. On the largest island, Eilean Mor, were the remains of a chapel said to have been dedicated to St. Flannan. When the crews of the visiting boats had reached a spot about twenty paces from the altar of this chapel they removed their upper clothes, which they laid upon a stone placed there for that purpose. They then prayed three times—the first prayer as they advanced toward the chapel on their knees, the second as they travelled sun-ways round the chapel, the third within the chapel itself. They were now free to collect sea-birds' eggs and the down from the nests of the eider duck.

Another curious custom was that, no matter how many sheep might be killed on the islands, no suet might be taken back to the mainland, for such fat was regarded as sacred. Again, no bird might be killed before landing, nor might certain things on the islands be called by their proper names.

This curious custom of avoiding all reference to places by their usual names was most carefully adhered to by the islesmen of the Hebrides when they sailed abroad, in order that no evil spirit of the ocean might overhear whither they were bound. Thus no one sailing to the Flannans ever mentioned them by name; they were known as The Country. In like manner the Isle of Muc might safely be named Tir Chraine, *the Sow's Land*, or the Isle of Eigg might be referred to as Eilean nam Ban-mor, *the Isle of the Great Women*, when to speak openly of them by their usual names while at sea would be to court disaster.

HM-23

A Hebridean croft in winter.

Using the cas crom (foot plough) on Skye.

A busy fishing port: Castlebay, Barra.

5

Birds Above All

Though Seton Gordon was an all-round naturalist, birds were his greatest lifelong study, about which he wrote prolifically in books and magazine articles. Nine of his twenty seven books were primarily bird books and most of the others contain bird chapters. He described nearly every Scottish bird over the years so this is a very selective choice. (Shorter, anecdotal notes have a separate section later.) First, there are several descriptions of how he and his long-suffering wife tackled the adventures of early bird photography; thereafter, a range of studies from schoolboy days ('The Water Ousel') onwards, taken from different books, in what proved chronological order.

A school day's picture of a robin's nest in a weeding basket.

Seton Gordon setting up a hide to photograph terns.

A START IN BIRD PHOTOGRAPHY

My first clear recollection of my interest in natural history is not of birds, as might be expected, but of the behaviour of fish. It was in 1895, one of the most severe winters in Scotland for more than a century, and I was nine years old at the time. The River Dee was frozen from its birthplace in the Cairngorm Highlands to the North Sea. Where the ice was smooth, curling matches were played, and spectators kept themselves warm by sliding. For a small boy, those long slides were formidable, and I remember being overtaken by a grown-up expert when, half-way down the slide, my own impetus exhausted. Before I was swept on in his arms I saw, through the clear ice, several salmon immediately below me. They were keeping station against the current, and for all the interest they took in the human intruders about four feet from them, they might not have existed.

Our home in my boyhood was near the River Dee, and one of the first birds I can remember clearly is the oystercatcher. These cheerful waders nested on a large island on the river. They searched the recently sowed fields of oats, for worms for their young and used to fly low over our house on their return journeys. I still have a distinct memory of one bird with an out-sized worm held firmly in its bill. How, thus handicapped, it was able to call, loud and clear, was a mystery to me.

When I was sixteen I found myself involved in the coronation of King Edward VII. A friend of the family had presented a flag to be hoisted on the lonely Hebridean island of St Kilda on coronation day, which was to be June 26, 1902, and I had been chosen to take the flag to the island. This was long before the days of wireless, and the Gaelic-speaking inhabitants were completely cut off from the world during the winter months. The steamer *Hebrides,* then a new boat, was making her first call of the season a few days before the coronation date, and a friend and I joined her in Glasgow. Early that day we had heard the news of the King's sudden illness and that the coronation had been indefinitely postponed. The people of St Kilda knew nothing of this, and greeted us with joy. It was arranged that the flag should remain on the island and should be unfurled when the coronation took place. St Kilda is the home of seabirds, which still nest in incredible numbers. My friend became lyrical as he saw these colonies. He wrote in a letter: "The puffins puffed, the razorbills raised their bills, the fulmars made fools of themselves".

Some years before I went up to Oxford my chief ambition was to find a ptarmigan's nest and photograph the sitting bird. It still surprises me that not one of my acquaintances had found this nest, although I asked many stalkers, ghillies and shepherds. For years I wandered across the high hills without success. It was a triumph therefore when, on May 27, 1906, I was successful. The day, month and year have remained clear in my memory for 70 years. It was a glorious morning of sunshine, after frost, and as I walked up the glen tree pipits were rising in song from the glen's outpost birches, still leafless. When I reached and passed the heather line, the sun flooded with dazzling light the high Cairngorm hills across the Dee Valley. Then suddenly, with snorting cries, a cock ptarmigan rose near me on his white wings and, after he had flown across a snowfield, hesitated and for a moment altered his flight line before continuing for more than 100 yards. I crossed the snow, and, when I had reached the ground where he had momentarily hesitated, to my delight I saw his mate sitting closely on her nest, so my climb had been well worth while.

The hero of my boyhood was Richard Kearton, and it was through his books that my love of birds was encouraged. It was helped also by the under-standing assistance of both my parents. I knew that Richard Kearton had never photographed a ptarmigan on her nest, and so I sent him a telegram (which cost sixpence in those days) to say I hoped he would come at once and share my good fortune. He arrived fresh and enthusiastic after a 600-mile train journey, and we set off for the high hills. He was very lame, and his large camera and a plentiful supply of plates were heavy. When I suggested that we should walk through the night (the path was good and there is little darkness in the Highlands at the end of May) he readily agreed. We reached the snowfield beside the ptarmigan's nest at six o'clock in the morning. The sun was already bright, and dew drops sparkled on the short grass and alpine flowers. I had told Kearton that a ptarmigan is usually a close sitter, and that if he advanced slowly he would probably be able to photograph her as she sat. He set out, his large camera on its tripod held in front of him. He advanced very slowly and I anxiously watched his controlled excitement as he neared the bird, pausing every few feet to take a photograph. At last he was only 9ft from her. So clear were his photographs that the dew drops can be seen on the ptarmigan's back.

It was about this time that I made acquaintance with my first pair of nesting golden eagles, birds that have been my favourites throughout my life. In the Old Caledonian Forest the eagle usually has her eyrie in a Scots pine. When I heard from a stalker friend that a golden eagle had her eyrie with two eggs in a pine which he thought I could climb, I lost no time in visiting him.

We set out from his house in the forest, where the capercaillie has his home. The stalker brought with him a short ladder to help me to reach the first branch on the massive tree. Alas, when we arrived at the tree and I climbed the ladder I was still several feet short of the first branch. My friend the stalker was a strong man. He lifted the ladder as I stood on it against the tree, lifting me up until I was able to stand from it on to the first branch of the tree. Climbing to the eyrie was not difficult from there, and I was able to photograph the great nest. The platform of the eyrie was built entirely of pine branches and shoots, their needles still fresh and green as on the day, several weeks before, when the eagles had broken them off one of the trees of the forest. In the cup of the eyrie were two large, handsome eggs, strong shelled and marked with reddish-brown spots, which after six weeks' brooding produced two white-downed eaglets.

My introduction to the golden eagle was associated with the kite, a bird that had disappeared from the Scottish Highlands for a hundred years. On our way to the eagle's eyrie I was shown a kite's nest built in a fork high on a Scot's pine. I was told that it was at least 40 years since the last pair of kites in that area had used it. I was also told an interesting story about the last kite. A local ghillie, fishing for salmon, wished to fish a pool of the river Dee from the opposite bank. He removed his socks and left them on the bank of the river and waded across in his shoes. On his return, he walked to where he had left his stockings, and was surprised to see that one was missing. Some weeks later the missing stocking was found in the kite's nest.

The golden eagle, ptarmigan and snow bunting have been my greatest bird friends on the high hills, and the dotterel has often been a wonderful companion. On the lower ground the songs of curlew and greenshank have a unique charm. On a July night – the year was 1909 – the Lairig Ghru was spanned by a lunar rainbow as I climbed to hear a cock snow bunting salute the dawn. A little later his mate arrived with food for a young bird. She had no fear of me and the photograph I took was, as far as I know, the first photograph taken of a British snow bunting at the nest.

Sixty-five years ago next June I had to sit my final examination in Natural Science at Oxford University. I was not too confident of success, but a Highland friend and I decided that we would spend the weekend before the examination on the Cairngorms, 600 miles north of Oxford. The examination at Oxford was on Tuesday, and to my joy I read on the printed slip in front of me the words, "Write all you know about the Alpine Flora of Britain". I wrote an essay of 2,000 words on this question, and can truly say that my visit to the Cairngorms brought me an Honours Degree from Oxford University.

(Country Life, April 1976)

BIRD HIDES

My wife always had a love for birds but during the four War years which followed our marriage we had few opportunities of photographing birds though I had many of observing them during my service on the west coast of Scotland on Admiralty Patrol Service, and later in Ireland in the Naval Intelligence Service. After the War [*World War One*] we set about photographing birds seriously, and to my wife's practical help and interest I owe a great deal. She and I have taken turns watching in the hides, and she has taken many of the photographs which form the illustrations of my books.

For the success of hide photography it is necessary that two persons should work together. Birds—with very rare exceptions—see no difference between one person and two people. This is fortunate for the observer who goes to the hide set up near the nest he wishes to photograph. He takes with him a second person, whose duty it is to screen him as he creeps into the hide and, after he and his camera are safely concealed, to make as ostentatious a departure as possible. The bird has seen two persons, which in its mind are registered merely as 'danger', approach its nest, and now sees one person, again recorded in its mind as 'danger', leave it. Reassured, it now returns to its eggs or young, the idea that a part of the 'danger' still remains never entering its mind. On the other hand, if the photographer approaches and enters the hide by himself, his hopes of success are very slight, for the bird has last seen the 'danger' uncomfortably near its nest, and now watches anxiously for the 'danger' to leave. It realizes that a human being is inside the hide and will not return until he has left.

Each bird photographer has his own ideas on the subject of hides.

There is no doubt that in hide photography the small observer has a considerable advantage over the large one. I stand over six feet in height, and in a hide am almost always in a cramped and uncomfortable position, which becomes increasingly painful with the passing hours. Ladies, being as a rule smaller than men, are more fitted to take long watches in hides. (My wife is comfortable in a hide in which I am unable to move.) Our longest watches are up to eight hours, and my wife once watched in an eagle hide for ten hours.

With certain birds—the raven, for example, and the peregrine falcon—the difficulty of photographing them lies mainly in finding a ledge near the nest sufficiently broad and accessible to permit of an observation post being built with an unrestricted view of the nest.

On one occasion when we were photographing a golden eagle's eyrie there was no ledge sufficiently broad for a proper hide, and I was obliged to stand motionless for hours on a narrow ledge with a cover of old sacking over me and my camera. The early summer that year was unusually cold, and one day I stood, not daring to move, in a bitter north wind and driving snow showers for nearly five hours with this flimsy covering over me scant protection against the cold. At the end of this watch at the eyrie I found that my legs had lost their power and that I was quite unable to descend the cliff. I stood there, perched high on the rock, with a curious feeling of helplessness until my wife, who was just recovering from a badly sprained ankle, climbed up and guided my feet into the footholds while I made a painfully slow descent.

Some of us who have Kearton's books may recall that he had the skin of an ox set up in a life-like position, and that he used to carry this ox about with him when he wished to photograph birds. He also made use of a stuffed sheep, but found that the inside of a sheep, or even an ox, was hot and airless. I do not think these forms of hides ever became popular.

30Y-36

BULLISH BIRD-WATCHING

My wife had an unpleasant experience when photographing a Slavonian grebe at the nest. The nest was in green reeds beside a small grassy island a little way off shore. On this islet the hiding-tent was set up and, having seen my wife into the hide, with camera in position, I waded ashore through the shallow, sun-warmed water and walked along the bank of the loch, being soon out of sight of the hide.

A couple of hours later I returned, and when I came in sight of the hiding-tent I saw that a herd of cattle had fed down to the shore of the loch near it. My anxiety was increased when, on a nearer approach, I saw that a bull of formidable appearance had noticed the hide and was disapproving of it in no uncertain manner. He was standing on the shore with head down, pawing the ground. The water between the shore and the island was only a foot deep and it looked as if any moment the bull might walk through the shallows and lift the tent and its unseen occupant, blissfully unconscious of danger, on his strong polled head.

I hurried forward at my best speed and took a short cut across to the island, forestalling the bull who now had become furious and was kept at bay with difficulty by our collie, Dileas. The dismantling of hide and camera was done on this occasion, as may be imagined, more speedily than usual and the farmer arriving providentially on the scene averted what threatened to develop into a crisis.

WBB-38

NESTING DIVERS:
THE PHOTOGRAPHIC PRACTICALITIES

We had given up the idea of attempting to photograph a black-throated diver on her nest for that season, when unexpectedly—for the nesting season was well advanced—we saw a black throat on a neighbouring loch swim ever closer to one of the islands, and at last clamber ashore and settle down on her eggs.

Unfortunately for us there was no boat on the loch, but we remembered the offer of a friend to lend us his collapsible canvas boat and at once went over to his house about ten miles away.

The boat we transported so far in a car, then my wife and I dragged or carried it across a seemingly interminable bog. But when we attempted to inflate the bladders of the boat we found that, through age, the rubber was perished, and having no repair outfit with us, there was nothing for us to do but to launch the frail craft with the bladders empty. My wife, being the lighter of the two, made the first passage to the island. She took with her the camera and plates, and as she paddled across I paid out a long line, one end of which was tied to the boat, so that I might be able to pull the boat back and paddle myself across in my turn.

When loaded with passenger and camera the frail craft was less than an inch above the water-line. It was a work of art to sit down in it without capsizing the whole outfit. But at last my wife commenced her passage, with the camera poised on her knees and toes to keep it out of the water—for the craft leaked as well as shipping the water over the low sides. After some tense minutes she reached the island. When I had pulled the crazy boat half back, the disconcerting discovery was made that the paddle remained upon the islet! Here was a pretty state of affairs. On the island was my wife, with only a paddle, here was I on the shore of the mainland with a boat, but no means with which to propel it, and no sticks to use as a paddle within thirty miles! The day was cold, and the prospect of swimming eighty yards and back again uninviting, not to say dangerous, as anyone who knows the coldness of the water of a Highland loch will believe. But the crisis was averted by our collie dog Dileas. She is a famous swimmer and, being called by my wife, swam across at once to the island. There my wife tied the paddle to her tail, carrying the weight to the water's edge and pushing it off as I whistled to Dileas from the mainland. The collie swam swiftly across the channel, towing the paddle behind her. She did not seem to be aware of it until she was leaving the water when, feeling an invisible something pulling at her from behind, she became filled with alarm, so that I had difficulty in untying the knot round her tail.

My own passage across was full of excitement; several times I shipped so much water that I got ready to swim for it but somehow righted the craft at the last moment.

T11-26

Seton Gordon's wife with a nesting dotterel in the Cairngorms.

THE WATER OUSEL

Every river and nearly every highland stream is haunted by this charming little bird; and as he rises at your feet and skims along the surface of the water uttering his cheery *Tzeet, tzeet*, he presents a very pretty picture. No moorland is too wild, no height too great for the Dipper: he will be found haunting streams almost at sea-level while at a height of 3,000 feet, where the mountain silence is broken only by the occasional croak of the Ptarmigan, the Water Ousel suddenly rises from the source of some moorland burn and flies rapidly off.

Although the Dipper's call note is to be heard any day, his song is comparatively rarely used, but is of extraordinary sweetness, resembling to a certain extent that of the Wren, but purer and more liquid. What gives it an added charm is the fact that it is uttered all through the winter months, when other birds are silent. Sometimes the Ousel sings on the wing as he wends his way rapidly above the stream but his favourite spot when singing is a large stone standing out into the stream. His song appears sometimes to be used for the purpose of calling his mate to his side.

During the winter, when the weather is severe and the moorland burns are to a great extent snow-bound the Ousels may often be seen on the rivers near their estuaries, where I have noted quite a number working the river together—a state of affairs which would not be tolerated during the nesting season when each pair of birds has a certain portion of the stream as their beat and trespassing Dippers are very soon driven off by the rightful owners.

The Water Ousel is perhaps as early a nester as any bird of the highlands. Last spring I watched a pair constructing their marvellous dome-shaped nest on the foundation-stone of an old disused bridge, about a foot above the burn. Both birds were busy carrying materials for the nest and it was a charming sight when they arrived together, the cock singing a few snatches of song to his mate to cheer her on her labours. The morning was very fine but towards noon heavy snow-clouds came down from the west and soon a dense snowfall commenced, the flakes being of exceptional size. I wondered what the Dippers thought of the storm and whether they imagined they had made a premature start in house-building.

Three weeks later the nest was finished and one egg laid, but when the young birds should have been nearly ready to leave the nest, a tremendous storm of snow and rain swept down from the north and the burn rose rapidly until it lifted the nest from its foundations and bore it seawards in its current. The last I saw of the nest was just before it was washed away but there were no signs of the old birds so perhaps they had succeeded in getting their brood to a place of safety.

The Dipper usually lays five eggs of a pure white colour but when fresh, the yolk shining through gives them a pink tinge. They are rather elongated, and are very similar in shape and colour to those of the Swift. The mother bird sits very close and often the first intimation you have of the nest being occupied is when your hand touches the brooding hen inside.

The Dippers seem to take longer to rear their family than most birds of their own size and six weeks after the eggs are laid the young may still be in the nest. Sometimes, when you have inserted your hand to feel how the young inside are progressing, the young birds pop out one after another directly it is withdrawn, and jump into the stream below, chirping loudly and swimming off in all directions. Then the parent birds immediately make their appearance and with loud cries of alarm endeavour to collect their scattered family.

A favourite nesting site is in the niches of a rock behind a small waterfall, the bird entering at the side, where the rush of water is almost absent; sometimes however the parent bird has to fly right through the fall. Often the nest is constructed under the arch of a bridge where a stone has fallen out and sometimes on a stone in midstream. In one of Mr. Kearton's books is a photograph of a nest in a tree about 10 feet above the stream.

The nest is a large domed structure, with a small entrance hole near the bottom and this hole is usually so small that it is almost impossible to feel the eggs inside without enlarging it somewhat.

The usual nesting materials are moss and leaves, and these are put together with such marvellous skill that, although the water is often dripping continuously on the nest, the inside is always perfectly dry.

The Dipper has often been accused—wrongly so, I think—of feeding on the spawn of trout and salmon in the bed of the stream. Although it is true the Water Ousel spends most of his time in feeding below the surface of the water, his food consists chiefly of the insects which have their home in the bed of the stream. It is also said that fish bones are found round the nest but that has never been the case in my experience.

When the frost is intense and the stream on each side is frozen over, the centre only remaining open, it is very interesting to watch the Dipper feeding. Standing on the ice's edge, he constantly dives into the stream, reappearing each time a yard or so further down and when his hunger has been satisfied he preens his feathers contentedly in the frosty sun.

As a result of nesting so early, the Ousel sometimes has his nest destroyed by the snow, and in one case that came under my observation the unfortunate birds had their home covered with a snow wreath many feet deep and when this had melted their nest had vanished. The birds will return to the same nesting place year after year but this particular pair have not returned to the spot since the snow destroyed their nest.

I have seen a Dipper disappear into the ground when flushed from a stream, the explanation being that, a short distance further up, the stream went under ground and was lost to view, the bird likewise disappearing and following the course of the stream.

I have found the Water Ousel at the Pools of Dee, between Brae Riach and Ben Muich Dhui, at the boundaries of the counties of Inverness and Aberdeen, where even the Grouse were left below and his only companions were the lordly Golden Eagle and the snow-white Ptarmigan.

Once I found in the month of May a Dipper's nest with half-grown young. On returning to the place some time later, I was very much astonished to find that a Spotted Flycatcher had built her nest on the top of the Dipper's, probably after the latter's brood had left, and had reared her young in this unique situation.

BLM-07

A NIGHT WITH THE GOLDEN EAGLE

It was to study the eagle with her young that a friend and the writer set off one early summer night for an eyrie not many miles distant from "Dark Lochnagar." Leaving the low grounds shortly after ten in the gathering dusk, we were accompanied for the first mile by a stalker, who put us on the track—very difficult to locate in the darkness—and wished us good luck before he returned to his cottage. The night was wonderfully clear, for though there was no moon the sky in the north never lost its glow, and even at midnight the hills could be made out without difficulty—the large snowfields looming out with almost startling distinctness.

Our way for the first three miles led up a rocky glen with a small burn hurrying down to the river below, and on the banks of the stream numerous birches made the night air fragrant with their sweet perfume. From time to time we scanned the westward heavens for Halley's comet, but that celestial visitor did not put in an appearance, and a view of him a few nights previous to the expedition was, we must confess, a very great disappointment. Not a sound save the subdued murmur of the water disturbed the intense stillness of the night as we made our way up the glen, but an occasional ghostly form was from time to time made out hurrying past in the gloom when we disturbed some stag or hind browsing on the rich grass near the burn-side.

It was now nearing one o'clock, and the light in the northern sky had increased considerably, so that one could read the time on a watch with ease. As we crossed the bog at the watershed the whistle of a golden plover as the bird flew past us in great alarm, sounded extraordinarily loud. This was the only note of any bird we heard during the whole of our climb. Descending to the "glen of the eagles," the giant pines were dimly visible in the dusk. The vicinity of the eyrie was reached about 1.20 A.M., and having chosen a tree with a good view of the nest, we made ourselves as comfortable as circumstances would allow and waited for daylight.

I was awakened from a somewhat uneasy sleep at 1.55 by the song of missel-thrushes. Several were singing loudly in various parts of the glen, and a few mergansers were flitting noiselessly up and down the stream. The eyrie was now faintly visible, and an indistinct white shape seemed to suggest the possibility of an eaglet, but the light was not yet bright enough for any certainty. Shortly before three o'clock chaffinches burst into song, and we now perceived to our intense satisfaction the golden eagle standing on the edge of the nest and guarding a solitary chick.

It is a noteworthy and curious fact that some 80 percent of nesting eagles lose one of their young during the first three weeks of its existence. Numerous explanations have been advanced to account for this, but they are all somewhat unsatisfactory, although we imagine that the supply of food is at times insufficient for both youngsters. The eagle was standing over her young with wings slightly raised, and the chick seemed quite contented with his head alone sheltered by his mother. Before the light had become clear confused movements were noted in the eyrie, and the youngster was in all probability having his morning meal. Occasionally the chick would raise his head and appear to beg his mother for an extra tit-bit, but this was refused him with gentle firmness.

Hour after hour the eagle stood motionless over her young with a look of tender mother-love in her eyes, quite unlike the usual fierce expression associated with the king of birds. The sky, shortly after two, had become quite free of clouds and the air was extremely cold, the touch of frost which had set in on the passing of the clouds being by no means conducive to our comfort. Almost exactly at four o'clock the sun rose in the north-east. He came over the brow of a hill looking red and angry, and for the space of fifteen minutes lit up the glen with a deep red light. The brooding eagle looked particularly beautiful in this light, being transformed for the while to a ruby red bird of prey, and the young bird also being faintly tinged with pink. The sun reddened the snowfields on crater-shaped Cairntoul with charming effect, but his reign was all too short, for ominous clouds come hurrying up from the west and soon the Cairngorms were shut in by the gathering mist.

I had intended to secure a photograph of the eagle leaving her eyrie, but the feeble light effectually put a stop to all efforts in the photographic line, and shortly before six the eagle slipped noiselessly off the nest and disappeared from sight.

In the eyrie were the remains of what appeared to be a wood-pigeon, and the breast-bone of a grouse was lying at the foot of the tree. Once we saw the eaglet—which seemed about a month old and was still covered with fluffy white down—walk unsteadily to the edge of the eyrie and peer over inquiringly. On one of these excursions he nearly lost his balance, and thereupon wisely retreated to the centre of the eyrie and lay down comfortably. When, after a wait of quite six hours, no signs of the parent eagle were forthcoming, and the weather had changed for the worse, we reluctantly gave up the attempt at photography and commenced our return journey. For a couple of miles our way led along the banks of a large mountain burn, which was running full on account of the melting of the snows, and at one point a hind on the farther bank gave indications that she had a calf in the vicinity. During the descent a grey wagtail was found and photographed on her nest near the 2,000-foot level, and several ring-ousels were disturbed from the head of a gorge. A dipper flew rapidly past, bearing food for her young ones, and as we reached the banks of the Dee the whistle of the oyster-catcher fell pleasantly on the ear.

COH-12

Golden eagle and chick.

THE DOTTEREL OF THE HIGH TOPS

Most fearless and perhaps most charming of all birds who have their homes about the high tops is the dotterel. There are certainly fewer than one hundred pairs in all Scotland.

So confiding is this graceful wader that in the Gaelic language he is known as An t-Amadan Mointeach, *the fool of the peat moss,* his absurd tameness seeming to the Highlander to mark him as a bird devoid of sense. But the dotterel is by no means a fool, although his eggs would be safer from the collectors who are so often on his track were he to borrow some of the wariness and cunning of the golden plover.

The dotterel is without exception the highest-nesting bird in Britain. Wintering far to the south of these islands, he nevertheless chooses as a nesting-ground the topmost slopes of the loftiest hills—expanses of wind-swept ground, too high for even the hardy ptarmigan or the elusive snow bunting.

Personally, I have never come across a dotterel nesting below the 3,000-foot line, and during June, 1920, had under observation a nest almost exactly 4,000 feet above the level of the sea where, up to the third week in May, the winter's snow remained unbroken. Even during a fortnight in June, when in the glens beneath the air was warm and the sun shone from a cloudless sky, the wind, often blowing with gale force, was bitterly cold at this dotterel's nesting-ground.

And little wonder, for a few hundred yards to the south of the nest was a great snowfield filling a wild precipitous corrie, and however warm the day at lower levels, the south wind, blowing straight from off the snow, brought always winter in its breath. Day after day the wind had swept the plateau with gale force so that the dotterel, when running about the nest in characteristic fashion, had frequently to crouch low, head to wind, with legs wide apart and firmly planted on the ground till the passing of the squall.

Very early on the morning of June 10 I first located the birds. They were feeding together on a ridge 4,100 feet above sea level, and for fully an hour and a half a companion and I watched them feed round and round us, entirely careless of our presence, even at a distance of a few yards.

The morning was a magnificent one. As far as the eye could see, the deep blue fields of the sky extended without a single cloud to dim them. Only the faintest of airs stirred on the hilltop, and even at this height the air was pleasantly warm.

In the case of the dotterel it is the hen bird who is the more brightly coloured of the two, and in this instance—it is an interesting fact that those birds nesting in the far north, or at great heights in this country, are more brightly coloured than their relatives of the south or of the lower grounds—both cock and hen were particularly handsome. From their behaviour we made certain their nest was near, but after a time both birds flew off and we saw nothing further of them that day. I was doubtful whether any bird would nest at so great a height, or in so exposed a situation and came to the conclusion that this pair had lost their eggs by some mischance when nesting at lower levels and the fine morning had tempted them to this wild plateau to feed only.

Late in the evening of June 16 we again visited the plateau. Snownelds still lingered here and little growth was apparent amongst the Alpine plants, although the willow of the high hills—*Salix herbacea*—was already opening its minute green leaves where the snow had gone. A chill wind blew across from the snow-filled corrie to the south and in the soft evening light the plateau bore a strangely remote and desolate aspect but one of a peculiar grandeur.

After searching some likely-looking ground with little hope of success, I was delighted to see a dotterel rise just ahead of us and flutter away a few yards in characteristic manner. A short search revealed the nest, a shallow depression scraped out in a tuft of wiry hill grass and lined with dried leaves of the previous season's Alpine willow. In the nest were three beautifully marked eggs which, on being tested in some running water near, showed that they had been brooded for some days at least.

The following morning we again visited the plateau. Though the sun shone brightly, a strong cold wind swept across from the south. It was hoped on this occasion to set up a hiding-tent but the force of the wind was such that the idea had to be abandoned.

The dotterel left the nest when we were still some distance away, running rapidly ahead of us. We remained silently near and it was not long before he—it is, as I have said, the male dotterel who incubates the eggs—came running back in fast spurts, from time to time stopping an instant to pick up a spider or a beetle. The wind was now blowing in fierce squalls so that he had more than once to stop and hurriedly face the blast, which he did in a half-crouching, tense attitude. On one occasion he twice attempted to pick up a beetle sideways, but each time was blown away and was obliged to turn half about and make a frontal attack on his prey. On the opposite slope his mate was calling from time to time with soft whistling cries and once she passed over with swift powerful flight, swaying, however, as the gusts struck her.

From the glens far beneath the smoke from several great fires could be seen rising—for the scorching wind had now blown uninterruptedly for many days, and the heather was dry as tinder. But now the weather was rapidly changing. Away to the south-west thunder clouds swiftly formed. In a very few minutes the sun was blotted out and the mutterings of thunder were heard while away westward the hills became dim and took on a curious copper-coloured appearance.

In the air was that acrid scent that so often accompanies a thunderstorm and it seemed as though we should have that interesting, though awe-inspiring, experience of a thunderstorm actually in the clouds, which were now touching the plateau. But the hills were so parched that there was no attraction for the vapours with their moisture and almost as soon as it had formed the storm passed and the sun shone out once more.

Crossing the plateau there appeared an unlooked-for visitor—a black-headed gull, a bird of the low country. Following the little burn, he soon reached the top of the precipice, when the wind caught him and lifted him vertically a full hundred feet into the air before he recovered his balance.

For a dotterel, the particular bird of which I write was not tame. One had to sit not nearer than fifteen feet from the nest to ensure his returning to his eggs without delay—far warier than a dotterel we had been photographing at a height of 3,000 feet but then that bird, even for a dotterel, was really absurdly confiding. From the first he showed no fear of us, allowing us to photograph him from a distance of six feet with supreme trustfulness and being obviously annoyed when, by approaching to within a foot of him we caused him to rise from his eggs and walk a yard or two away—to wait with obvious impatience for our going. This nest was liberally lined with lichens. By June 22 the chicks were hatched out and had left the nest. But on this date the nest at 4,000 feet did not show any signs of hatching.

The fine weather had now gone from the hills. A strong southerly wind brought with it white drifting mists so it was not easy to locate the nesting-ground.

By now plant life, refreshed by the rains, was at length stirring on the plateau. The cushion pink was everywhere opening its flowers, some of the deepest crimson, others of a pale pink. The grasses were tingeing parts of the plateau a fresh green, good to see as a harbinger of summer.

The dotterel on this day let us approach to within a few yards, when he fluttered off with tail outspread and wings drooping and quivering, all the time calling plaintively. He then disappeared into the mist, but soon returned and flew straight to his eggs, having, I think, lost trace of us in the clouds. We watched him awhile and after a little he flew away to a grassy part of the plateau a hundred yards away where he was in the habit of feeding.

On this day, at a height of about 3,800 feet, we passed a mother ptarmigan with her brood strong on the wing, and met with another family at the unusually low level—for this hill bird—of 1,800 feet. The next occasion on which the nest was visited was on June 24—Midsummer's Day.

For the first time since the nest was discovered it was found possible to set up the hide and both my companion and I entered it. The hiding-tent was not more than twelve feet from the nest and though we entered it in full view of the dotterel he returned without suspicion and settled down confidently on the nest. He seemed, however, to find the task of hatching out his wife's eggs a dull and wearisome business and went off to feed no fewer than four times during the three hours we had him under observation. On these excursions he was away about twenty minutes at a time but on the last occasion he had already been absent from his eggs a full half-hour when we—the light having become too poor for photography—left the plateau for the day. Next morning brought mist and rain to the hill-tops but towards evening the weather cleared and the following day saw us once again at the 4,000-feet level. The nest was reached at 9.45 a.m. but the bird was off feeding and the eggs none too warm. The chicks, however, could now be heard tapping vigorously on the walls of their prisons and a few minutes later Mr. Dotterel returned from his leisured meal, running rapidly over the ground and ignoring the hiding-tent which we had just erected eight feet from the nest. Even when we both sat inside the hide talking to each other in ordinary tones our presence was unnoticed. The attitude of this obligingly confiding bird seemed to be, "Out of sight, out of mind," for he took not the slightest notice of our conversation, and several times dozed on his eggs.

Once he stood up in the nest and pecked hard at a chipping egg, apparently removing a small piece of the shell. He permitted my companion to approach to within twelve inches of him and then ran off, holding up one wing as though wounded. Once when shamming injury he shrieked aloud, but soon forgot his anxiety and began to feed unconcernedly only a few yards away, returning to the nest within ten minutes and at once falling asleep.

There was a great charm today in being on the roof of Scotland. Although the sun was hidden, the air was extraordinarily clear and, a rare thing for these altitudes, not a breath of wind stirred. Over all was a great silence, save for the distant sound of a waterfall in the corrie below and the song of a snow bunting from some neighbouring scree.

For the last time we visited the dotterel at his home amongst the clouds on June 27. The air was still on the plateau, and the sun shone from a deep blue sky. What a magnificent view may be had from this wild country! From Lochnagar, in the Balmoral forest, away to the conical peaks of the hills about Knoydart on the Atlantic seaboard, the shape of each hill was clear. Only on the summit of Ben Nevis were clouds resting. Away beyond the Moray Firth could be seen the blue smoke from some moorland or forest fire.

On reaching the nest we found two chicks already hatched, one of them crouching about a foot outside the nest. They were quite dry, and had evidently hatched out during the night or small hours of the morning; the third egg was addled.

The father dotterel appeared very pleased that his monotonous duty had been crowned with success, and whenever the chicks moved under him, purred with a curious though pleasing note. During the course of the morning a pair of dotterel which had apparently lost their eggs fed up close to him. He thereupon flew off the nest with feathers ruffled with anger and fiercely drove away the intruders. By midday both chicks could run actively and made excursions from the nest, returning obediently when called by their father. A little later they left the nest for good.

For some little time the parent bird was unwilling to leave the addled egg. On two or three occasions he returned to it, brooding it for a few seconds and listening intently for the tapping of a young bird. But the egg was unresponsive and so he each time hurried back to his two chicks and, after a while, gave up this brooding as an unprofitable business and returned to the egg no more. An interesting point was that, although he fed a good deal himself he never made any attempt to feed his young nor to instruct them how to feed. The chicks nevertheless actively picked up minute objects and one swallowed or tried to swallow a blade of grass as long as itself.

An interesting discovery which we made, and which I have never seen chronicled before, was that the young dotterel leave the nest, run actively, and even feed—or at all events pick up things—before their eyes are open! Indeed one of the chicks which we examined in the afternoon had even then, after several hours of wandering, its eyes still almost closed. We had noticed before that they seemed to be uncertain on their feet, frequently falling over, and stumbling against stones, but considering that their eyes at this time were still closed their movements were nothing short of marvellous.

The fine weather was of brief duration. About two o'clock the sun was obscured, and grey clouds drifted in ever-increasing masses across the plateau from the south-west. One by one, the big hills to the westward were blotted out, and the wind blew chill from out the advancing mists.

The dotterel called his two chicks to him, for they were feeling the cold—curiously enough, the hen had never once put in an appearance even on this auspicious occasion when her family first saw the light—and made a charming picture as he brooded them in the shelter of a tiny tuft of green grass, a plant of cushion pink with rich red flowers blooming profusely only a few feet from him.

And so we left him, wishing him well with his family cares in that wild snow-splashed country of the high hills and dark lochans, the home of the mists and of the four winds, and where the foot of man rarely treads.

WON-21

The "companion" through many dotterel-watching years was Seton Gorden's wife. At one site in hot weathers, with two eggs laid, the female bird was feeling the heat and continuously panted with wide open bill. A snow bridge spanned the bed of a hill burn a few hundred yards from the nest, and I brought up a large snowball which I placed a few inches to windward of her. Almost at once she stopped panting and dozed in the grateful coolness.

On another occasion, he wrote, I had taken with me a small box of worms to see whether I could induce my bird to feed from my hand. It was the male who was brooding on this occasion, for once the third egg had been laid the male has the entire responsibility of hatching them. He was so tame that when I placed my hand over the eggs he attempted to brood it: he fearlessly picked up insects two feet from me yet he took no interest in the worms I offered him and did not seem to realize they were good to eat. Incidentally I discovered that half an hour's exposure to bright sun and cold wind killed a lively worm stone-dead.

ISNB-41

THE NATIVITY OF THE STORMY PETREL

(illustrations, p. 280)

On July 1, in an old ruined wall, I found a stormy petrel brooding a fresh egg, white and glossy. This little petrel is the latest of all our sea-birds to nest and in the Hebrides it is useless to look for their eggs until July. I returned to the island just fifteen days later, and found that the egg had in some way been swept from the shallow nesting hollow and now lay, cracked and deserted.

After lifting their creels and fishing for pollack for bait, the fishermen and I went into a small thatched bothy on the island to pass the short hours of the summer night. At three o'clock in the morning, as I dozed on the earthen floor I was awakened by the caresses of wings on my arm and head, I opened my eyes and could hardly believe them when I saw a stormy petrel fluttering about me. The little bird had, I believe, come in at the open door to visit his mate brooding her egg hidden away in the bothy-wall (We heard her from time to time). The new-comer had been dazed by the candle which still burned brightly and so had been unable to find the entrance to the nest. The candle was extinguished and in the darkness I hoped the stormy petrel would be able to find his nest and mate. About half an hour before sunrise when I opened my eyes the first object they rested on was a stormy petrel, its night flying over, in the very act of climbing moth-like up the wall just outside the bothy door and disappearing into its narrow nesting hole.

On August 23, when I visited the island, I looked into the hollow where the deserted petrel's egg had lain and was interested to see that the bird had laid a second egg and was sitting closely.

The young petrels grow very slowly, and in order to see, if possible, on what they were fed, my wife and I pitched our camp near the colony on September 4. It is only by watching at night that the feeding of the growing petrels may be observed for the birds do not visit their young during the day and sleep away the hours of sunlight far out at sea. The night we camped was very mild and dark. There were two young stormy petrels in crannies where they could be watched without moving any of the stones of the old wall, and every few minutes we flashed a small electric torch into these crannies to see whether the parent birds had flown in to visit and feed them. From dusk until midnight no petrels came in from sea, but just at midnight we saw through the deep gloom the dark form of one outlined against the night sky. With swift swallow-like flight it passed and repassed us only a few feet away. We imagined the bird had just come in to feed its chick, but it was not the parent of either of the two young birds. When we looked into their holes they were still unattended. From 9.15 p.m. until 2 a.m. we sat near the hole where one of the young petrels was crouching. Every ten or fifteen minutes we flashed a torch into the hole but never saw the parent bird there. I also went from time to time to the chick in the other part of the wall and each time found it lonely.

The stormy petrel is so fearless at night of a human being that I do not think the fact of our sitting near their nesting colony was the reason of the birds' absence. I believe the young birds are fed only once, or at the most twice, during the night, and of course not at all during the day. This meagre diet would account for the slow rate of growth of the petrel chicks. A stormy petrel is a smaller bird than a blackbird. A young blackbird, fed liberally and frequently, is fledged within a fortnight. A full eight weeks pass before a young stormy petrel takes wing!

On September 27, a beautiful day of early autumn with a light wind from the north-east, I crossed over with the lobster fishermen and found that the bird which had lost her first egg had now hatched out her second egg successfully. The nest contained a lively chick clothed in warm grey down and about a fortnight old.

By now the other petrel chicks (they had been hatched from first layings so were well in advance of this youngster) were feathered. One of them had its white rump showing. Its head was clear of down but there was down on the back and also on the lower surface of the tail. Another young stormy petrel, as it lay on the ground within the wall, stretched one wing, eaglet fashion, to its fullest extent, then preened the base of the wing quills, its shoulders, its breast, its feet. Finally it twice lifted its beautiful long, pointed wings high above its head, as a dotterel or a dunlin might have done.

My next visit to the home of the petrels was on October 11. There were wild showers borne on a strong wind and about a mile from the island on our outward passage a heavy squall struck us. The wind velocity was so great that some kittiwakes flying near us were driven to the sea, and we were obliged to reef our sails still further. Despite the cold and the fact that it was unattended (the stormy petrel does not brood its chick except during the first few days of its life) the little petrel was cheerful and lively. It felt like a small hot-water bottle when I held it in my hand. The wing feathers were growing, but there was no appearance of feathers elsewhere.

The winter birds had by now begun to arrive at the island group. On the rocks a purple sandpiper was feeding and as we sailed for home with a gale astern of us and the sky wild and momently becoming more threatening, a pair of long-tailed ducks crossed our bows.

After a full month of rough weather I crossed to see the young petrel on October 31, a calm sunlit day of great beauty. Barnacle geese were now on the islands in numbers. They were wild and unapproachable and as they passed high overhead their calling was impressive. There was an astonishing change in the last-hatched petrel chick. Three weeks ago it had been a downy youngster. Now the wings were well grown and the white rump was showing. Indeed the only down visible was on the back. The petrel uttered little chattering cries of anger when I took it into my hand. The last of the petrels from the first layings had now left.

The weather after this one good day became even worse, and the fishermen did not lift their creels at all during the week beginning November 10. We did indeed attempt the passage on November 15, but the seas became heavier and we had to run for harbour. It was not until November 17 that I had an opportunity of crossing.

The surrounding hills were snow covered as we sailed over the sound in the low winter sun. On the petrels' island we found barnacle geese more numerous than ever and around the petrels' nesting wall were numbers of migrating thrushes. The young petrel had gone.

For at least eight weeks its world had consisted of a few feet of the interior of a wall, dim even at noon, intensely dark at night. Beyond its vision was the sea which it may have heard on stormy nights but knew nothing of. Creeping to the entrance of its nesting crack in the darkness of night in the midst of winter storm, the petrel must have launched itself out on its wonderful and perilous first flight. In a very few minutes the gale must have carried it far from land and until it alighted upon the angry waters it must have drifted along amid flying spume and spindrift.

A stormy petrel never approaches land after its first flight until the following summer, and thus is compelled to battle day and night throughout the winter with wind and wave.

ITH-31

THE GREENSHANK

Amid the ancient pine forests and out on the open moors of the Central and Northern Highlands the greenshank has his summer home. He is a bird larger and taller than the redshank and his cry is deeper-toned and more musical. His song is rarely heard yet in certain respects it is the most beautiful and certainly the wildest of all the bird songs of Britain.

Before singing, the greenshank climbs into the air to a height of perhaps a thousand feet and then, dashing madly backwards and forwards across the sky at varying heights, or flying in wide circles, sings perhaps for half an hour his wonderful song—a continuous rhythm of bold and musical whistles flung to the air and thrown back to him by the echoing pines far below.

So high does the greenshank mount during his song that on one occasion when I was watching him through a telescope he touched the clouds which, as I could tell from the neighbouring hills, were 2,000 feet above the ground. On this occasion the greenshank when he had finished his song dropped towards the ground with a swift, falcon-like stoop and settled on the highest branches of a pine tree.

It is impossible to set down the greenshank's song in words. It is usually uttered in groups of two notes, the first two notes in a low key, the second two in a higher. They are somewhat as follows: *teuchi, teuchi, clever clever.* On returning home after having listened for half an hour to a greenshank's song I found that the notes could be reproduced closely on the chanter of the Highland bagpipe. There is an old pipe tune on the notes of the storm petrel, and the song of the greenshank might well be taken as the theme of some *piobaireachd* or piece of classical pipe music.

The nest of the greenshank is hard to find, for the sitting bird is exceedingly shy and wary. It is curious, therefore, that she should utter a series of loud and distinctive notes immediately before she settles on her eggs. These notes often betray the nesting site yet even when they are heard they are difficult to locate for the greenshank is a ventriloquist and the notes are always puzzling and sometimes impossible to track.

The home of a certain pair of greenshanks was on a boggy clearance in a pine forest. Because of the wetness and the acid soil the pines were small and stunted so the impression was of a treeless district, with tarns and peaty pools of water. I had reason to believe that a pair of greenshanks were nesting but repeated searchings failed to locate the nest and therefore my excitement was great when one evening as I sat watching at the edge of the forest I heard the familiar cry of a greenshank about to brood her eggs; *tchook tchook tchook, tchook tchook tchook* continued without pause for fully two minutes. The elusive sound was difficult to locate and for thirty minutes I searched in vain for the nest, although I found a *scrape* at the foot of a felled tree. I then retired to the only tree near and had my tea beneath its scanty protection. I was about to give up when Dileas our collie pricked her ears and I heard the note of a greenshank on my left. This bird flew over and at the same time I heard the same cry as before, now much nearer. The bird was standing on the top of a stunted pine and when I showed myself she became very agitated. Fifteen paces from the tree where she had stood I found the nest containing four beautiful eggs.

A hide was put up near the nest and for several days the bird was nervous and impossible to photograph. I give below some notes from my diary:

May 29. The bird was suspicious and would not come to the nest. The day was brilliant and very warm, and dark thunder clouds gathered in the afternoon. We saw two pairs of greater spotted woodpeckers in the neighbourhood.

May 30. We went before six o'clock to the greenshank's nest. A thick mist lay over the land and was hopeless for photography. I took a watch in the hide and had been left alone only a few minutes when the hen greenshank arrived and after a short, chortling cry settled confidently. Half an hour later the male bird flew over and when he called his alarm note she looked round in disquiet. The cock settled in a tree, and continued to call in a less vehement manner. All at once he must have imperceptibly changed his cry, for she stood up in the nest after standing for a moment and ran quietly away. She was apparently expecting that the male would now take his turn of brooding but he was so wary that, although he walked up near the nest and called with the *tchook tchook* note for several minutes without a pause he did not venture to come to the egg.

May 31. As we approached the greenshank's nest we were interested to hear a cock chaffinch working into his song a clever imitation of a greenshank's call!

Ten minutes after I had been left in the hide, a greenshank returned but instead of settling on the eggs chortled for half an hour from the top of a small pine. I chanced to look through the peephole at the front of the hide. To my astonishment I saw a greenshank sitting closely on the nest which was less than twelve feet from me. The explanation was, I think, that the male had been brooding the eggs before my arrival, but that his courage had subsequently failed him and he had flown off leaving the eggs to the care of the more serene-minded mate. She sat quietly, regardless of the noise of the shutter when I photographed her, and dozed on the eggs in the bright sunshine. When a grey crow flew close over the hide, uttering a loud and harsh *craa* the greenshank was at once on the alert but did not move. Sometimes she pecked absently at the grasses surrounding the nest, and as the sun increased in power she panted and gasped. From time to time she shuffled the eggs and when a cool breeze sprang up she dozed contentedly or slept with her head tucked away beneath her feathers.

At 1.20 the male greenshank approached the nest, bowing as he did so. The hen on the nest answered him with a very soft cry: *Oich oich cloich*, her bill firmly closed, her whole body vibrating as she called. The morning had been fine but rather before noon heavy rain began to fall, followed by thunder. Dileas our collie was anxious for my safety and came to the hide, alarming the greenshank for a short time. It became very dark, the thunder rattled overhead and the rain fell in torrents. My problem was to take Dileas from the hide without alarming the sitting greenshank, and so I very quietly crept out at the back and kept the hide between myself and the bird until I had moved a considerable distance away from her. When I returned to the hide the male bird, who had evidently seen me leave it, stood on the wee fir tree about twenty yards off and *chip chipp chipped* without pause but I succeeded in entering the hide without the hen being aware of it. The cock then swooped in anger at the hide and flew farther off and his mate at once began whistling, not loudly, in a high key *chee chee chee, chee chee chee chee*, evidently the signal for the chicks to run about and enjoy themselves. The hen then rose from the nest and walked away, for she obviously considered it the cock's turn to look after the young family. The male greenshank since he had seen me creep into the hide was very nervous, chip chipping repeatedly. When I had despaired of him coming to brood the chicks he walked confidently on to the nest and I photographed him facing me with a chick standing by his side.

The thunder rolled among the hills but overhead the sky had cleared and the light was now brilliant. The brooding greenshank's feathers soon dried, and the young were contented in the warm sunshine.

That afternoon we moved the hide, with happy memories of pleasant hours spent at the nest of one of Scotland's most delightful and beautiful birds.

30Y-36

THE GREY WIND

One September day I recall when the Grey Wind was the bearer of white drifting mists of unusual density. I was abroad on the open moorlands on this day and walked through a dim and ghostly world. Occasionally overhead the mist momentarily thinned and one saw the dim orb of the sun shine wanly upon the heather that was still rich in colour although the season of its flowering was almost at an end. Every ditch was overflowing; every burn was a torrent; every heather stem and blade of grass was saturated with moisture. And there seemed to brood on this day a spirit of sadness—that sadness which uplifts rather than depresses and is peculiar to the sea-pervaded shores of the Isles.

Who has not crossed to the Outer Isles from the western mainland on a day when the Grey or the West Wind has been blowing, and as he crossed the Minch felt the spell of western seas? How silently the fulmar petrels glide on such a day! For a moment only they are seen, sailing on wings which seem held always so stiffly, so rigidly, and then, almost before the eye has realised their presence, they are gone, steering an unerring course through mist-held aerial seas. How wild the scream of an Arctic skua on a day such as this; how dark its swift-flying form that seems always to cleave the air with almost supernatural strength!

Should the Grey Wind advance with its silent mists at the season of autumn, how hazardous is the journeying of the migrating bird-people which steer southward above perilous seas at that time! These bird-travellers lack the unerring sense of direction which the fulmars and some other sea-birds possess, and on dark misty nights countless thousands must find a watery grave.

I shall always remember the account which one of the lightkeepers at the lonely rock-station of Skerryvore gave me of the destruction caused by the lantern to the migrating bird-armies one autumn night when the Grey Wind was abroad. On such a misty night birds travel low and the lantern rays have an irresistible and fatal attraction. They press in upon it in clouds, striving to reach the fierce ray that, like some fierce sun-spirit, draws them with compelling strength. Many birds that night struck the lantern and fell wounded to the rock below. Many more glanced off the smooth glass and perished in the sea—if indeed they were not dead when they reached the grey, heaving waters. The majority of the birds that night were fieldfares. These field travellers—for such is a translation of their name—had voyaged from the birch forests of Norway, like the Vikings who subdued the Western Isles of old, and were doubtless making for the Irish coast. Many, many of them fell, and the darkness resounded with their cries of alarm, wonder, and excitement as, too late, they attempted to save themselves from striking that deadly wall of glass.

But in spring and early summer the Grey Wind comes seldom. Rather it is the Crimson Wind from the east or the Black Wind from the north that drifts across the Isles bringing with it blue skies and crisp, exhilarating air, so that the breeze is laden with the scents of innumerable growing things. The Black Wind, traveling down to the Isles from the frozen seas that approach the Pole, sweeps away the mists and the haze so that distant hills seem near and the jagged, snow-flecked spires of the Cuillin rise sharply into a fairylike horizon.

But although the Grey Wind may slumber long, the day will come, sooner or later, when once again it will advance from the west, will obscure the blue skies and each hill, high and low, and with its soft moisture will refresh the land.

T11-26

The rare picture of a pair of greenshanks at their nest.

6

Hill Days

Seton Gordon was a formidable walker. Desmond and Carrie Nethersole-Thompson encountered him first on the Cairngorms and noted the slow, steady, tireless hill stride of the tall thin man with bonnet, tweed jacket and kilt — instantly recognised. He walked everywhere in pursuit of wildlife or historical places of interest. Summits were incidental and often kept for clear days to allow hours on top of the widespread world he knew so intimately. 'Morven in Snow' tells of a teenage day but, forty years on, his 1945 diary, quoted later, shows the lure of the hills as strong as ever.

The Old Man of Stoer.

MOUNTAIN DAWN, MEALL NA SUIREANACH

The beauty of sunrise is appreciated the more when it is seen at the end of a long walk, arduous and sometimes wearisome, across moors and hill slopes during the shadowy hours of a Hebridean summer night. That night, sunset behind the hills of Harris had been at twenty minutes past ten, visibility had been good and it seemed that a clear sunrise might follow. Half an hour before midnight Morag, the Cairn terrier, and I left our home in the north of Skye. Had Morag known that our destination was the small cairn on Meall na Suireanach above the Quirang, 1779 feet above sea level, she might have shown less enthusiasm for a night walk.

Of the thousands of visitors who have climbed to the Quirang, few have stood on the hilltop close to and almost immediately above it for the rocky face is inaccessible and a long detour is necessary in order to reach the cairn. The night was warm after a day of sunshine when a shade temperature of seventy-five degrees (the highest reading for two years) was recorded. Across the Minch came the friendly flashes, in threes, from the lighthouse on Glas Eilean on the island of Scalpay. The scent of a myriad early July flowers lay above the sun-warmed moor: large white moths drifted past, seeking nectar from these flowers.

The crofters of Skye believe in burning the midnight oil although, now that electricity is supplied them, oil is almost a thing of the past. Half an hour after midnight I could see in the distance a number of houses still brightly lighted. The Hebrides lie so far west that even by Greenwich Time the clock is half an hour ahead of the sun. During Summer Time, the clock is an hour and a half ahead of the Small sun—the Islesman calls it an hour and a half 'fast'.

At 1 a.m., therefore, twilight was still deepening. We were then approaching the shore of dark Loch Sneosdal from which Creag Sneosdal rises almost one thousand feet. On this precipice there is a geological fault which appears like a great wall, at least twenty feet high, built almost vertically up the cliff. Its local name is Garadh na Fèinne, *the Fingalians' Wall*. When an old lady of the district was asked what reason those half-mythical Celtic warriors, the Fingalians, had for building that great wall she replied, 'Maybe they had nothing better to do.'

It is said that these heroes were so tall that they were able, as they sat at the top of the precipice, to cool their feet in the waters of Loch Sneosdal.

There is a strange atmosphere in the neighbourhood of this loch. Here, it is said, the dreaded *each uisge* or water horse has his home and there is a pass here known as Bealach na Beiste, *Pass of the Beast* or *Monster*. Had we been at home Morag would have been sound asleep at this hour, but as she sat beside me on the shore of the loch she would not rest, but started often to her feet, ears cocked, as she gazed intently through the dusk.

The moon, past the full, was obscured by clouds that drifted past slowly from the south. As the moon showed herself for a moment, her pale light mingled with the afterglow on the far northern horizon, whence came a single stab of white light from the lighthouse on Tiumpan Head close to Stornoway, forty miles distant. Later the clouds dissolved and I found that the dazzle from the low, unclouded moon made walking more difficult. The moon, a few of the brighter planets and stars, and the afterglow creeping imperceptibly northward produced a soft twilight through which the hills of the Outer Hebrides could be seen rising faintly on the horizon.

Dawn was breaking as I reached the watershed and came in sight of the island of South Rona and the powerful flashes from its lighthouse. There was no hint of chill in the midsummer dawn. Faint currents of wind, fragrant with the perfume of hill flowers and plants, drifted across from the south. At 3.45 a.m. a meadow pipit rose into the air and flew waywardly higher and higher in the direction of the waning moon until lost to view. The dawn, as I could see, was strengthening behind the hill top, but there was no hint of sunrise from the south slopes. It was therefore a surprise when I reached the small cairn to find that I was only just in time for sunrise. On the far north-east horizon rose the hills of the Reay Forest. One of them, Farraval, eighty miles distant, a hill usually of no great distinction, was now dark and imposing against a red, glowing sky, the time being just sixteen minutes past four.

As I sat and watched this scene of changing beauty I noticed that Morag, now beyond the influence of the haunted loch, had curled herself in a tight ball and was fast asleep. A golden plover arrived and stood only a few feet from me, uttering his mournful flute-like whistle. The far north-east horizon brightened and at 4.26 a.m. the sun's orb, enormous and with tenuous clouds streaked across his red disc, climbed very slowly above the horizon and seemed to fill the strath of the far distant Dionard River. The sun had travelled far since, six hours before, he had dipped behind the summit ridge of Clisham in Harris, and his coming signalled a new day of warmth and sunshine. When next I noted the hour the time was 4.39 a.m. and the sun was poised above the long hill of Foinne Bheinn and now threw a golden pathway on the sleeping, almost windless, ocean. Farraval, lost its glory and was almost invisible in the haze of distance. The pillar of reflected sunfire on the sea became more glowing and gained in distinction when the sun for a few seconds was hidden by a distant cloud. By five o'clock the hills of the Reay Forest had become dim in haze but the sea near Rudha Reidh, a promontory of Wester Ross, was afire in the sun's rays and a dark red glow burned on the cliffs of Beinn Eadarra [Edra] of Skye. Before sunrise Trodday and the Shiant Isles had been dark and very clear; now, although the sun shone on them, they were less distinct and the magic of the sunrise hour had faded from the scene.

It is a peculiarity of the common ling or heather that it flowers earlier on hill tops than at lower levels, and well-formed pink buds were showing on the hilltop while fifteen hundred feet below on the low moors not a bud showed.

Larks were joyously soaring and cheerful families of wheatears were passed during the descent that morning. It was seven o'clock when I again approached Loch Sneosdal and rested awhile on its shore. The loch was no longer gloomy and mysterious and the morning sun shone brightly on the water and on the high rocks, which are in sun only in the early morning. Small trout were rising to a hatch of fly, or were sunning themselves in the shallows. A sandpiper flew out over the loch, the waters of which, near the far shore, were still opaque from a cloudburst towards the end of June.

Before that cloudburst the Isle of Skye had been for many days an isle of sunshine. The rain, that evening of June 23, gradually became of tropical violence. Hill torrents appeared where none had been known before. Darkness descended before sunset and in three hours the rain gauge recorded two and a half inches. Early next morning the sun was shining on hill and sea. The grassy face of Creag Sneosdal was changed in a remarkable manner. Here two great scars showed where thousands of tons of rocks, earth and grass had slipped like an avalanche down the hill face. They will remain for many years, perhaps for centuries, to commemorate that tremendous rainfall of 23 June, 1955.

A heat wave in early June is marred by neither of those two Highland pests, the midge and the cleg. A hot spell in early July encourages them both. The cleg or gadfly gives the walker, or the worker in the field, no peace and its bite is more formidable than that of the midge. Fortunately it is not wily and should a first attempt to slay it fail, it returns at once, and is usually liquidated. The name cleg is an unusual one; I used to think it was Scottish until I heard it was used in Norway. It may be a relic of the Norse occupation of the Hebrides.

The small cairn from which I had seen sunrise is named Carn Mhic an t-Sagairt, *Cairn of the Priest's Son*. On my way across the common grazing at the foot of the hill I passed near Buaile an t-Sagairt, *Sheepfold of the Priest,* and Clach an t-Sagairt, *Stone of the Priest*. It would seem that, like the cairn on the hilltop, these names commemorate a priest of olden times. Saint Maolrubha was known as the Red Priest of Applecross and he was often in Skye; the names may commemorate him or one of his followers.

Earlier I mentioned the sunrise burning dull red on the high rocks of Beinn Eadarra. It was some months later in the year when a friend and I, this time accompanied by Dileas the collie and Morag, climbed the hill, which is just two thousand feet high. October gave summer warmth that year. Although the heather was over, hill violets were flowering out of season. The grass was green beside a clear stream where stand the foundations of summer shielings more than one hundred years old. The people of the glen lived in these shielings during the summer months, taking with them their stock in order that the grass on their small fields might recover from the close grazing of the winter months. These small ruins tell of a way of life that will return no more. High above these shielings, on stony ground almost two thousand feet above sea level, were a number of wheatears, pursuing insects with quick, fluttering flights, or playfully chasing one another. These were almost certainly Greenland wheatears, held up by the south wind after a hard oversea migration, and finding a plentiful food supply and unexpected warmth. Near the hilltop, where black-faced sheep had cropped the grass close as a lawn, rosettes of cyphel were green. The cyphel *(Arenaria)* has very small green-tinted flowers without petals, close to the ground to withstand the gales at this height. A raven, sailing high over its mountain territory, turned joyfully on its back, then closed its dark wings and dropped like a stone behind the east-facing precipice. A few minutes later excited croakings were heard, and we saw a thrilling sight for birdlovers. Close overhead a golden eagle appeared, the raven, seeming no larger than a blackbird by comparison, in hot pursuit. Both birds were heading into the strong breeze and the eagle was driving himself forward by powerful thrusts of his strong, broad wings. In less than half a minute raven and eagle disappeared from sight behind the line of cliffs; shortly afterwards the raven returned, to sail backwards and forwards above its territory as before.

HD-63

AN TEALLACH

From Braemore one has a glorious view of one of the most inspiring of Scottish mountains—An Teallach. I had often looked upon An Teallach. From Skye and the Outer Hebrides I had seen it rise to the clouds that so often drift above the high mainland hills when the islands are bathed in sunshine. From the Cairngorms I had looked, times without number, across the intervening bens to its rocky spires, and from the high ground of Sutherland I had seen it guarding the gateway of ocean. From whatever quarter it was viewed An Teallach had always been graceful, always distinctive, so that I was hopeful of exploring it more closely.

At length came a spring afternoon when I was on the Diridh Mór (*the Great Ascent*) which climbs away eastward from Dundonnell to Garve and, standing on the road in the setting sun, looked over brown moorlands to where the snowy corries and majestic peaks of An Teallach rose to the silver-edged clouds that idly drifted above its summit. As I was spying the hill-top a full six miles away through my telescope I saw a golden eagle sail across the ice-plastered cairn and soar magnificently, with careless grace, out over the great precipices of Loch Toll an Lochain.

The sun was shining and the air was clear and calm when I left the hospitable inn at Dundonnell on the shore of Little Loch Broom the next morning. The first thousand feet of the ascent are steep, but a good path makes walking easy. As I climbed I looked back from time to time to admire the view. Across Little Loch Broom rose shapely Beinn Ghobhlach, *the Forked Hill*, well named because of its two peaks and as I mounted higher Ben Mór Coigeach appeared to the north with its long and inviting summit ridge holding, here and there, a field of snow. To the east of me was the high hill known as Sgùrr Eideadh nan Clach Geala—*the Peak of the Garment of White Stones*, but on this April morning of strong sunshine these white stones were deeply hidden beneath an unbroken covering of virgin snow. For the first thousand feet of the climb I had been out of sight of the main peak of An Teallach, but now I came suddenly in sight of it. Stately and aloof, it rose to the deep blue of the sky. Upon its dark rocks snow lay thickly and the mounting sun shone so dazzlingly upon these spotless snow-fields that, even at a distance, it pained the eye to look upon them.

Yet, did one look west, one seemed on the instant to be transported from winter to summer. Eilean a' Chléirich (*Priest's Isle*) and the Summer Isles rose from a blue serene sea and faint and hazy in the far distance was the coast of Lewis. At a height of 1,500 feet above sea level I reached the snow. None but those who have actually walked on newly-fallen snow in late spring or early summer have any idea of the intensity of its reflected light. The eyes of the climber unless they are protected by snow glasses, suffer acute discomfort. A long walk over this type of snow may produce snow blindness. I remember on one occasion walking on the Brae Riach plateau on the Cairngorms in late May. The previous day there had been a heavy snowfall and the sun shining with almost midsummer power rendered the unbroken snowy surface so dazzling that my friend and I, after stumbling forward half blinded for a time, were compelled to sit down beside a few rocks from which the snow had melted. Here we waited until a cloud had obscured the sun. Snow blindness is a painful thing. It may render the sufferer totally blind, and may compel him to remain in a darkened room while sight slowly returns.

I was fortunate to find areas of snow-free ground on my climb up An Teallach. There were sun-warmed terraces of red sandstone on which cushions of sea thrift were stirring into life. It is a peculiarity of this plant that it is equally at home beside the tide or on the high hills. On An Teallach it is more plentiful than on any other Scottish hill I have climbed, and takes the place of the cushion pink, the usual flowering plant of the high tops.

The summit of An Teallach is marked on the map as Bidein a' Ghlas Thuill, *the Peak of the Green Hollow*. It is 3,483 feet above sea level. The last few hundred feet of the peak are steep and stony and frozen snow made climbing more arduous. As I neared the hill-top the weather was changing. Gathering clouds hid the sun and from An Teallach rose vaporous mists like smoke from some giant forge. An Teallach indeed means the forge, and the old Gaelic name may have been given to the crowded summits which form its *massif* because of the mist that so often eddy about them. A wandering whirlwind caught up a column of frozen snow and carried it over the hill-side just beneath me. The breath of the north wind was keen. Across the snow led the track of a fox. A golden eagle, perhaps the same bird that I had seen from a distance the previous day, sailed across the hill in the teeth of the breeze, a dark, determined form. It was early afternoon when I stood on the hill-top beside the ice-encrusted cairn and looked over the vast precipices to where dark Loch Toll an Lochain lies in the heart of this mighty hill.

Across the abyss, where the eagle soars and the ptarmigan at times flies like a drifting snowflake, rose the awe-inspiring turrets and slender spire of Sgùrr Fiona, just nine feet lower than the hill-top where I stood. From Sgùrr

Fiona the slopes of an-t-Sàil Liath, *the Grey Heel*, led down to Strath na Sealg, home of swamps and rushes and resinous bog fir. Loch na Sealg, *the Loch of the Hunts*, lay invisible in its deep glen. East and south storms of snow and hail had formed, and the Cairngorm Hills which I had hoped to see were invisible.

Nearer at hand, across Gruinard Bay, I could see Rudha Mór, where lies Loch na Béiste, *the Loch of the Monster*. The supernatural creature was often visible. It appeared even to some elders of the church of a Sunday morning. This audacity so terrified the people of the district that they persuaded the landowner to drain the loch in order that the beast might be destroyed. But the loch could not be dried and after long months of fruitless efforts it was decided that the monster must be killed in his lair—a deep hole in the middle of the loch. To this end fourteen barrels of lime were emptied into the hole—with much trepidation. The creature evidently submitted tamely to being limed in, for today it is seen no more!

The clouds thinned, and overhead the sky once more was blue. Northward the clouds rested lightly on Cuinneag, and the slopes of Ben Mór Coigeach took on that deep blue which so often foretells a change of weather. Away on the northeast horizon rose the great bulk of Ben More Assynt, a remote hill that is the mother of the Oykell River. The dazzling glare had left the snow-fields near me; An Teallach was now bathed in soft lights. A pair of ptarmigan and a wandering deer had the hill to themselves but when I had descended below the snow-line and walked again by the shore of Little Loch Broom many birds were calling in the quiet of evening. Here was warm sunshine, but looking back I watched a great storm gather on An Teallach. Inky clouds, bearing in their depths both snow and hail, dropped lower and yet lower upon the snowy cones of the mountain group and I thought of the eagle grasping some rocky pinnacle with his strong talons as he awaited the storm, and the ptarmigan crouching in the shelter of some protecting rock, and the hind hastening with whitened coat to the lower corries.

H&BW-35

LOCH COIRE A' GHRUNNDA:
A HIGH CUILLIN TARN

There are few lochs in the corries of the Black Cuillin. Loch Coruisk, Loch na Creitheach, Loch an Athain—all are in the deep glens and lie less than a hundred feet above the Atlantic surf. In Coire Lagan of Sgurr Alasdair is a dark pool but it is so small that it can scarcely be called a loch: the only hill loch of the range in the true sense of the word is cradled in a delightful corrie 2400 feet above the sea. This corrie is Coire a' Ghrunnda, *the Corrie of the Ground or Earth*. It lies between Sgurr Alasdair and Sgurr nan Eag, and the loch is in its basin.

From no part of the low ground is Loch Coire a' Ghrunnda visible; it is guarded closely by the conical peaks of Sgurr Alasdair and Sgurr nan Eag.

Loch Coire a' Ghrunnda lies high, yet its climate is not cold, and one April day when the lochs of the Cairngorms were beneath snow and ice a friend of mine bathed in its clear waters! The spring sun shines strongly here and from the hard winds out of the north and east the loch is sheltered by the hills that rise steeply from it. On the second day of May I have seen the blaeberry plants near the loch in full leaf, and the purple mountain saxifrage in blossom.

One day I saw a gathering of golden eagles here. In brilliant sunshine the first eagle sailed easily above the narrow ridge, east of the loch. From a different direction a second eagle appeared, then a third, fourth, and finally a fifth. High above the corrie the five magnificent birds met, flying up from north, south, east, and west. In the deep blue of the sky they soared awhile, gliding as steadily as aeroplanes. One pair, rising into the easterly wind, swung in circles to an immense height. A white cloud was hanging fully 4000 feet above the corrie, and into the cloud one of the eagles sailed mysteriously, gliding into its billowy depths. The male bird of the second pair swiftly dipped towards his larger mate. She, crossing above the barren cone of Sgurr Dubh, dropped, plummet-like, earthward in two magnificent headlong dives of frightful impetus. Finally this pair of eagles sailed leisurely across the smooth rock walls of Sgurr Sgumhan, casting dark shadows on its glistening snowfields. One after another the five eagles disappeared from view and the sky was void of bird-life as before.

There is no more delightful walk in the Cuillin than the climb to Loch Coire a' Ghrunnda and the hills above it. Beneath the climber the ocean swell rolls in gently. On the Atlantic are many islands—Rhum, Eigg, and Canna, the Outer Isles, Mull of the Hills. It is always inspiring to see them rise from the restless plains of the ever-changing yet changeless ocean. At the mouth of Coire Lagan the climber crosses a stream of clear water with steep heathery banks where stunted hollies cling, then crosses moderately level ground at a height of 1000 feet and reaches the base of Coire a' Ghrunnda where great slabs of brown rock alternate with pleasant heather-clad ground.

The symmetrical basin of Coire a' Ghrunnda lies behind steep, rocky slopes; there is just sufficient difficulty in climbing the approaches to the corrie to give a feeling of satisfaction when the climber reaches the loch.

In a series of falls a burn drops swiftly from the loch to the low ground. On grassy ledges beside the burn of Coire a' Ghrunnda the shapely golden-rod blooms late in summer, and cushions of *arabis* brighten the scree. In July the bog asphodel flowers here, and sprays of golden St John's-wort mingle with it. *Achlasan Chaluim-chille* is the Celtic name of this graceful flower, since St Columba always carried it on his person. It was specially prized by the people of the Isles when found in the folds of the flocks, for it was an omen that the animals would prosper throughout the ensuing year. It was believed that the St John's-wort kept all evil from the person who, finding it unexpectedly, plucked it and carried it always in a secret place of safety.

The eastern shore of Loch Coire a' Ghrunnda is of dark sand that is the colour of earth. The sand stretches far out into the water and may give the corrie its name. On the surface of the submerged sand furrows are sometimes seen. In appearance they resemble minute wavelets, and are formed by the pounding of the waves on a day of storm. Above the sandy beach the rocks are bright with alpine flowers. Moss campion, cushion pink, rose root, sea thrift, starry saxifrage, and milkwort—all these flowers grow beside this loch of the hill Cuillin. From the loch a small rocky island rises. There are crannies in its rocks where alpine plants grow, and on its crown the hill grass is delightfully green. On the waters beside this islet water-beetles row themselves backwards and forwards, but no trout lives in this lonely lochan.

One quiet day of summer when I climbed to Coire a' Ghrunnda the mist closely enfolded the hill. So dense was the cloud that the farther shore of the loch was invisible. A chill breeze brought wavelets from out the unknown to break at my feet with faint music on the low shore. At times the cloud overhead became less dense and it seemed as though the mist would lift. But always fresh clouds arrived from the invisible peaks and the corrie remained a place of ghostly vapours.

I had rested an hour beside the loch when the sky overhead changed from grey to blue. In little more than a minute the mist had rolled away, not only from the loch itself, but from the Cuillin that lean above it. The summit of Sgurr Alasdair is just 1000 feet above the waters of Loch Coire a' Ghrunnda, and it was a memorable experience to see the mist swiftly draw back and dissolve, revealing the silent loch, the rocky slopes of Sgurr Alasdair clear to the summit, and the sun upon Sgurr nan Eag. Faint clouds for a few minutes longer lay just below the crest of Sgurr Alasdair then they too faded and the sun was supreme. The last of the mist-laden breeze died away and the small hill loch lay calm as a mirror.

From the ridge, 400 feet above Loch Coire a' Ghrunnda, later in the day I looked down upon the loch. There were many colours upon it. In the centre of the lochan the waters were pale grey. Near the northern shore, where the depth was greater, they were inky black, while above the sand they were dark brown. This day no eagle's wing darkened the surface of the tarn, but a mountain pipit rose from beside me and sailed easily down to the loch across great boulders of volcanic origin. Flying daintily across the loch, the small bird was reflected faithfully in the quiet surface.

Once more the mist began to enfold the hills. Where I stood was the dividing line between cloud and clear weather. Far below me Loch Coruisk lay. Often it is a loch of gloom and darkness, to-day the sun shone upon it and upon the waterfall that leapt eagerly from the loch to the mother ocean so that peace and happiness replaced the greyness of twilight. The waters of Loch Scavaig, flooding submerged sands, were emerald. From these waters green, grassy islands rose, sun-bathed all of them.

From time to time a curtain of mist rolled up the *bealach* from the Garbh Choire, and a cold air-current of its own making glided with it over the dun stones as it shut out that scene of sunshine in Coruisk below. The mist crossed the pass and slipped into Coire a' Ghrunnda. It strove to reach the loch but was ever dispersed by the warm air in the corrie where the scent of the wild thyme lay. Eager breezes more than once ruffled the calm surface of Loch Coire a' Ghrunnda. They were the herdsmen of the mists and since the mists were lost to them they crossed the lochan aimlessly, as the clan of dreams that take their departure at sunrise. But the hills, although it was full day, continued to dream, and everywhere was a silence so intense that it could be felt—a silence broken once by the croak of a raven high among the rocks of Sgumhan. Sun-glow upon hill mist is always a wonderful thing. The clouds to-day were so thin at times that the sun, penetrating them, burned faintly upon the hillside below the mist. A few yards from me rose Clach an t-Sionnaich, the *Fox's Stone*. This great pillar of rock was mist-encircled, faint and hazy, yet glowed as though afire. One minute it rose thus, with intangibility upon it, the next the mist dissolved and the rocky tower, clear-cut and no longer mysterious, stood with the full light of the summer sun upon it.

Towards evening the view from the corrie was such as the west alone can give. From a sunlit sea the Cuillin of Rhum rose steeply, light clouds resting upon their summits. Red sandy beaches alternated with dark headlands on that island of green pastures and heavy stags. Canna, Eigg, Muck, the point of Ardnamurchan, the Isle of Mull—all were clear, while upon Soay a thunder-shower gathered, then passed westward.

In Coire a' Ghrunnda itself there is little view southward, for Sgurr nan Eag rises steeply above it, but from the hill-slopes below the corrie the houses of Elgol could be seen and the boats that were anchored in its bay. There was shade here, but away beyond Loch Eiseord the promontory of Sleat rose with sunlight upon it, and the ocean here was afire.

Evening brought a breeze from the north. It bore the last of the clouds from the hills and when, an hour after sunset, the full moon of burnished gold climbed from the sea beyond Sleat, her light shone undimmed upon the lonely waters of Loch Coire a' Ghrunnda.

COS-29

The view to Coire Lagan has not changed – unlike outdoor clothing!

MORVEN IN SNOW

About six miles north-west of Dinnet, Morven, *the Great Hill* (2,863 feet above sea-level), lies midway between the valleys of the Dee and Don, and from the summit cairn a view of surpassing beauty is obtained in every direction.

At the time we make the ascent the new year is yet only a few days old, but a succession of warm southwesterly winds has caused most of the traces of the recent snowstorm to disappear. Motoring from Aboyne, we have, at the old mill of Dinnet, to take the car through a field, as an immense drift, which a day or two ago was estimated at 20 feet in depth, lies across the roadway. The route is by Ordie and Loch Davan, and two wreaths have to be cut through to reach Morven's base. The air is soft and mild and extraordinarily clear but a gale blows from the south-west and it is not easy to progress against it.

The hill is wonderfully clear of snow but one huge drift is noted in a low-lying corrie and the fence is completely hidden by the snow. The first white hare is seen just below the 2,000 feet level and he runs off, looking for all the world like a small snow wreath as he is spotlessly white with the exception of his ears. Just before reaching the mossy plateau lying about the 2,000 feet line we put up several Ptarmigan. These mountain dwellers are rarely met with below 2,500 feet, but we have noticed them several times at this spot, even during the nesting season, which is rather interesting, seeing that on Lochnagar, Ben Muich Dhui, and their other strongholds they do not descend much below 3,000 feet. All round the plateau pack after pack of Grouse get up and, rising against the wind, gradually swerve off and fly down-wind at express speed. The birds are exceptionally wild and take wing while we are yet several hundred yards from them.

Although it is only two o'clock the sky to the south-east, from Mount Keen to Kerloch, is lit up a beautiful pink, as though the sun has already set. Morven's southern slopes have many deep and soft wreaths on them but we strike off to the right and gain the summit plateau at the eastern cairn, which is partly of natural formation. Before reaching the summit, however, we have some snow climbing to do, as a drift some 200 yards long and exceedingly steep bars the way, and at one point we are almost blown from our scanty footing by the force of the gale. On the distant wreaths coveys of Grouse stand or run weirdly about, looking very comical on the snow, and a number of hares run quickly for safety from their natural enemy. Several roosting hollows of the Grouse are discovered, some containing fresh droppings; a bed on the snow, must prove rather chilly when there is so much bare ground all round.

As we emerge on the summit plateau the wind blows with hurricane force; but at length we gain the shelter of the cairn, about 400 yards distant, and gaze our full at the glorious view. During the ascent a thin grey mist has at times passed over the higher reaches of the hill, but has been borne onwards by the gale. We have climbed Morven many a time, but never has the view been such as it is today. Due south, Mount Keen (3,077 feet) and the Braid Cairn, a few hundred feet lower, are comparatively free of snow. The summit of Clach-na-Ben is clearly seen, as are also Kerloch and Cairn Mon Earn. Evidently there is less wind further down the valley, for the smoke of Banchory is lying above the village and the North Sea is hidden by the smoke of Aberdeen.

Due north, Ben Rinnes is bathed a most glorious pink by the setting sun, and here the sky is of surpassing loveliness. Northwest the blue is tinged with green; this gradually merges into dark blue, and still further east the sky is tinged with pink. The Brown Cow (3,000 feet), between Gairn and Don, carries an immense drift on its south side, locally known to the natives as the 'Brown Cow's White Calf.' To the northwest, about eleven miles distant, the road from Cockbridge to Tomintoul is seen winding up the hill and filled with huge drifts. Ben Avon and Cairngorm are occasionally hidden by mist, and at times the giant stones on the former's summit are the only part of the mountain left visible.

The setting sun shining on the westward slopes of the hills to the north-west has a marvellous effect and we seem to be transported to a fairy world. Above Strathdon the road appears to carry a considerable depth of snow but between Dinnet and Donside the road is comparatively free of drifts. Looking south-west, ice-bound Loch Muick is seen nestling amongst the mountains, and Lochnagar and the Cuidhe Crom make a beautiful picture with the setting sun behind them.

Suddenly a mist envelops the cairn behind which we shelter. We strike down the south side of the hill. We hoped to have been rewarded with some glissading but unfortunately the snow is comparatively soft and after several unsuccessful attempts we have to give up.

For another hour at least the sunset continues, each minute receding further west, where for long the sky is lit up with a crimson hue impossible to describe. The Grouse rise startled at our feet, calling loudly in alarm, and darkness rapidly descends on the mountain; while the glow in the west becomes gradually fainter and fainter, until at last night reigns supreme.

BLM-07

The lochan in Coir' a' Ghrunnda, Skye.

A FOINNE BHEINN DAY

It is one of the charms of a November day that unexpected legacies of summer are sometimes seen in unexpected places. One day early in that month I climbed Foinne Bheinn, the highest hill of the Reay Forest in North West Sutherland. My way had taken me first along the banks of the salmon-haunted Dionard river, where the dark shapes of fish could be seen in the amber-tinted pools. When I reached Dugal's Pool I left the river and climbed to Dugal's Corrie where lies Dugal's Loch. I wondered then, as I have since, who was this Dugal for his name remains long after all record of him has been lost.

Sarove Dugal's Corrie the radiant peak of Foinne Bheinn in virgin snow rose against the blue of the sky. In the corrie the grass was brown, the heather bloom long since withered, and the sodden ground newly imprisoned beneath a crust of frost, yet a single scabious flower, large and deep blue, rose from these sere acres and gave me, as it seemed, a message of summer days when the sun was warm, the air heather-scented and the grass of the corrie soft and green.

A flower, unexpectedly seen, sometimes brings back to me the memory of my mother. She, like the mother of W. H. Hudson, loved flowers, for she had a love for all that was beautiful. During my early wanderings if I came upon a wild rose with a specially fragrant scent or a spray of bell heather of an unusually lovely red, I used sometimes to take those flowers home to her. But with the passing of the years I am inclined to leave a flower on its stalk, although I often stoop down to breathe in the fragrance of a wild rose, or a scented orchis, or the honey scent of a clustered head of the rosy moss campion, opening its hardy flowers close to the blinding glare from some snowfield of the high Cairngorms. The most exquisite pictures of flowers photographed on and stored by the mind are the blossoms that grew free as the air they breathed and not gathered into a vase within the confines of a room. In his poem *Forbearance,* Ralph Waldo Emerson asks 'Hast thou named all the birds without a gun? Loved the wood-rose, and left it on its stalk?'

With some of us our love of flowers continues unchanged, and even intensified, with the passing years; the beauty of a flower, a bird, a cloud, sunset and sunrise, evoke in us the same response in later, more anxious years as in the fullness of youth.

When I had climbed through Dugal's Corrie to the ridge of Foinne Bheinn I saw ahead of me a young stag feeding, then lost sight of him. When I reached the ridge the young animal received the fright of its life, for I suddenly appeared beside him as he rested, chewing the cud, on a grassy sun-warmed bank.

Beyond the ridge the snow was continuous; on it were the tracks of fox and hare and, more unexpected, the footprints of an otter. The ridge lay between the two salmon rivers, Laxford and Dionard, and the otter had perhaps crossed the high pass of Foinne Bheinn from the rocky pools of the Laxford and as an expert fisherman was hoping to try his luck in the Dionard. Otters in a river pool strike terror into the hearts of the salmon inhabiting it, for they know that this land animal is their master even in their native element.

One day a friend and I were walking beside the river Feshie not far from its source amongst the Cairngorms. On the banks of a pool we found a freshly killed salmon, untouched except for a bite taken out of the shoulder—that part of the salmon which is the otter's favourite cut. My friend took the fish home with him, and it provided him with supper and breakfast for several days.

Near the otter's tracks on the snow of Foinne Bheinn a ptarmigan rose on white wings and disappeared over the ridge into the corrie. Alas, before we could reach the hilltop the mist swept in on the north west wind. Fog-crystals in beautiful fern-shape grew from the rocks: the frozen moisture in the fog fell as delicate spicules of ice. Here, at nearly three thousand feet above the sea, the frost was sufficient to freeze the water vapour in the air. To freeze the spray of the waves—a sight never witnessed in Scotland—an immeasurably more severe frost is necessary. A friend of mine, the captain of one of His Majesty's Ships, told me that when on escort duties with a convoy bound for Murmansk the spray from the great waves that broke over his vessel reached the bridge as ice—the spray froze in less than three seconds when suspended in that bitter air.

Behind the cairn that marks the highest point of Foinne Bheinn I waited in a mist-filled land. From time to time for a few brief seconds black cliffs showed, then were blotted out again in the grey, blue-tinted cloak of mist. Although during these periods the gloom lightened and the blue of the sky showed overhead the hilltop remained for the rest of that short November day hidden in cloud and when on my descent I had at length passed beyond the zone of cloud I could see that the hills to the east—Ben Hope, Ben Loyal and Morven—were, each one of them, shrouded in a white mist cap.

HY-44

BEN VORLICH OF LOCH EARN

It is interesting that there should be two hills at no great distance from one another as the eagle flies, each bearing the name Ben Vorlich. Ardvorlich, on the shore of Loch Earn (from which Ben Vorlich takes its name), is the Gaelic Ard Mhurlaig, *Promontory of the Sea-bay*. This country is the home of the Stewarts of Ardvorlich, an old Highland family who have held their lands for 350 years.

In the house of Ardvorlich is preserved the family talisman, the celebrated Clach Dhearg, *the Red Stone*, which was held to have miraculous properties. If the stone were dipped in a pail of water and moved thrice, *deiseil* or sun-wise, round the pail, the water would then have healing powers in the illnesses of cattle. So renowned was this crystal that people walked great distances to carry back to their ailing cattle water in which Clach Dhearg, no doubt with appropriate incantations, had been dipped.

The west wind was shaking the leaves in russet showers from the stately old trees which surround the house of Ardvorlich and was raising white-capped waves on Loch Earn that autumn morning when first I climbed Ben Vorlich. I had last looked upon the hill in clear April weather when this hill of lovely curves rose to the unclouded blue of the sky at sunrise, a picture so rare and inspiring that I hoped some day to set foot on its summit. But when actually I did achieve my ambition the weather was dark and boisterous, with a rugged wind whistled through the most sheltered corries with cold, clammy breath.

At first as my friend and I walked up Glen Vorlich there was shelter from the west wind, and we watched sun and shade rapidly pass across the hill and the mists rise and fall on the cone of Ben Vorlich, which bounded the horizon ahead of us. On the sheltered slope above the glen a stag and a few hinds were feeding, the stag — for it was the rutting season — anxious and restless. The bloom on the heather was past its best but here and there a small yellow tormentil flower caught the eye, and beside clear hill streams pink blossom-heads of the lousewort showed that summer had not entirely gone. We climbed by way of an old *bealach* across which cattle from the Highlands had been driven for centuries to the Falkirk markets. We passed a nameless stone that marks the last resting-place of the body of an unknown traveller who long ago lost his life here during a winter blizzard. Near the watershed between Ardvorlich and Glen Artney we saw two old cock grouse chasing one another so furiously and flying at so great a height that it was difficult to recognise them as red grouse.

We were now in wild storm-swept country and watched a pair of ravens fly high overhead and a buzzard rock as the wind-gusts struck him. Through the *bealach* the wind swept with the strength of a gale and made us realise the conditions which were likely to be experienced on the hill-top, 1,300 feet above. We watched, perhaps a couple of miles to the east, the gusts of wind sweep down upon a small loch, dark and lonely beneath the stormy autumn sky.

The name of that wind-vexed tarn is Lochan na Mnà, *the Woman's Loch*, and the strange story of the naming of the loch was told me by the descendant of the woman of the tragic tale, as the rough wind tore past us on the steep slopes of Ben Vorlich.

The first Stewart of Ardvorlich married, towards the close of the sixteenth century, the daughter of Drummond, the King's Keeper of the Royal Forest of Glen Artney and Steward of Strathearn. A party of MacGregors on their way home from the Lowlands took the opportunity of killing some deer in the royal forest. They were caught and, instead of being hauled before the sheriff (as they would have been at the present day), their ears were cut off and they were sent home gory and muttering threats of vengeance.

The MacGregors brooded on this insult. They made their plans for revenge and set out to capture the King's Forester when hunting alone in Glen Artney. They surrounded and slew him without mercy and carrying his head wrapped in a plaid, they crossed the *bealach,* made their way down Glen Vorlich, and heading for Balquhidder, chanced to hear that Stewart of Ardvorlich was away from home, so knocked at the door of his house and asked for food and drink. The lady of Ardvorlich saw the rough, travel-stained men at her door, and from their tartan she no doubt recognised them as MacGregors. She must have been well aware of the feud between that clan and her father, yet the law of Highland hospitality was binding, and she called them in, placed bread and cheese and oaten cakes on the table before them, and then left the room.

When she returned she saw, set upright on the centre of the table, and with a piece of bread and cheese in its mouth, the blood-stained head of her father. Shrieking, she fled demented from that house of horror; as she made her way wildly up the glen the tumult of her wailing became softened by distance and then was no more heard.

Ardvorlich returned soon afterwards and he and his people searched the glen and the hills beyond for his missing wife, with no success. But some days later, those who at the time were living in the summer shielings at the head of Glen Vorlich — the ruins of these shiels can be seen at the present day — became aware that their cows were giving little milk. Some suspected the fairies but a watch was kept at night and a woman was seen milking the cows. She was quietly followed and was discovered sheltering near the shore of the tarn which has ever since been named Lochan na Mnà, *the Woman's Loch*. Moaning pitifully and temporarily bercft of her reason, the poor lady was borne down the glen to her home. Soon after she gave birth to a son, James, who throughout his life bore the stamp of the terrible experience which had befallen his mother. It was this James Stewart of Ardvorlich who, growing into a strange and moody youth, murdered Lord Kilpont in a brawl in Montrose's camp before the battie of Inverlochy.

The MacGregors who had committed the murder were from Balquhidder, of the outlawed race known as the Children of the Mist. They carried the gory head along the wooded shore of Loch Earn and when they had reached Balquhidder sought out their chief, Alasdair of Glenstrae, then a young man of twenty-one, and flung themselves on his protection. Glenstrae took their side. He summoned the clan, and in the old church of Balquhidder a grim scene was enacted. The head of the King's Forester was placed upon the high altar and the chief, walking forward, laid his hands upon it and swore that he would defend with his life those who had done the deed. His clansmen followed his example, and the hearts of the murderers were lightened as they saw that they would not go friendless.

The wrath of the Government in Edinburgh was roused. On February 3, 1590, " the Lords of Secret Council, being credibly informed of the cruel and mischievous proceedings of the wicked Clan Gregor, so long continuing in blood, slaughters, herships, manifest reifs and stouths", outlawed and condemned to death the whole clan. John, Lord Drummond, was one of those who were granted letters of fire and sword against the MacGregors.

We mused on these days of desperate vengeance as we sat in shelter from the October wind. For some time Ben Vorlich had been clear of mist, but the clouds, moving in from the west at the speed of an express train, reached the hill-top before us. Mist and gloom enveloped the summit when at length we gained it. Across the narrow ridge the west wind rushed furiously. In gusts its speed must have reached a full ninety miles an hour and its power was hard to withstand. Twilight brooded on that tempest-swept summit and the cold was intense. We sought a way out of the cloud and my friend, with his local knowledge, found the correct slope of descent on the farther side of the hill.

Jostled and shaken by the wind, we ran before it and soon reached the heathery slope that is known as Sgiath nan Tarmachan, *the Ptarmigan's Wing*. We emerged below the cloud-cap and saw that the slope had been well named, for a covey of ptarmigan which had risen unseen from the ground now swept past us down-wind. They remained in our view only a few seconds but their snow-white wings against a background of gloomy rocks were singularly beautiful. Into the dark east-facing corrie of Ben Vorlich the ptarmigan sped: as they alighted and folded their white wings they became at once invisible.

It was strange to peer into that deep corrie and to pass in a moment beyond the power of the wind. As I looked down on to rocks several hundred feet below I saw a creature resembling a wild cat prowling here, perhaps stalking one of the ptarmigan.

That day, even below the mist, Ben Vorlich gave no view, but six months later my friend and I again climbed the hill at sunrise on a May morning and, although the Lowlands were then hidden in haze, the view west and south-west was clear, and extended as far as the peak of Goat Fell in Arran.

On this autumn day it was necessary to hurry down the hill at our best speed in order to bring warmth again to our numbed hands. At an elevation of 2,200 feet above the sea we passed the burrows of a mole. I cannot recall having elsewhere seen mole-heaps on ground so elevated.

Down in Glen Vorlich we escaped the bitter wind, and that evening when the fire burned cheerfully on the hearth in the old house of Ardvorlich and the moon showed fitfully through the storm wrack, the piper tuned his pipe and played a *pìa-baireachd* of the past, telling of days when broken men haunted these hills, and when human life may have been of little account. As he played, the piper thought perhaps of that nameless piper of long ago, he who is commemorated in two place-names of Ben Vorlich — Sgiath a' Phìobaire, *the Piper's Wing* or *Slope*, and Uaimh a' Phìobaire, *the Piper's Cave*.

H&BC-48

7

Western Isles

Both World Wars saw Seton Gordon based on or travelling extensively throughout the Inner Hebrides. This is a minimal selection from a vast amount of material but we return for a third section on islands later – testimony to their endless attraction to Seton Gordon.

A tourist sailing to Staffa.

John Mackenzie, the famous Cuillin guide.

CROSSING THE SOUND OF IONA

I shall always vividly remember the first occasion on which I crossed the sound. The season was near the shortest day and incessant storms had swept in day after day from the Atlantic so that the swell was strong on the rocks. But as the ferry-boat pushed out from the little harbour of Fionphort the wind was not too fresh and we soon covered the mile of sea and made Iona without difficulty.

Toward sunset the wind veered to south-west, increasing momentarily in force, with a wild sky of green framed in black storm-clouds to windward. When the boat set sail, with every reef in, on the return passage, a gale was sweeping the waters, so that some of those in the boat—and there were many crossing because the mail-steamer had failed to call—were of opinion that "There was no safety in the sound."

But all trusted themselves to the fine Highlander who, often single-handed, has sailed the passage these forty years back; and with many farewells from the shore the sail was filled and the boat shot forward with the wind.

Almost at once we were in a heavy sea and the wind blew with such force that all idea of crossing to Fionphort was quickly abandoned and, sailing before the gale, the course was set for the sheltered creek near the little fishing village of Kentra. Things looked serious for we were shipping the waves which broke white-topped and menacing around us—the tide runs strong in the sound and when moving against the storm renders the swell doubly dangerous. Each person had perforce to lie at the bottom of the boat so that the ferryman might see the more easily to avoid the overfalls of the heaviest waves. Some feared that the mast would snap before the strain but all went well and it was with much gratitude that we reached harbour and many a word of well-deserved praise and thanks did the ferryman, soaked to the skin by the breaking waves, receive from his Gaelic-speaking passengers.

LHG-20

A DAY ON THE WHIRLPOOL ISLAND
OF SCARBA

The sun set in splendour behind Muile nam Mór Bheann, *Mull of the Great Hills* and the young moon, golden and benign, sank very slowly beyond the rocky coast of Jura of the Caves. North of Jura rose the high island of Scarba, still clear-cut but dark as night. The evening breeze awoke, gently shepherding small waves over the silent, sleeping sea and arousing it from its dreams.

The wind of dusk was short-lived; next morning the sky was without a cloud as we sailed across from Craignish on the mainland to Scarba. This is a distinguished but lonely island, its one hill, approximately 1,500 feet in height (and haunted by adders) being a landmark from afar. Sir Donald Monro, High Dean of the Isles, wrote of Scarba in the year 1549 as 'an high, roughe yle, inhabit and manurit (cultivated), with some woodes in it'. Little is known of the early inhabitants of Scarba; they have long left.

Mary MacLeod, the celebrated Gaelic poetess whose father was a cousin of the chief of the clan, and who in the course of her long life of 105 years, acted as nurse to five chiefs of the MacLeods was here. As a punishment for a satire she composed on him, the chief banished her for a time to Scarba, where she wrote some of the finest of her songs. When the distinguished traveller Thomas Pennant landed on Scarba in the year 1772 he found forty inhabitants living on the island. His vessel anchored beneath the 'vast mountain of Scarba' which he climbed under the guidance of 'Mr Macleane' who at that time owned the island. Pennant records that the climb was 'through heath of an uncommon height, swarming with grouse'.

Martin Martin, who published his book *A Description of the Western Islands of Scotland* in the year 1703, mentions that only two years before he wrote, a woman 'lived sevenscore years on the Isle of Scarba, and enjoyed the free use of her Senses and Understanding all her days'. The island at the present day (1970) has a population of sheep, red deer and wild goats. There is now only one house, which has not been lived in for some years. At the landing place on the east side of the island we found the sea calm and very clear; jellyfish of various sizes drifted slowly past and there was an unbroken silence over land

and sea. The east shore of Scarba is comparatively sheltered and trees grow almost to the tide-mark. We climbed on a rough track, past bracken five feet high and through a thick wood of deciduous trees, Even in the strong sunlight this wood was dark, except in one place where the clustered berries of a rowan tree were brilliant red. Near the upper margin it was unexpected to find the remains of an avenue of silver firs (*Abies nobilis*): old trees, still erect and stately, but their tops are lifeless; the salt-laden gales may have been too much for them. High above the deserted house, near which several fallow deer were grazing, a pair of kestrels soared and dived like swifts.

We followed a path which had been made more than half a century ago. It rises gradually to a height of some 800 feet above the sea and after passing near a scattered wood of planted Scots firs leads round the island. The heather bloom on Scarba is remarkable; in places there was white heather growing close to the path. Through the clear air we looked upon the many hills that formed the horizon east and north-east. The twin, shapely tops of Ben Cruachan (the name in true Gaelic form is Cruachan Beann which, translated, means *Haunch of Peaks*) were prominent, and at the head of distant and invisible Loch Etive we saw Beinn Starav, home of the ptarmigan, and Bidein nam Beann, highest hill in Argyll. Across the blue Atlantic northward rose Ben Buie, Creach Bheinn, and Ben Talaidh—hills of Mull. The silence was broken by a sound now rarely heard in Britain—the song of the grasshopper, a rustling music that is associated in my memory with summer days of long ago. Grasshoppers cannot resist pesticides; it is good to know they have a retreat on Scarba. A less attractive resident on this island is the adder. We did not see one but at the side of the path was an adder's thin delicate skin, recently cast.

Scarba is celebrated for its whirlpool, which is near the Scarba shore in the mile-wide strait which separates Scarba from Jura. The whirlpool's name is Coire Bhreacain, *Breacan's Cauldron*, named after a prince of Norway whose galley was overwhelmed here. Breacan loved the daughter of a great Highland chief who may have been the Lord of the Isles. The chief told him that he could marry his daughter if he succeeded in anchoring his galley for three nights in the formidable strait. Breacan returned to Norway and a seer of that country told him to take with him three cables, one of hemp, one of wool, and the third made from maidens' tresses. Breacan was handsome and popular and the maidens of Norway were glad to present him with their cherished hair.

Breacan sailed from Norway to the Hebrides. He anchored his galley, held by the three cables, near the whirlpool. The first night the hemp cable parted, on the second night the cable of wool gave way. The third night came and Breacan knew that his life depended on the hair of the maidens of Norway. The seer had warned him that this hair must come only from maidens of spotless reputation. The night was almost past but as the dawn broke one strand of the cable parted. This was the beginning of the end. The galley was never seen again, but Breacan's body was brought ashore by his faithful hound to the sandy bay of Jura, on the south side of the strait. Martin Martin (1703) tells us that Breacan is buried in a cave in the north of Jura, 'as appears from the stone Tomb and Altar there'.

One would give much to know more of this cave, but island tradition is now silent as to the whereabouts of Breacan's grave. On the August afternoon of sunshine when we rested above the blue strait in the sun-warmed heather the Atlantic was at rest and the whirlpool slept, yet all the time the air was filled with a volume of deep sound as of a great river as the flood tide passed through the strait. When a westerly gale fights with that tide, the sound of their battle is heard on the mainland of Argyll, sometimes at a distance of twelve miles.

A friend of mine arrived in his yacht off the west entrance to the strait one afternoon in early March. A gale from the west was blowing and driving snow almost hid the land on either side of the strait. The skipper and owner was a daring character; he decided to continue on his course through the gulf of Coire Bhreacain. The gale urged him on; the strength of a spring tide was against him. For a few minutes he was able to see, through the whirling snow-flakes, the rocky coast of Scarba and was amazed to find that although he was steaming at ten knots he remained stationary. He increased speed to eleven knots, his engines running at full throttle, and anxiously watched the shore. After a time he was thankful to see that the yacht was creeping forward, literally foot by foot. The roar of the sea, the flying spindrift, the whirlpool with the noise of pistol shots spouting high into the air only a few hundred yards from the ship, the currents and eddies that seized his vessel and terrifyingly altered its course; all these things made the passage a hair-raising one. A native of Jura who was a master mariner, when he heard the story, at its close remarked solemnly and emphatically, "That man should never be alive." After what seemed an age the ship cleared the strait and passed beyond the ten-knot current. Dusk was falling and anchor was dropped in the lee of Jura.

The Rev. Donald Budge, who was minister on Jura for many years, tells us in his valuable book, *Jura,* of the strange disappearance of a cabin-cruiser without trace in the whirlpool of Coire Bhreacain on a mid-summer day in the year 1951. The engine failed; the passengers and skipper took to the small boat and when last they saw their vessel she was being drawn irresistibly towards the whirlpool; she vanished completely and no trace of her was ever found.

On this August afternoon as the tide ebbed we watched a low, rocky island slowly emerge from the white foam near the centre of that great tidal river. It is said that occasionally at low water in the rutting season stags swim across from Jura to Scarba and rest awhile on this island. There are other isles, near the Jura shore. During the clan fight when the Campbells of Craignish killed all but two of the Macleans of Jura, a Maclean survivor escaped by swimming, in a strong tide, to one of these isles.

The path on Scarba, high above the whirlpool, continues westward until the walker sees ahead of him, out on the blue Atlantic, the Garvelloch Islands, sometimes known as the Isles of the Sea. These are a chain of small islands, and on one of them are beehive cells and a stone on which is incised a cross. There is a tradition that this stone marks the grave of Eithne, mother of Saint Columba whose mystic Isle, Iona, can be seen from the high ground of Scarba on a clear day. Scholars believe that Saint Brendan founded his monastery of Ailech here before Columba arrived on Iona.

A light air current kept off the midges but when we turned for our long walk to the jetty that air current was with us and they were able to attack in numbers. We passed a hill loch where trout were rising and from here saw the white sails of a ketch moving on the tide through the Dorus Mór or *Great Door* which marks the tide-beset passage to the Crinan Canal. Far below us was the small wood we had passed that morning, when we at last reached it a pair of buzzards showed us that, like the wren who later scolded us, we were regarded as unwelcome visitors to their territory. All that day we saw no red deer; they, like the wild goats which are said to kill the adders with their hooves, were on the rocky Atlantic side of the island.

We had the last of a favourable tide that evening for the passage across to Craignish and as we reached deep water a pair of fulmars circled the boat, and shags dived in the tidal stream. The hills of Mull became faint in the evening haze. The piper tuned his *Pìob Mhór* and played one of the most beautiful of all pipe tunes, 'Lament for Mary MacLeod', and we looked back upon Scarba where she had lived in temporary banishment three centuries ago.

HS-71

SOAY

When the Norsemen a thousand years ago added the Hebrides to their crown and named them Südreyar, *South Isles,* many of the islands received Norse names. Such a name is Soay, *the Isle of Sheep.*

At least three islands of this name lie off the west coast of Scotland: one is beside Iona, the second is far out in the Atlantic and forms one of the St Kilda group, the third is off Skye and lies in the shadow of the Black Cuillin

One winter afternoon, as I stood in deep snow, upon the narrow summit of Gars Bheinn, most southerly of the Cuillin, where the roosting hollows of a covey of ptarmigan showed grey beside me, I saw a small heather fire lighted on the shore of Skye, opposite Soay. It was a signal for a boat and the smoke had coiled into the still air but a few minutes when a boat passed out from Soay and crossed the strait for that lonely unseen traveller. But although I had often looked upon Soay from the Cuillin I was long in setting foot upon the isle. My opportunity came one day of May.

The previous evening I had rested upon the top of Sgurr nan Eag, three thousand feet above the Atlantic. The air was warm. There was no wind. South and west lay the ocean, pale grey and hazy in soft primrose light. Above the hill-top a butterfly fluttered. A bumble-bee, flying fast across the hill, steered unerringly for Loch Coruisk, three thousand feet below. Immediately beneath me—so close that it seemed as though a stone might be thrown upon it—the island of Soay lay. On its heathery crown lochs of various sizes reflected the blue of the sky. In a crescent on the shore of the eastern bay stood the small village, its buildings from this great height seeming like dolls' houses. Beside the houses were the small cultivated patches, green with young grass. On the bay a number of small boats were moored, and the steamship *Hebrides,* even as I watched, left the isle and steered west through sunlit waters.

The following day came my opportunity of visiting Soay. A boat had crossed to Skye for the doctor and the owner of the boat—a seaman and piper—kindly gave me a passage to the island with him.

The sun shone brilliantly upon the blue Atlantic and the sands of Loch Brittle as the engine was cranked up, the anchor weighed, and we sailed out through sparkling waters.

Arriving at Soay from the north one enters a fine natural harbour that is sheltered from every wind but which it is not possible to use at low tide because of a shallow bar across its mouth. The shores of the harbour are delightful. Feathery birches grow to the tide and beneath the birches is a carpet of wild hyacinths, primroses, and violets.

It is a half-mile from the landing-place to the village. The track is rough and narrow and is slippery with stones. The people of Soay have petitioned the authorities for a road—so far without success.

The first people to live here were, it is believed, shepherds in the employment of the MacAskall of Rudha an Dunain. These shepherds were sent to Soay in the sixteenth century. There is a tradition that the first two shepherds on Soay allowed their peat fire to die out. They had no means of rekindling it, nor had they a boat. They thereupon boldly swam the Sound of Soay to the nearest point of Skye—a distance of fully a mile—and then walked across to Rudha an Dunain for tinder for their fire. But the shepherds must have left Soay before the time of the compiling of the *Old Statistical account* (1795), for it mentioned Soay as uninhabited.

At the present day there is grazing on Soay for several hundred sheep. There are no horses on the island and so the land cannot be ploughed in the usual way. Soay is one of the few places in the west where the old-fashioned *cas chrom* (a plough-shaped spade, worked by hand) is still in use. It is an unwieldy implement in the hands of an amateur but those skilled in its handling make light of it, and they will tell you that it delves deeper than the plough and gives better crops.

On the island of Soay there is no telegraph. When the doctor is needed a motor-boat must cross to Glen Brittle, six miles distant. Thence a man must walk nine miles to the telegraph office at Carbost to summon the doctor who lives at Struan. A telegraph or a telephone would be of inestimable value to the people of Soay.

Should a man of Soay cross to Skye and wish, a few days later, to return to his native isle, he must light a fire, and by means of a thick smoke cloud seek to attract the attention of his people.

Soay receives most of its mails from Mallaig, twenty miles distant, by sea. Each Tuesday morning a motor-boat leaves Soay for Mallaig, returning the same night with mails from the mainland.

By the overland route the traveller crosses the lower slopes of the Cuillin from Glen Brittle and when nearest to Soay lights a fire, taking care that there shall be as much smoke as possible. When the smoke is observed from the village on Soay the village is perhaps two miles distance from where the fire is lighted. An answering fire is sometimes kindled.

Until recent years each family on Soay had their own knoll for the kindling of fires so that those upon the island at once knew who was waiting for the ferry. But now the old distinctions have gone and since the various knolls have no longer any special significance a fire is lighted wherever there is suitable heather for burning.

Twice my friend and I crossed the three miles of boggy moorland that lie between Glen Brittle and Soay in an attempt to reach the island. On the first occasion our fire was not a success. There had been heavy rain the previous day and the heather was wet and sodden. At the end of an hour and a half, since there was no answer to our feeble smoke, we returned to Glen Brittle in a gathering storm.

Bad weather persisted for a week then at last came a lessening of the north wind and, as we crossed the moor towards the island, Sgurr Alasdair rose clear against a cobalt sky. We found it hard to make a fire. The island missionary had inadvertently set the hill ablaze during dry and frosty weather the previous Christmas and it was only after a search that we discovered a small area of old heather. When this was fired a dense volume of blue smoke rose into the air. We watched its effect on Soay.

The island lay below us in brilliant sunshine. Through a stalking glass the inhabitants could be seen cutting their peats and in a few minutes we saw an answering column of smoke rise from the heathery crown of the isle. Soon after that a boat crossed the Sound of Soay for us. The tide was at the full as we embarked. Oyster-catchers called shrilly and flew close to the boat. We were hospitably received. The people of Soay are crofters and most of them are lobster fishers. They are hard workers. The houses are slated, and lack the primitive appearance of the houses of the Outer Isles.

At sunset I climbed the heathery hill above the village. The sky was clear. Across the Sound the Cuillin towered. Upon Sgurr Alasdair, upon Sgurr Dearg, the shades of night descended. Clear-cut and shapely rose Blaven against the evening sky. Between Blaven and Gars Bheinn the lesser hill of Sgurr na Stri was dwarfed by its giant neighbours.

Sgurr na Stri is *the Hill of Contention*. It was named thus because, of old, MacLeod and MacKinnon strove for its possession. At last, in 1730, the two chiefs met amicably on Sgurr na Stri and after a conference agreed to a new march between their lands. It was decided that this new boundary should run northward from the sea at a small bay called Port Sgailen, some four hundred yards from where the river from Loch Coruisk enters Loch Scavaig.

Since it was of importance that the new march should be known beyond doubt by the local people, a boy from Soay was taken in a boat across to Port Sgailen. Here, in the rude fashion of the times, he was thrashed to within an inch of his life in order that the exact spot should be engraved indelibly upon his memory. Willow charcoal (which is imperishable) was also placed on a knoll beside Port Sgailen to mark the new boundary.

On this peaceful night the stars one by one appeared behind the hill. West, on the far horizon, rise the bens of Uist. Above the distant island peak of Hecla the new moon shone; beneath it was the orange afterglow. From Hyskeir, beyond Canna, came rhythmic flashes from the lighthouse. The evening sky was faultlessly mirrored in a moorland loch near me. A light air swayed the heads of the feathery bog-cotton. Near me a grouse crowed cheerily as he settled down for the night. Darkness came, and below the waning western glow shone, faint and star-like, the distant light of Uisinish.

COS-29

Drying peats at an extensive cutting in Trotternish, Skye (Beinn Edra behind).

RAASAY

The rugged island of Raasay, at which the Skye mail-boat makes a call twice daily was, at the time Dean Monro visited it (near the middle of the sixteenth century) an isle, 'having twa fair orchards … and maney deires'. There are now few deer on the island and little remains of the twa fair orchards. The Dean adds that 'the isle pertains to McGyllyChallan of Raarsay by the sword, and to the Bishops of the Iles by Heritage'.

MacGille Chaluim, MacLeod of Raasay, was head of a very old Highland family who held the lands of Raasay from time immemorial. This family considered themselves as important as the MacLeods of Dunvegan, and free to choose their own path in Highland history. When the MacLeods of Dunvegan decided to support the Government against Prince Charles Edward, MacLeod of Raasay threw in his lot with the Prince, and suffered for his chivalrous action. Almost the whole male population of Raasay took arms under their chieftain in the Prince's cause. The island must at that time have been the home of many pipers, for it is traditionally said that no fewer than twenty-six pipers went to that war from Raasay, and that ten of them were lost. Raasay himself was wounded on the field of Culloden but escaped from his enemies and succeeded in making his way back to Raasay. The patronymic of the eldest son of MacLeod of Raasay was Rona, a name taken from the adjoining island of Rona which Dean Monro sadly asserts to have been the home of 'thieves, ruggars, and reivars', who made a living by the 'spulzeing of poure pepill'. Rona was too young to take part in the rising, later claimed the estate in a court of law. His father had taken the precaution of making over the estate to his son before leaving for the war and Rona swore that his father was 'below the ground' and that he had 'walked over him'. The court accepted this testimony, delivered on oath, as proof that Raasay had died and therefore made the estate over to the young man. Rona had indeed sworn truthfully yet had the court known that when Raasay was 'below the ground' and when his son had 'walked over him' the father had been hiding in a cave, their decision would no doubt have been different.

Rather more than forty years after the rising of 1745 MacLeod of Raasay hospitably entertained Johnson and Boswell on his island, at which they had arrived, not without adventure, by rowing-boat from Skye. The great Samuel Johnson was highly pleased by his reception on Raasay. Hear what he says of it in his book, *A Journey to the Western Islands:*

> We found nothing but civility, elegance and plenty. After the usual refresh-ments, and the usual conversation, the evening came upon us. The carpet was then rolled off the floor; the musician was called, and the whole company was invited to dance, nor did ever fairies trip with greater alacrity. The general air of festivity, which predominated in this place, so far remote from all those regions which the mind has been used to contemplate as the mansions of pleasure, struck the imagination with a delightful surprise.
>
> When it was time to sup, the dance ceased, and thirty persons sat down to two tables in the same room. After supper the ladies sung Erse songs, to which I listened as an English audience to an Italian opera, delighted with the sound of words which I did not understand.

Johnson paid his visit to Raasay in the year 1773. He records that the lands of MacLeod of Raasay had not at that time gained or lost a single acre during four hundred years, and that besides owning the islands of Rona and Fladda, the family held an extensive estate in Skye. MacLeod of Raasay who entertained the travellers had thirteen children: three sons and ten daughters. There was a tutor for the sons, and the Lady Raasay educated the girls.

The island of Raasay is celebrated for the excellence and size of the trees which still grow around the old house. Even at the time of Johnson's visit the trees were remarkable for the visitor records that 'the laird has an orchard and very large forest trees grow about his house'.

Johnson places on record a curious custom, which at the time of his visit still continued. MacLeod of Raasay and 'MacDonald of Sky' had long been in close alliance. It was the custom that the survivor inherited the sword of the deceased, and as Johnson remarks, 'on the death of the late Sir James MacDonald, his sword was delivered to the present laird of Raasay'. This custom may indeed have continued until the MacLeods of Raasay sold their ancestral island in the year 1823.

Before the MacLeods took possession of Raasay, no doubt by the sword, an armed expedition from Norway arrived by sea at the island, to harry and plunder it. The great war-galley went aground in shallow water at Eyre, near the south end of the island, and the Norsemen were killed to a man—only their leader, Storab, escaping with his life. This solitary survivor, son of the King of Norway, escaped to an island on the loch which still bears his name. His height and strength were such that he was able to leap from the island to the shore and go by night to a woman, who gave him food. The men of Raasay set about draining the loch in order to reach their enemy and, seeing his retreat becoming insecure, Storab, under cover of darkness, left the island. He later made his way along the burn which bears his name, but when he had reached a crossing-place now named Ath Storab, *Storab's Ford*, he was shot by a herd who aimed his arrow from the bank above. The arrow pierced Storab between the shoulders, inflicting a mortal wound. He was buried on a grassy mound, where two old sycamores now grow and his grass-grown grave is still easy to find. A stone slab marks it and, an inch or more beneath the short-cropped grass, are small stones—the Cairn of Remembrance set up by Island hands a thousand years and more ago.

In some way news of the fate of Storab and his men reached Norway. His sister Bjornal sailed then to Raasay with a fleet of war-galleys, wasted the isle, and set fire to the forest which at that time covered it.

On the sombre April morning when I stood beside the lonely and wind-swept grave of Storab, the sycamores had not yet burst their buds, but primroses were opening on banks which faced south. The stems of the sycamores were pale as the hill grasses which lay prostrate towards the north after the searing winter gales. Across the Sound rose the peaks of the high Cuillin of Skye on which the clouds were gathering after an early morning of sunshine: the snows of winter still lay in the shelter of the corries. Beyond the Bay of Portree rose the black precipices of Beinn Storr; farther north were the bastions of Quirang, on the north wing of Skye.

Leaving Storab's grave, I crossed the high ground of Raasay and, when I had reached the eastern face of the island, looked down upon the ruins of the ancient castle of Brochel. This castle is part of the rock on which it stands for in places solid rock forms the walls. Remarkably little is known of the history of this castle. It is said to have been built in very early times to accommodate the whole island population during an enemy raid. Its date may be fourteenth century or even earlier. The castle suffered after the Forty-five, when it was bombarded and destroyed by a Government frigate. Had the MacLeods of Skye been less circumspect it is likely that the historic castle of Dunvegan would have shared the fate of Brochel.

Brochel was built above the cold, east-facing shore of Raasay and the scene here this April morning was sombre and wintry. The birches were still in their winter nakedness, although on the opposite shore their branches were already covered with small green leaves of a most delicate perfume. A cold breeze blew from the sea, wind-tossed and leaden, which separated Raasay from Applecross on the Scottish mainland. I was greeted by a raven who was sailing high above the castle: he made his characteristic roll as though to salute the old place then soared southward into the grey heavens until lost to view.

In order to realise the true grandeur of Raasay it is necessary to traverse the island above the long and lofty cliff which rises from the uninhabited eastern shore. The ocean lies far beneath—so far, indeed, that the gannet I saw fishing seemed no larger than a herring gull. A young stag which I disturbed above the eastern cliff trotted with little alarm across the heather-covered ground, keeping away from the edge of the rock. South rose Crowlin Island and west of it the low island of Pabbay, now treeless, but in Dean Monro's day 'full of woodes' which, as he says, were 'a maine shelter of thieves'. The name Pabbay is of interest since it indicates that Culdees lived on these islands in the days before the Norsemen conquered the Hebrides. Pabbay is Norse and means *Priest's Isle*.

From the eastern rock-girt coast of Raasay, Dùn Caan, the island's highest hill (known to seamen as Raasay's Cap) rises in a stately manner. A pair of buzzards soared, mewing, high above this flat-topped hill, which in appearance is not unlike the smaller of MacLeod's Tables in Skye.

Rain was spreading fast over the sky as I reached the almost level summit plateau of Dùn Caan. This rain had already hidden the coast of Skye and dimmed the Cuillin; the coast of Lewis was almost blotted out, although the mainland hills for a time remained clear and the Sisters of Kintail mist-free.

Below Dùn Caan is a small loch named Loch na Mna, *the Loch of the Woman*. A young woman was, it is averred, killed here by a fierce *Each Uisge* or Water Horse, who had his haunt deep in the peaty waters. This water monster, in the guise of a handsome youth, made love to the lass and then, changing into a black stallion, bore her into his watery lair. The maiden's father laid plans for revenge. Knowing that the Water Horse was fond of flesh, he killed and roasted a sheep near the loch, with the wind blowing on to the loch from the roast. The monster, smelling the savoury smell, emerged from the depths, and (since his human enemies were carefully hidden) unsuspectingly advanced to the sheep and fell into the trap set for him. The *Each Uisge* was at last killed by a blacksmith with his red-hot irons, and when examined after death was seen as a large jelly-like mass.

From Dùn Caan a damp, moss-grown track winds beside a burn to the old beech-woods which shelter Raasay House. Wind and rain drove against me on that walk; in hollows sheep were sheltering, for winter had returned with the storm. But in the beech-woods violets and primroses were in flower, and the grass, already green, showed that the coming of summer was near. After Culloden the House of Raasay was fired but was later rebuilt on the old site. Here can be seen the room in which Johnson slept during his visit; the bed is said to be the one which he used. On one of the low rocks on the shore below Raasay House a cross is incised. At one time eight crosses marked the *girth* or Sanctuary of the chapel behind the house; but they have gone the way of the crosses of the Sanctuary of Applecross. The prospect from the House of Raasay is magnificent. Beyond the trees the Sound is a blue foil to the great range of the Cuillin Hills which, rising beyond that sea channel, have the appearance of a hill-range of Norway rather than of Scotland.

AH-50

Ben More, Mull.

THE LAND OF TIREE

Some seventy miles north of the Irish coast, and about nine miles to the north-east of Skerryvore, lies a green and fertile island, Tiree by name.

As to the origin of the island's name much uncertainty exists. The most widely held opinion is that it signifies Tir-i, *the Land of Iona*, as in olden times the monks were said to get most of their grain from here, and across in the Ross of Mull is a district known as Pot-i, *the Larder of Iona*, where the monks were wont to obtain their meat. Another suggested meaning is Tir-an-eorna, *the Land of Barley*, and a derivation which has of late held favour is Tir Eadh, *the Level Land*.

Unlike most of the Hebrides, this island is composed mainly of great stretches of level green pasture land lying only a few feet above the height of a spring tide and, except along its south-west shores, there is none of that characteristic rugged and bleak appearance which is so typical of these western isles.

There is an old saying that "only for paying two rents, Tiree would yield two crops in the season," referring to the extreme rapidity of growth which all cereal crops make on this favoured island, where barley put into the ground in the last days of May is ready for reaping by August, and where the vegetables of the gardens spring up as if by magic. Indeed, so fertile has the island always been, that it bears for its arms a sheaf of corn.

On Tiree the conditions, to my mind, in many ways closely resemble those obtaining on the great plateaux of the Cairngorm Hills. In fine weather these conditions are indeed magnificent, for the sun shines with intense power, and his rays are reflected from the sea with additional brilliance. But of shelter there is none so that even in midsummer one may vainly seek some protection against the north wind which sweeps down from the Minch with winter, even at this season, in its breath. And the potato haulms may, even in June, be flattened and rendered black by the gale.

Tiree is famous for its sands. These extend for miles at a stretch and are of a remarkably white colour for they are composed entirely of the remnants of shells. When the sun shines on them, their dazzling whiteness is such as to tire the eye, and the dark form of the skua, as he stands in wait for the tern and its catch near the water's edge, seems even darker by contrast. Of all the sands the longest is Traigh Mhor which extends in a great crescent to a distance of several miles. Here in summer terns glide and wheel and in winter many shore birds find feeding at the edge of the tide. One sees turnstones, dunlin, sanderling, purple sandpipers, and godwits on this wide shore, while a little way out to sea solans hunt and long-tailed ducks ride buoyantly. Farther west lies Traigh Bhagh where terns have their eggs and where the small burn from a chain of lochans enters the sea at its eastern end. Here at times grilse and sea trout attempt to run in from the sea but there is rarely sufficient water to cover them so they pass on to the streams of Mull maybe, or to the far-distant Irish coast. At the south end of the island are the beautiful sands known as Traigh Bheidhe, from where the dark rock of Skerryvore can be seen and the tall lighthouse that rises there.

At the extreme south-western end of the island Stands the hill Ceann a' Bharra. But the name, as written at present, is held to be meaningless. Here the coast is wild and rocky and abounding in caves where rock doves have their nest and where much driftwood is cast by the tide. After the wind has blown strong from the south-west the great Atlantic swell thunders on these rocks. Slowly and with a great stateliness the long waves, clear and blue in the sunshine, roll forwards towards the half submerged rocks. They do not break fussily and abruptly as the wavelets of the North Sea or Irish Channel. Gradually curling over, they crash on the black rocks with tremendous power, throwing the spray high in the air to fall to leeward in a slow cascade of shining whiteness. And when the sun is sinking on the western horizon behind grey storm clouds, and when the ocean wind blows freshly, then it is that on the breeze may be carried the pungent smell of the burning seaweed, coming from Saundaig maybe or from Green, and around all the outlying rocks there lies a thin grey mist, arising from the breaking of the great waves which, despite the wind, seems to hang motionless above the surf.

Many sea birds have their home on Ceann a' Bharra. Here the gentle but somewhat foolish guillemot broods her one egg during the long days of June, choosing as a site for her hostage to fortune a ledge so insecure and slippery that disasters are frequent. Here too the wise razorbill, though in small numbers, finds for her egg a more safe resting-place, usually a cranny hidden away amongst the rocks. Green cormorants are here too, and from time to time the peregrine and the raven nest in the cliffs, and the grey crow builds her home of the stems of the giant seaweed.

Tradition has it that long ago a party of witches were passing Ceann a' Bharra on their way to Ireland, sailing, as was their wont, in egg-shells. A native of the island, seeing that his own wife was of the party, and therefore a witch, and knowing that they were in the spell of the evil one, wished them Godspeed on their journey. Instantly the egg-shells were sunk and the man's witch wife drowned.

Fairies were not so long ago held to have their dwellings beneath the grassy slopes of Ceann a' Bharra. These 'silent people' were said to come always from the west, for they could pass with equal ease over the ocean as on the land. When travelling they moved in little eddies of wind. When wind and rain came from opposite directions—that is on a sudden change of wind after a shower—it was possible to bring down the fairies in a body by throwing a piece of horse-dung against the breeze.

On a clear day of sunshine early in May Ceann a' Bharra is at its best. By now the grass is springing up fresh and green and wild hyacinths are tingeing the southern slopes of the hill with blue, while many primroses blossom in the sun-bathed and sheltered crannies, and throw out their scent far across the hill. Away to the east the high corries of Ben More Mull, still deep in snow, throw back the sun's rays, while in the Passage of Tiree trawlers are busy fishing, their mizzens set to steady them in the gentle swell. Far beyond Skerryvore and Dubh Hirteach the views extend, as far indeed as the track of the big ships, as they make for the Irish coast.

Nestling between Ben Hynish and Ceann a' Bharra is the little crofting township of Ballephuill. Here many of the older generation "have no English," as they quaintly put it, but will greet you in the Gaelic and offer you the hospitality of the Highlander. On the small crofts the land is green and fertile and besides the harvest of the land there is the harvest of the sea.

The bracken, *raineach* as it is known in the Gaelic, is so plentiful and wide-spread throughout the western coast that it is curious to find it almost entirely absent on Tiree. Only in one spot have I seen it; on the slopes of Beinn Hough, a round grassy hill standing on the northwestern shores of the island. Its absence is no misfortune for once this quickly spreading fern gains a footing on the land it is extremely difficult to eradicate and it thrives best where the soil is richest.

Beyond Beinn Hough lies the wildest part of Tiree, Craignish Point. Here the land runs out in a narrow peninsula and for miles to the westward there stretches wild broken water with jagged reefs of rocks where the grey seals rest and round which there swim great copper-coloured lythe of an August evening.

Born and bred by the sea, some of the finest seamen of the west come from Tiree. In their small boats the men put to sea at any time throughout the year when the weather is favourable. In summer they are perhaps after saithe, *piocaich* as they term them or they may perhaps be trolling for lythe for kippering for the winter months. Then there is the lobster fishing which takes up much of their time from early summer up to December and even to the New Year should the weather be fair. In winter and early spring there are long lines to be set for cod and ling and there is also the herring fishing which of late has brought much money to the island.

Since there is now no peat on Tiree, the natives were wont to sail their small skiffs across to the Ross of Mull, over twenty miles to the south-east of the island, where there is an abundance of moss and peat bogs. But more than one accident occurred on the passage across and more than one boat was lost so that the custom has been discontinued and coal and drift wood have taken the place of peat.

Lying as it does well out into the Atlantic Tiree is visited by many birds during the time of their migration. In the early days of May whimbrel and white wagtails halt awhile here on their journey north and many flocks of golden plover, resplendent in their nesting plumage, feed on the grass fields before moving on to the Arctic with swift and powerful flight. Hence the proverb, "Cho luath ris na Feadagan," *As swift as the whistling plovers.* One season a pair of cuckoos took up their abode on the island for more than a month, so it is probable that the hen bird laid her eggs in some of the many nests of the meadow pipits. Amongst the children of the island the cuckoos were a source of not a little excitement. The birds were to them quite unknown, and their call was universally a matter for talk.

Amongst the Gaels the cuckoo is spoken of as Eun sith, *the fairy bird* and this name has been given to it from the fact that it was said to have its home underground like the fairies. To this underground retreat it retired on Midsummer's Day—surely rather an early time this for one's winter sleep!—and so was ranked with the wheatear and the stonechat as one of the Seven Sleepers.

In autumn many wild swans visit the island, coming perhaps on the arms of a gale from the nor'west when even the solans have difficulty in facing the squalls and rise and dip aslant the gale. The wild swans have great power of flight and it is a fine sight to see them forging their way in a line against the storm, each bird seemingly unaffected by the gale save that its progress is slower. The first of all the winter migrants to take their departure, the wild swans leave the island during the very earliest days of spring, when, away to the northward, the Cuillin Hills of Skye still stand out clothed in a mantle of unrelieved white and even the lesser heights of Mull and Ardnamurchan are snowclad.

Later in the season, when full spring is come, the air is at times of a wonderful clearness and hills at a very great distance are visible. From Tiree to Ben Nevis is a distance of just over sixty miles yet I have frequently seen this, the highest of Scottish hills, of an early May day when the mountain was still of an unspotted white and so contrasted vividly with the deep blue of the sky. At such times, through the glass, every rock of the Cuillin is distinct and the hills about Knoydart seem to lose a little of their sternness as the stong sunlight floods them.

I think there can be no island more open to the winds than Tiree. In winter across the island there sweep a succession of gales from the south and south-west that continue for days without a moment's intermission so that even the sanderling and dunlin are driven from the sands and the curlew are no longer heard. Tiree has no safe harbour or anchorage so that the mail boat is often unable to call and the island sees its mails and bread being carried off once more to Tobermory or Bunessan.

Amongst the older generation of the island it was always held that the wind the old year left behind would be the prevalent wind for the ensuing year. Thus on Hogmanay, many anxious glances were cast at the sky, and pleasure was expressed if it were seen that the wind was from the south, for the Gaelic saying has it:

> Gaoth deas, teas is toradh
> Gaoth tuath, fuach is gaillionn
> Gaoth 'n iar, iasg is bainne
> Gaoth 'n ear, meas air chrannaibh.

> South wind, heat and produce;
> North wind, cold and tempest;
> West wind, fish and milk;
> East wind, fruit on trees.

When on Tiree I have often tested the saying that 'When the wind is lost, you may look for it again in the south' and have found it almost always correct. Often after a fierce storm from the north the winter's dawn breaks without a breath of wind. The surface of the sea is like glass yet the sky shows a dull leaden look which portends nothing good. Towards midday, or maybe earlier, a puff of air comes away from the south. Within half an hour a fresh breeze is blowing, and before the afternoon is old a whole gale of southerly wind is sweeping up from Islay and the north Irish coast, sending in seas which thunder on the white sands and causing the herring drifters to seek what shelter they can find.

For this reason it is held that the first day of the south wind, and the third day of the north wind, is the best time for crossing the dangerous, tide-swept Sound of Gunna which divides Tiree from neighbouring Coll. But to cross safely one must reach the ferry early even on the first day of the south wind and I have had a wild crossing through arriving at the ferry too late in the day. The tide flows so swiftly that the wind raises a heavy sea almost at once and although the ferryman knows every rock and tide rip intimately it is impossible for a small boat to cross in a storm. But in the summer months the south wind can blow softly and steadily, though at times it may bring with it rains and mist from the sea. Indeed, to the Gael the south wind is sometimes spoken of as *the Gateway of Soft Weather.*

No channel that I know of is so frequented by the solan as the Sound of Gunna. The birds are here throughout the year, with the exception of the dead of winter, and I suspect that from here they make their way with their catches of herring and mackerel to their great nesting-ground on Borreray of St. Kilda, just under one hundred miles to the north-west.

In full summer there is little darkness in the Land of Tiree. I have crossed at midnight that great stretch of level land extending across the island from east to west near its centre and in the dusk have heard the trilling cries of many curlew as they swept in from the sea. From the swampy ground at such times come the curious and pleasant cry of the dunlin and the harsh notes of the corncrake. And before two o'clock the song thrushes have been singing their loudest, perched on the top of some wall or on some storm-scarred gorse bush, for on Tiree are no trees of any kind. And then the air would be sweet with the music of countless larks, for I think this sweet songster is more plentiful than in any other district I know, although their numbers are thinned by the fierce peregrine and their full-grown young have been borne off in my view by herring and black-backed gulls. Then on the *reef* the tribe of the green plover are to be found in their thousands, from early spring to midsummer, and with their peevish cries there mingle the soft melodious notes of the unobtrusive ringed plover.

It is said that during very clear weather the northern coast of Ireland can be made out from the summit of Ceann a' Bharra. I have never had the good fortune to see it, but the distance from this point to Malin Head is not more than sixty-five miles so I imagine that the higher hills of that district should be visible at times.

Since no trees can grow on the wind-swept island wood is dear and difficult to obtain, so that most of the crofters' dwellings are constructed of driftwood, carried, maybe, thousands of miles on the Atlantic tides. To withstand the great gales of winter these houses have strong walls of exceptional thickness, with small windows set far back. The old earthen floors have been replaced by coverings of wood and stone, and one can now very rarely obtain a *cruisgean* or old-fashioned lamp burning fish oil.

One by one the old beliefs die out—the fairies are now no more than a name; the water-horse no more inspires a superstitious dread; the half human, half fairy being known as the "Glastig" is no more seen abroad of dark and stormy nights. Yet the natives of this wild island retain all their charm, and in them the true Highland hospitality is still strong, for their lives are lived close to the very heart of Nature and they have as their companions all the four winds and the restful spirit of the everchanging ocean.

LHG-20

During the First World War Seton Gordon visited Tiree regularly, something that was to be repeated in World War Two. Afoot in the Hebrides *has another chapter on the island; interesting to compare 1920 and 1950.*

IONA

We crossed the Sound of Iona in the light of the November full moon which had risen as the last of the sunset ebbed on the ocean horizon towards the south-west. The tide was high and a fresh breeze from the north contended with the tidal stream in the Sound. The motor-boat bore up close to the shore until under the lee of Eilean nam Ban, showers of salt spray beating on our faces like hail. From Eilean nam Ban (*Isle of the Women*) we stood out westward across the Sound and arrived after a quick passage at the little slip where the two passengers and the island mails were landed. The moon, at first golden, became silver as it climbed high into the heavens.

Late that evening, from our comfortable quarters beside the low shore of Traigh Mór, my friend and I walked, in clear moonlight, to the White Sands at the extreme northern end of the island. On the roadside MacLean's Cross stood dark, graceful and slender. This beautiful cross, ten feet in height, is carved on a thin slab of schist: it is believed to date from the fifteenth century, and may have been erected in memory of one of the Chiefs of Duart, although some authorities think the cross is much older.

We passed below Dùn I, which St Columba often climbed, and now saw ahead of us the intensely white sandy area which lies upon the machair at the northern end of the island, before the machair gives place to the rocks of the shore. Machair is the name given to flat grassy pasture-land on the Atlantic seaboard of the Isles. As we approached this sand its whiteness became more bright so that it now resembled a sheet of new-fallen snow. So clear was the moonlight, the pale-green waters of the sea above submerged sand were coloured almost as faithfully as in the light of the sun. Iona, *I Chaluim Chille*, the sacred island, seemed to lie beneath a spell.

It is said that beneath the full moon visions of past events are seen sometimes here—the galleys of the Northmen approach the shore, their inmates leap into the shallow water and quickly draw the galleys beyond reach of the waves. The invaders are seen moving in silence towards the abbey church and, after an interval, they return, enter their boats, and are soon hidden by the night, their dark deed re-enacted before those who have the 'two sights'.

We returned to the southern end of the island towards midnight. The moon, now a shining disc in the high heavens, was moving towards the south-west. On distant Tiree a beacon flashed rhythmically; here on Iona the tide had ebbed far and the wet sands gleamed coldly. One thought of that night before Christmas in the year 986 when a party of Danes or Norsemen slew the Abbot of Iona and fifteen monks on the dark, steep-sided rock, Sgeir nam Mart, bounding Traigh Bhàn, *the White shore.*

The night passed, and an hour before the orb of the sun appeared over Erraid, across the Sound, the eastern sky was bright with colour where the sun-fire burned upon lambent clouds. On Traigh Mór a flock of grey crows and greater black-backed gulls searched the deep-drifted seaweed for food; from it came the strong and not unpleasant smell of the sea. Starlings, too, probed the weed with activity. We crossed the machair, green even in winter—the cows where we lodged, although they had not yet been taken in at night, gave rich, creamy milk—and climbed a low pass which led near Coire Siant, the Bespelled Corrie; here we found ourselves looking down upon the historic bay, Port na Curaich, *Harbour of the Coracle,* where Columba with his twelve followers landed on that far-distant day in early summer of the year 563. There is a tradition that his *curach* (coracle) is buried here, a short distance beyond the reach of the waves. On the stony shore are heaps of stones of various sizes which, writes Pennant, were made by the monks as penances: he says judging by the size of some of the cairns, certain of the monks must have been given a heavy penance indeed. Port na Curaich has a shore of small stones, some of them pebbles of translucent green serpentine, known as Iona stones. These were believed to be a charm against drowning at sea. Martin quaintly observes that 'these pretty variegated stones in the shoar … ripen to a green colour, and are then proper for Carving. The Natives say these stones are Fortunate, but only for some particular thing, which the Person thinks fit to name, in exclusion of everything else.'

To the north-west of Port na Curaich the ground is high and rocky and on the highest eminence is a small cairn said to have been built by Columba, or by his personal orders, which has the name Carn Cúl ri Éirinn (*Cairn with the Back towards Ireland*). We reached the cairn as the lamp was lighted in Dubh Hirteach lighthouse on its deadly reef on the southern horizon. Mist hid the hills of Mull, but between drifting showers the Dutchman's Cap, Lunga, and Staffa were clear. A flight of grey geese passed overhead, flying towards the south below a thickening cloud-canopy, and a raven made his way to his roosting ledge. For fifty years and more, in the memory of old people, a pair of ravens have nested on the sea cliff near Carn Cúl ri Éirinn. The mother bird, as she broods, looks out towards Éire, invisible below the horizon of the sea over which the *curach* of Columba sailed.

The rugged, rock-strewn country adjacent to Carn Cúl ri Éirinn might be expected to be the haunt of snakes, but since the time when Columba prophesied that no serpent should henceforth harm any living thing on Iona the island has been without adders and grass snakes. I heard the story of a man who, to test this belief, brought a serpent to the island in a bottle but when liberated the creature quickly died. It is also believed that no flea can live on Iona.

Adamnan, Columba's biographer, relates of the kindly treatment Columba ordered to be given to the weary crane which he prophesied should arrive from Eire on the isle and which appeared on the day he had foretold. In the Latin text the word is *grus*, meaning a crane, a name sometimes wrongly used in the west Highlands at the present day for the heron. There are now no cranes in Ireland but there are reasons for believing that in former centuries the crane nested in that country.

It is evident from Adamnan's *Life* that the Atlantic seal at that time had its home on an uninhabited island—perhaps Soay—in the neighbourhood of Iona as it still has today, fourteen hundred years later.

It seems that the monks were accustomed to eat the young seals, for it is recorded in Adamnan that a certain 'robber, Erc Mocudruidi', who lived on the island Colosus was in the habit of killing the seals. One day Columba called two of the monks, and spoke thus to them:

'Sail over now to the Malean Island [Mull] and on the open ground, near the sea-shore, look for Erc, a robber, who came alone last night in secret from the island Colosus. He strives to hide himself among the sand-hills during the daytime under his boat, which he covers with hay, that he may sail across at night to the little island where our young seals are brought forth and nurtured. When this furious robber has stealthily killed as many as he can, he then fills his boat, and goes back to his hiding-place.'

The brothers preceded across the Sound, discovered the robber in his hiding-place and brought him to Columba, who asked him:

'Why dost thou transgress the Commandment of God so often by stealing the property of others? If thou art in want at any time, come to us and thy needs shall be supplied.'

The inference is, I think, that the community of monks considered the seals to be their property and perhaps killed them for their flesh and for the oil which they gave. The description of 'the little island where our young seals are brought forth and nurtured' clearly describes the Atlantic seal for the common seal is not a communal breeder. The saint bore the robber no ill-will, and when later he saw in spirit that the man's death was at hand, he had a fat sheep and six pecks of corn sent him as a last gift.

No visitor to Iona can fail to be impressed by the beauty of its crosses. There are at the present day only two crosses entire. MacLean's Cross is on the road-side, between the ruins of the nunnery and the cathedral; that noble monument, St Martin's Cross, fourteen feet high, stands opposite the west door of the cathedral.

Also near the cathedral is St John's Cross. This cross must in its original form have almost equalled in beauty of design St Martin's Cross, but only a portion of the original cross remains, and the restoration is heavy, inartistic work. The fourth cross is St Matthew's, standing near St John's Cross; it has suffered the same fate, for it was broken by the hands of vandals long ago. It will perhaps never be known who destroyed these early creations of beauty. It would appear that both St Matthew's and St. John's Cross had already been destroyed when Pennant visited the island in the summer of 1772, for he does not mention them, and the fragments were probably lying concealed by the mass of vegetation which then covered the cathedral precincts. An insight into the conditions prevailing at that time is given by his statement that the floor of the cathedral, then without a roof, was covered 'some feet thick with cow-dung, this place being at present the common shelter for the cattle, and the islanders are too lazy to remove this fine manure, the collection of a century, to enrich their grounds.'

If we believe the manuscript *A Short Description of Iona, 1693,* supposed to have been written by Jo. Fraser, Dean of the Isles, and which Pennant mentions as being, in his day, in the custody of the Advocates Library, Edinburgh, 360 crosses were standing in Iona at the time of the Reformation, but, as Pennant remarks, 'immediately after [the Reformation] they were almost entirely demolished by order of a provincial assembly, held in the island'. Mr Sacheverel, Governor of the Isle of Man, who visited Iona in 1688 when engaged in attempting to salvage the wreck of one of the Spanish Armada in Tobermory Bay, states that 'the synod ordered sixty crosses to be thrown into the sea'. Reeves, that distinguished Irish scholar, is of the opinion that these early statements are gross exaggerations, and that at no time were more than two dozen crosses standing on Iona. But even if his statement is correct, all but two of these two dozen crosses have been destroyed or irretrievably harmed.

We do not know what happened to the famous Iona library. Pennant quotes Boethius as recording that Fergus II, King of Scotland, assisting Alaric the Goth in the sacking of Rome, brought away as his share of booty a chest of books, which he presented to the monastery of Iona. The account that mentions the destruction of the crosses also states that the registers and records of Iona were destroyed after the Reformation which took place in 1561. There is a tradition that the Iona library is buried deep in the earth of Carn a' Burgh, one of the Treshnish Islands, the priceless books having been taken in secret from Iona at the time of the Reformation.

There are old records which show that, like other holy places, Iona had its *Girth* or Sanctuary, in which no fugitive from justice could be slain. It was customary to mark a Girth by crosses set at intervals in the ground. Presumably there was a circle of crosses at one time marking the Iona Girth; yet nothing is now known of it. It shares the fate of the last cross which marked the Girth at Applecross. That stone, more than eight feet high, stood on the *dun* at Camusterach: on the western face of the stone were the traces of an incised cross. A mason who was repairing the Free Church of Applecross broke the stone into pieces with his big hammer, believing it to be a relic of Popery. It is likely that the Iona crosses shared the same fate. Thus it is that Iona is full of disappointments, for it shows the beauty of spirit, the beauty of design to which the human race can attain, and it shows the depths to which fanatic zeal can descend. It demonstrates, also, what effect the neglect of centuries can have upon a holy place. Many of the beautiful recumbent gravestones are overgrown with moss and many of them have been moved from their original sites.

There are indeed few recumbent stones on Iona at the present day which are definitely known not to have been moved. The red granite stone, without inscription, said to record the burial-place of a king of France, can be seen at the present day, but whether it is on its original site is doubtful. Martin records that even in his time (about 1700) the inscriptions on the shrines where the kings were buried had been 'effaced by the Hand of Time'. Fortunately, when Sir Donald Monro, High Dean of the Isles, visited Iona in 1549, he was apparently able to read the inscriptions, for he records the presence of three tombs in the form of little chapels, and that on one were written the words TUMULUS REGUM SCOTIAE, where 'layes fortey-eight crouned Scotts Kinges'. King Fergus, according to Pennant, was the founder of this Mausoleum, and directed that it should be the burial-place of his successors. On the southern side of this tomb was another bearing the WORDS TUMULUS REGUM HYBERNIAE, in which 'ther wes fourc Irland kinges cirdit'. The most northerly of the three tombs (by being buried on the northern side they were nearer their own country) was TUMULUS REGUM NORVEGIAE, in which 'ther layes eight kings of Norroway'. Monro does not mention the stone of the King of France.

If all the Iona crosses except two were indeed destroyed or broken in an excess of fanatical zeal after the Reformation, Dean Monro must have been just in time to see them standing, and it is curious that in his notes he does not mention them. But neither does he mention the beauty of MacLean's Cross, nor of St Martin's Cross, so that his omission proves nothing. Martin Martin, as might have been expected, was more observant, for he mentions both St Martin's Cross and MacLean's Cross, so the inference is that these were the only two crosses standing in his day, St John's Cross not having been restored at that time.

Martin mentions that the Lords of the Isles are buried on Iona, also that the MacKinnons, MacQuarries, MacLeans, MacAllisters and other great families are interred in the sacred earth of Reilig Odhráin. He also records that 'there is a heap of Stones without the Church, under which Mackean of Ardnimurchin lies buried'. Is it to be inferred that this man was forbidden burial within the sacred precincts? Was he the great sea rover who had one side of his galley painted white and the other black, from the thwarts to the water-line, so that it might not be recognised from hostile shores when he returned from one of his forays? Or was he perchance the first Maclain, son of Angus MacDonald, Lord of the Isles—he who was known far and wide as Iain Sprangach and who founded the family which ruled Ardnamurchan from their stronghold, Mingary Castle, until, in the year 1624, the Campbells wasted Ardnamurchan and reduced the castle of Mingary?

The burial-place of Columba, from whom the isle received its sanctity and renown throughout the ages, is not known. It is traditionally believed to be the little cell, now open, near the west wall of the cathedral. The grave must have been opened when the saint's relics were removed. Adamnan records that the stone pillow which Columba used was set up as a monument at the grave. The stone traditionally said to be his pillow is rounded, with a cross incised on it. A corner of the stone, now in the Abbey Church, is broken. In this cell, a small ruined chamber 10½ feet by 7½ feet, attached to the north-west corner of the nave, Columba and his attendant Diormit are said to have been buried. The tomb is now empty and open to the four winds, and to the rain and hail of winter storms.

Pennant, and other writers, mention a celebrated family of Iona, named Clan an Oister, who were Ostiarii or door-keepers to the monastery. Pennant, writing of the end of the Clan an Oister, says that—

> the first of the family came over with Columba, but falling under his displeasure, it was decreed, on the imprecation of this irritable saint, that never more than five of his clan should exist at one time; and in consequence, when a sixth was born, one of the five was to look for death. This, report says, always happened till the period that the race was extinguished in this woman.

Martin mentions that the tradition of the place was that, in the life-time of St Columba, thirty of this family, which he names 'the Tribe here call'd Clan Vic n' Oster, from Ostiarii, for they are said to have been Porters', lived on Iona, and that because of some misdeed, Columba called down a curse upon them.

One would give much to know the fate of the Black Stones, which are mentioned by Martin and other early authors. These sacred stones lay rather to the west of the cathedral, and Martin Martin is careful to state that they were grey (not black) in colour, but received their name because of their effect upon anyone who was guilty of perjury after swearing an oath upon them. MacDonald, Lord of the Isles, upon bended knees on the Black Stones and with uplifted hands, delivered the rights of their lands to his vassals, and solemnly swore that he would never recall those rights. This, Martin proceeds to tell us, was instead of his great Seal. 'Hence it is that when one was certain of what he affirm'd, he said positively, I have freedom to Swear this Matter upon the Black Stones.'

Nor does tradition say what was the fate of the stones known as Clachan Bràth. In Pennant's day they reposed upon the pedestal of a cross. It was considered propitious to turn each of these stones thrice *deiseal* or sunwise. Pennant quotes Sacheverel in saying that the stones which he saw replaced 'three noble globes, of white marble, placed on three stone basons, and these were turned round; but the synod ordered them, and sixty crosses, to be thrown into the sea. They are called Clacha bràth; for it is thought that the *brath* or end of the world will not arrive till the stone on which they stand is worn through.'

The ruins of Teampull Odhráin (Chapel of St Oran) recall a curious tradition. It is said that when Columba attempted to build this chapel, the walls built during the day were found demolished on the following morning. It was then revealed to the saint that they would never stand until a human sacrifice had hallowed the spot and driven out the hostile spirits. His follower, Odhrán or Oran, offered himself, and was accordingly buried alive. At the end of three days Columba, wishing to see his friend once more, had the earth removed, when Oran spoke the following words: 'Heaven is not as has been written; neither is hell as is commonly supposed'. On hearing so dangerous a doctrine from one who had literally risen from the dead, Columba at once gave orders for the grave to be filled in once more. The tradition that Oran sanctified the ground by permitting himself to be interred alive is given in the *Irish Lives of the Saints.*

Can this account be the still earlier legendary tradition of a human sacrifice by the Druids, before the arrival of St Columba on Iona? There are still names on Iona associated with the pre-Columba period, place-names such as Dùn Mhannanain, *Mannanan's Fort*, on the west side of the island. Mannanan mac Lir was, in the old Celtic mythology, God of the Sea: the Isle of Man is named after him. It has been suggested that the Druids, because of their anger against Columba, invented and spread this story in order to discredit the saint. Oran was of noble family and a kinsman of Columba. Whatever the truth concerning the manner of his death, it is, I think, correct to say that he was the first person to be buried in the graveyard which bears his name. Reilig Odhráin *(Oran's Burial Ground)* must be a very old name, for it appears, almost in its present form, in a note in an eighth- or ninth-century Irish MS. This saint gives his name to Tiroran, a district at the head of Loch Scridain in Mull, the word meaning *Oran's Land.* Teampull Odhráin and Reilig Odhráin were considered to be places of unusual sanctity, where the fugitive from justice was safe from those who sought his life. A Girth or Sanctuary, marked by crosses, doubtless surrounded this small chapel.

Were it not for Adamnan's scholarly yet simple biography, we should have no literary record of the life of Saint Columba. Adamnan was a Connaught man, born in the year 624, and as Columba died in 597, his memory must have been fresh when Adamnan was a young man. He was fifty-five years old when he was elected Abbot, and in his abbacy Maolduin, King of Dalriada, bore the expense of repairing the monastery. It is recorded that Adamnan led an expedition of twelve coracles to the mainland to tow back a number of trunks of oak trees, probably to assist in the repairs of the monastery.

Although Adamnan is immortalised because of his *Life of Columba,* he wrote a book also on the Holy Places of Palestine, from the description of a French bishop by name Arculf. This bishop, being driven out of his course by a storm, reached Iona, and there Adamnan wrote out his story. Adamnan, who was, in the words of the Venerable Bede, 'a good and wise man, and most nobly instructed in the knowledge of the Scriptures', was successful in his efforts to abolish the old custom of women fighting in battle.

No chapter on Iona would be complete without some short account of the Iona Community. The Cathedral, or as it should more correctly be termed the Abbey, of Iona was in the year 1900 presented by the 8th Duke of Argyll to the Church of Scotland. It was then a ruin, but, except for the refectory and other lesser buildings, was restored through public subscription during the years 1902-12. In the year 1938 the Trustees of the Abbey granted permission to the Iona Community to set about the restoration of the refectory and other ancient buildings in the vicinity of the Abbey on condition that the cost of the work should be borne by the Community, who accepted that condition with enthusiasm. The Iona Community is a body of men, ministers and craftsmen who, each summer, give up three months of their time to the restoration of the Abbey and its attendant buildings, so far as is possible, to their original state. Their leader, the Rev. Sir George F. MacLeod, M.C., D.D., has seen the membership of the Community grow until it now numbers more than 7,000 'Friends', drawn not only from the Church of Scotland but from the Roman Catholic Church, the Greek Orthodox Church and the Society of Friends. During the other nine months of the year, when not engaged upon work on Iona, the Community seek to apply to modern industry the principles of labour which they have learned during their self-imposed task upon Iona, the Saintly Isle.

AH-50

The Kilchoman Cross, Islay. Mrs Gordon and Francis Cameron-Head.

8

The Unrestful Past

Scotland, like most countries, has had a restless history, which is perhaps a somewhat euphemistic way of describing some of what Seton Gordon narrates of Highland feud and foray. Landscape and man's doings – geography and history – are inextricably twined and how much more interesting a walk or a visit can be when we know what went before. Seton Gordon makes the perfect guide.

A 'Sanctuary Cross' on Islay.

A LOCH EARN FORAY OF LONG AGO

Near the east end of Loch Earn is a small wooded island, Eilean nan Naoiseach *the Neishes' Isle*. There are old ruins on the island and, could they speak, they might tell of a grim deed when bloody vengeance was wrought by the MacNabs upon their hereditary foes the Neishes.

More than a hundred years before the event of which I write a grim fight had been fought in Gleann Bualtachan (Glen Boltachan), in the Loch Earn district, between the MacNabs and the Neishes. In this conflict the chief of the Neishes had been slain and his clan almost wiped out. It is possible that the survivors then decided to retire, for greater security, to the island of Loch Earn. Here we find them one day towards the festive season of Christmas, in the reign of King James V.

The MacNabs, who lived over the watershed to the north, at the head of Loch Tay, had need of wine and delicacies for that Christmas season. They sent their servants across the old hill track to Loch Earn, thence to make their way to Crieff, or perhaps to Perth, to make their purchases. The Neishes from their island saw them pass and a few days later, when they returned heavy-laden, they were set upon and despoiled of the Christmas cheer they were carrying, When MacNab was told of the deed he became, "of an unsocial humour"! He called to him his twelve sons, recited the unpardonable wrong which had been done to their house and ended his tale with words which have become historic, "To-night is the night if the lads were the lads".

The chief who spoke these words was old; his sons were quick to take the hint. Hurriedly arming themselves with pistol, dirk and claymore, they launched their boat upon Loch Tay. Beneath the frosty stars Loch Tay lay dark and still. High above the snowy cone of Ben Lawers the North Star shone. With lusty strokes of the oars the MacNabs swiftly rowed down Loch Tay and in little more than an hour had drawn up the boat on the shore at Ardeonaig. From Ardeonaig an old and well-worn cattle track leads across the broad watershed to Loch Earn, and no doubt at that time cattle drovers from the West Highlands were accustomed to take their herds to the markets of the south by this track. On the autumn day when I crossed from Ardeonaig by this old track I visualised the twelve sons of MacNab striding eagerly up the glen, relays of them taking it in turn to shoulder the heavy boat. In the darkness of a winter night it could not have been easy to have kept to the track near the watershed, where the hill country is a maze of peat hags and black lochans: snow may have lain thick on the ground, and the MacNabs may have sunk thigh-deep in snow.

Before I actually saw the country I imagined that the descent to Loch Earn was by Glen Tarken but the broad watershed is separated by rough and uneven country from the head of that glen and I have now no doubt that the boat was carried down to the loch by way of Glen Beich. Even at the present day the country here is lonely. Looking back one sees Ben Lawers and other great hills; south Ben Vorlich and Ben Ledi rise on the horizon, but north or south, east or west, no house is seen.

Even those twelve stalwart sons must have been weary when they at length reached Loch Earn and their stealthy row of four miles down the loch must have seemed pleasant in comparison with the arduous walk with a heavy boat on their shoulders. All was dark on the island stronghold of Neish. Cautiously the boat was grounded, and the eldest son, he who was known as Iain Min Mac an Aba, *Smooth John MacNab*, thundered at the stout door. It is said that old Neish, dozing beside the open fire of wood and peat, was aroused by the tumult. "Who is there?" he called in a quavering voice. "Who is it you would like least to be there?" came the menacing reply from the gloom without. Neish, with icy fear at his heart, after a moment's thought replied, "Iain Min Mac an Aba." "If he has hitherto been Smooth," came the same fateful voice, "you will find him rough enough for this one night." The door was forced open, and the MacNabs rushed into the darkened room with claymores drawn. They saw the old chief swaying before them and his family and retainers lying in a drunken stupor for they had tasted freely of the "choice wines" of which they had despoiled MacNab's servants.

The MacNabs gave no quarter. All they saw they slew, so that the water which lapped the isle became tinged with crimson. Old Neish's head they cut off, wrapped it carefully in a plaid, and once more embarked in their boat, thinking that they had left none alive to tell the story of that night of horror. Unknown to them, a young grandson of old Neish, had hidden away and lived to remember deeds which must have influenced him throughout his life.

And what of the murderers? Carrying their grisly trophy with them they rowed back along the loch. The laggard December morning had perhaps dawned ere they once again shouldered the well-tried boat and climbed the long slopes of Glen Beich. Near the watershed a great weariness overtook them and in that wild hill country they left their boat and, thus lightened, made their way across the shoulder of the hills to their home. Old MacNab eagerly awaited their coming. They entered the house and silently unwrapped the plaid, exposing to their father's view the head of their hated enemy. MacNab looked long upon it, then, turning to his sons, he said, "The night *was* the night, and the lads *were* the lads."

Miss Isabel MacDougall tells me that her grand-uncle, who was tenant of Dall in 1854, had seen the remains of the MacNabs' boat lying, deep-embedded in peat and heather, on the watershed 'twixt Earn and Tay. She believes that, even as late as 1894–5, the winter of the severe and prolonged snowstorm, a few stays of the boat still remained there.

To add insult to injury, the MacNabs, after the beheading of Neish, took his head for their crest. Iain Min later distinguished himself as a soldier and was killed in 1651 at the battle of Worcester; he had been a great supporter of Montrose and had commanded Montrose's castle of Kincardine.

H&BC-48

A Skye crofter's home.

THE LOCH OF THE SWORD

On the rugged watershed between Lochaber and Rannoch is a small loch, by name Loch a' Chlaidheimh, *the Loch of the Sword*. Many travellers must have had a fleeting glimpse of this peat-stained lochan for the West Highland Railway passes close to it but few are familiar with its name or its history. This loch lies at the march between three great Highland counties— Inverness, Perth and Argyll—and received its name from an old-time incident, the story of which was told me by Cameron of Lochiel, direct descendant of the Lochiel who figures in the story.

Lochiel and the Earl of Atholl had a dispute regarding the boundary of their respective lands, and arranged to meet at Loch a' Chlaidheimh to settle the controversy. It was mutually agreed that each chief should be accompanied by one man only. Lochiel set out from Achnacarry, but had not travelled far when he was met by the Witch of Moy. "Lochiel, Lochiel," said she, "Turn back, Lochiel. Where are your men?" Lochiel answered her that he could not with honour take men with him after the compact which he and Atholl had made. Unheeding his reply the Witch of Moy thrice repeated her warning, and Lochiel, thinking over the matter, came to the conclusion that it were prudent to take some of his clansmen with him. But before he reached the Loch of the Sword he told his men to remain in hiding in the heather, and not to show themselves unless he turned his coat outside-in as a signal that they were needed.

He then went on with only one man and met the Earl of Atholl who also had one man with him. At first the discussion as to the march was conducted in a friendly manner but as time went on tempers became frayed, argument became heated and at last Atholl with a sudden movement blew a shrill and long note on a whistle. To Lochiel's astonishment a number of men rose from the peat-hags where they had been in hiding. "Who are these?" asked Lochiel. "These," was the reply, "are the Atholl wedders, come to graze on the Lochaber grass." Lochiel did not speak, but quietly turned his coat outside-in, and this act had scarcely been completed when a strong force of Camerons sprang from their concealment. "Who are these?" said the Earl of Atholl. "These," said Lochiel, "are the Lochaber dogs and they are gey hungry for the flesh of the Atholl wedders."

Seeing that he was outnumbered, Atholl gave way to Lochiel, and in order to ratify the agreement which was then reached, a sword was thrown into the loch. There for centuries it remained until, in the year 1812, it was found in a curious manner. In those days there were summer shielings in that moorland country where no house now stands and one summer day, when children were paddling in the loch a girl cut her foot on some sharp object. A search was made and the old claymore, rusty and peat-stained, was found. It was taken to Fort William, but when the leading inhabitants of that place heard what had happened they decided that the claymore must be returned to the loch. It was therefore carried with fitting solemnity by twelve men back to the Loch of the Sword, where it was thrown far out over the waters. For an instant as it sped its trusty blade turned to glowing bronze in the sunlight then, like Excalibur, it sank from sight.

AWP-37

THE LOSS OF GAICK

Gaick was unenviably renowned because of an event which is known by the Gaelic-speaking natives of Badenoch as Call Ghàig, *the Loss of Gaick.* The story is a strange one. It is given in Scrope's *Days of Deer Stalking* and in other Highland records.

Captain John MacPherson of Ballachroan, with four attendants and several strong deer-hounds, at Christmas-tide of the year 1799 went up to a bothy in Gaick on a deer-hunting expedition. The day after the party had gone, a fearful storm of wind and snow broke over the hills and when the hunters did not return a search party set out up the glen. Through gigantic snow-wreaths they fought their way but when at last they reached the site of the bothy—somewhere below Loch an t-Seilich, beneath a steep slope now partly covered with birch—they saw no sign of it. After a careful search they found that the bothy was not merely blown down but quite torn to pieces: large stones, which had formed part of the walls, were found at the distance of one or two hundred yards from the site of the building; and the wooden uprights appeared to have been rent asunder by a force that had twisted them off, as in breaking a tough stick. From the circumstances in which the bodies were found, it appeared that the men were retiring to rest at the time the calamity came upon them. One of the bodies, indeed, was found at a distance of many yards from the bothy; another of the men was found upon the place where the bothy had stood, with one stocking off, as if he bad been undressing.

Captain Macpherson was lying without his clothes upon the wretched bed which the bothy had afforded, his face to the ground and his knees drawn up. To all appearance the destruction had been quite sudden; yet the situation of the building was such as promised security against the ulmost violence of the wind : it stood in a narrow recess, at the foot of a mountain, whose precipitous and lofty declivities sheltered it on every side excepting the front, and here, too, a hill rose before it, though with a more gradual slope.

The fact that in so sheltered a spot the bothy was swept away seems to have been taken as a clear instance of the supernatural: no one apparently thought of an avalanche, and yet it seems certain than an avalanche caused the disaster. Indeed in or about the year 1922 an avalanche swept down the hillside at this same place and killed several hinds.

H&BC-48

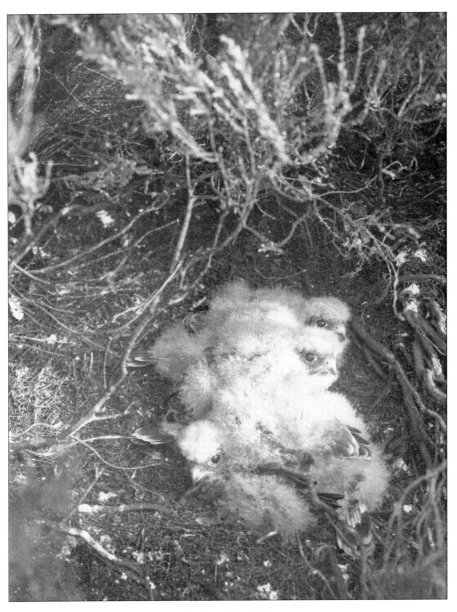

A merlin brood in their nest.

CORRIEYAIREAG: A HIGHLAND PASS

Near the headwaters of the Spey a road, made by General Wade and now long disused, leads through the heart of the hills from Badenoch to Fort Augustus on Loch Ness. This old road, skilfully constructed, crosses the Pass of Corrieyaireag, 2,500 feet, in a wild and lonely country far beyond the sight of any house.

The road across the Pass of Corrieyaireag seems to have been completed in the summer of the year 1731, for a gentleman of the name of MacLeod who crossed the pass in the autumn of 1731, saw six great fires, at which six oxen were being roasted whole as a treat for the five hundred soldiers who had that summer completed "the great road for Wheel-carriages between Fort Augustus and Ruthven, it being October 30, His Majesty's Birthday".

The Hon. Mrs. Murray, who has left a record of her travelling in the Scottish Highlands in the year 1798, crossed Corrieyaireag by coach in the late summer of that season. Before she began her journey she met, at breakfast with the Governor of Fort Augustus, an Oxonian who had crossed the pass on horseback the previous day. He gave her a depressing account of Corrieyaireag, a pass

> of wild desolation beyond anything he could describe; and the whole of the road rough, dangerous and dreadful, even for a horse. The steep and black mountains, and the roaring torrents rendered every step his horse took, frightful; and when he attained the summit of the zigzag up Corrieyaireag he thought the horse himself, man and all, would be carried away, he knew not whither; so strong was the blast, so hard the rain, and so very thick the mist. And as for cold, it stupified him.

Mrs. Murray tells of a woman with an infant at the breast who succumbed when endeavouring to cross the pass; the infant, being covered with snow, was still alive when found, and the governor's lady at Fort Augustus restored it to health. The same chronicler mentions that soldiers often perished on the pass, partly because "they over-refreshed themselves with whisky before the climb".

Prince Charles Edward crossed Corrieyaireag at the end of August 1745, at the beginning of his campaign. He had heard that Cope was encamped at Garvamore, on the Badenoch side of the pass, and was anxious to engage him as soon as possible. That morning, as he pulled on a new pair of brogues, he said happily, "Before I throw these off, I shall meet with Mr. Cope." The Prince sent ahead two of his officers to see whether they could get into contact with Cope's force, but when they reached the watershed "not a creature was to be seen", although a little later in the day forty deserters from General Cope's force were viewed ascending the zigzags on the Badenoch side of the pass: these deserters at once took up service with the Prince. Cope thinking discretion the better part of valour, had turned aside near Dalchully at a place still known as Cope's Turn, and was making towards Ruthven Barracks. At Corrieyaireag the Prince was joined by "Ardshiel (commanding the Stewarts of Appin), Glengarry and Glenco".

It is a century and more since the road across Corrieyaireag carried the last of its wheeled traffic but it is not so long since sheep and cattle were driven over it to the markets of the south. Mrs. Grant of Laggan, in her *Letters from the Mountains,* writes in 1781 from Fort Augustus:

> This district is divided from ours (Laggan in Badenoch) by an immense mountain called Corryarrick. That barrier is impassable in the depth of winter, as the top of it is above the region of clouds, and the sudden descent on the other (Spey) side particularly dangerous not only from deep snows concealing the unbeaten track of the road, but from whirlwinds and eddies that drive the snow into heaps; besides an evil spirit which the country people devoutly believe to have dwelt there time out of mind.

I was twice on Corrieyaireag in 1938. In the spring of that year I climbed to the summit of the pass on a cold April morning, when I met beside the Spey a party of motor-cyclists who (unknown to me at the time) had that day made history by crossing the pass from Fort Augustus: the wheel-tracks of their machines remained for many a day to tell of their exploit.

That morning I approached Corrieyaireag from the east. General Wade's road is still in use in the Spey valley, for about ten miles from its junction with the main Fort William-Newtonmore road to the stalker's house at Meall Garbh Ath, the *Hill of the Rough Ford.* The old road leaves the Newtonmore-Fort William road west of Laggan Bridge, passes near Dalchully, one of the hiding-places of Cluny Mac-Pherson of the '45, then follows the Spey past Glen Shirra and Loch Crunachan and crosses the river (here is a particularly fine Wade's bridge) beside the old barracks at Garvamore. At the present day the road is rough, and there are a number of gates to open and close again, as far as Meall Garbh Ath or, as it is now written, Meall Garbha; beyond that house the track is not in use; it is grass- and heather-grown, and usually very wet.

The scene ahead of me was wild and lonely as I set out into the heart of the hills. Even the glen of the Spey was bare and wintry, although here I had seen golden plover and heard the trilling of curlews. From now onward to the summit of Corrieyaireag I saw no bird, save a skylark which flew ahead of me low above the track but when I had almost reached the summit of the pass I saw and watched a pair of ptarmigan dozing on a warm, grassy bank.

At a time when, in certain parts of the Highlands and Islands, the Ministry of Transport were narrowing the existing roads as they reconstructed them, to a width of 10 feet, it was interesting to discover that General Wade made this road over the hills a width of 14 and in some places 15 feet. Here and there a cloud-burst had carried down earth and stones on to the track: perhaps the same flood washed away the first stone bridge after the stalker's house is passed, and did its best to sweep away the second. Icicles hung from the rocks of the corrie, and a cold northerly wind was bringing into the corrie the smoke of a distant heather fire, which burned far out of my sight somewhere beyond the watershed in the neighbourhood of Loch Ness.

Scars heal slowly in hill country, and I saw gravel-pits and banks and passing places and even old metal broken to repair the track. The road is well engineered, and there are few steep gradients, except at the zigzags.

When I reached the summit, 2,500 feet, the wind was so cold that I could not long remain to admire the view. To the north-west I could see Loch Garry, and the high hills beyond the loch, half hidden by snow showers, while south-west Aonach Mór and Ben Nevis raised their snow-filled corries to the passing clouds. I returned to Meall Garbha with the wind at my back and was overtaken by more than one snow shower which for a time whitened the hill slopes.

Very different were the conditions on the October day when a friend and I crossed the pass from Fort Augustus to Glen Truim in Badenoch. That autumn was continuously wet and stormy; our walk was through rain and mist, and the most pleasant memory of the day was the hot bath provided, along with a dram of *uisge beatha,* by our Highland host. It was already noon when we stood in the small room in Fort Augustus Abbey where Lord Lovat of the '45 was for some days a prisoner, and saw the old tree outside the abbey planted by Government officers to commemorate Cumberland's victory. A late start on a long walk is rarely justified, and throughout that day we were hurrying to reach Badenoch before the darkness of a moonless night closed in on us.

The way is first along Glen Tarff and in the mist and gloom it was impossible to tell through which upland glen we were ultimately to climb in order to cross the watershed to the Spey. Following weeks of rain, the track was sodden and the hills ran water. The most pleasant part of the climb was at Lagan a' Bhainne, *Dell of the Milk* (called by the Government troops Snugborough). Here weeping birches were scattering golden leaves into the peat-stained stream and a golden eagle, rising from near the ruins of old houses, flew close past us down the glen, showing clearly (it was a young bird of the year) the white marking on wings and tail.

General Wade's bridge spanning the stream at Lagan a' Bhainne has fallen away at the centre, and a foot-bridge has recently been erected here by the Scottish Rights of Way Society. We now climbed more steeply. Through dense mist we plodded, wind and rain driving in our faces and as we traversed this country of gloom heard invisible stags roaring about us. Our view was restricted to a few yards but the old road was a sure guide and at length we found ourselves descending into Badenoch. As we descended the steep zigzags, now running water, we finally passed out of the fog and saw ahead a sombre country which lay dark and dreary in the dusk of a day of rain. In the half light a peregrine falcon rose from a knoll where she had perhaps decided to spend the night: she flew backwards and forwards low above the moor, then swung high into the air and was lost to view in the deepening dusk.

Making the best speed possible, we reached the stalker's house and were glad to see the lights of the car which our kind host and hostess of Glen Truim had sent to meet us at Meall Garbha.

Were it possible to recall the past, there would surely be stirring sights to see on Corrieyaireag — the Prince's army streaming, to the loud strains of the great Highland pipe, eastward into Badenoch, travellers on horseback breasting those same slopes, and now and again a stately, horse-drawn vehicle belonging to some dignitary slowly making its way up the steep zigzags, or perhaps some lonely soldier, during a wild winter crossing, toiling onward until slowly overwhelmed by the choking drift and lying down to sleep the sleep that knows no earthly awakening. Surely this hill pass keeps many secrets in its bosom, but now its busy life has gone and it sees only the red deer and the hardy ptarmigan and perhaps a wild cat stalking a red grouse.

A strange visitor of late did indeed for a time make its home in the neighbourhood of Meall Garbha. This white-plumaged bird, large and unusual in appearance, preyed on the partridges which live beside the Spey here. It was unfortunately shot and was found to be a Greenland falcon, a wanderer from that distant snowy land which gave it birth.

H&BC-48

"YOU HAVE SLAIN YOUR PRINCE"

In summer the high road through Glen Moriston leading from Loch Ness to the Isle of Skye is thronged with cars. Most of them pass, at speed, a small cairn at the side of the road near Ceannacroc, a cairn which commemorates an act of devotion on the part of a Jacobite officer in the rising of 1745. The officer's name was Roderick MacKenzie and his grave, on the opposite side of the road to the cairn and close to the bank of the river, is marked by two rough stones. His brave dying act has won him a place among the immortals.

Roderick was one of Prince Charles Edward's bodyguards. After Culloden when those of the Jacobites who had escaped death were in hiding, our hero was in Glen Moriston, perhaps at the time when the Prince was in the care of the Seven Men of Glen Moriston, in Uamh Ruairidh na Seilg, *Cave of Roderick the Hunter*, high in Coire Dho between Glen Moriston and Glen Affric. These were indeed dark days for the inhabitants of Glen Moriston. Cumberland's soldiers mercilessly ravaged the glen, killing young and old. In a contemporary account it is said that 'the militia from the Isle of Skye' (it will be remembered that the MacLeods were hostile to the Jacobites) were urged by their officers to plunder the glen when the Earl of Loudoun, accompanied by MacLeod of Dunvegan and Sir Alexander MacDonald of Sleat, marched through Glen Moriston some little time after Culloden.

It is said that every man has a double, and Roderick MacKenzie was the Prince's double. When he was in hiding and a party of soldiers found him, their joy must have been great at the thought of the reward they would obtain on his capture. Roderick, no doubt hearing their excited shouts that they had found the Prince, and seeing that escape was hopeless, determined not to surrender but to fight and die where he stood. When at last he fell, mortally wounded, he had the courage and the presence of mind to say, "Alas, you have slain your Prince."

The soldiers severed his head, which they bore in triumph to Cumberland at Fort Augustus and we can imagine the commotion and the excitement there when the men's trophy was displayed. An officer of the garrison, no doubt by Cumberland's orders, approached MacDonald of Kingsburgh who was a prisoner there, and with great earnestness asked him if he would recognize the Prince's head if he saw it. Kingsburgh replied, "I would know the head very well, provided it be on the body." The officer then asked him, "What if the head be not on the body?" Kingsburgh replied. "In that case, sir, I will not pretend to know anything about it." The officer did not trouble him further, but the Duke of Cumberland, having satisfied himself that the head was indeed that of the Prince, set out in haste for London to acquaint the authorities there of the good news. He took the head with him. One of the Prince's servants, Richard Morison by name, was a prisoner at Carlisle, under sentence of death. He was sent for immediately but was unable to travel through illness for some little time. When at last he arrived, the head was beyond recognition. There is no doubt that Roderick MacKenzie's heroic action gave the Prince a period of much-needed respite.

HD-63

On the Shiants – Garbh Eilean.

CASTLE AT THE GATEWAY TO SKYE

At daybreak across the quiet waters of Loch Duich the snowy peaks of the Sisters of Kintail rose cold and stern at the head of the loch. On a low, rocky promontory a heron stood as though carved in stone. The ground rises steeply from the south shore of the loch and it is February before the sun shines on the houses of the small township of Letterfearn.

Beyond the sheltered house of Druideig old trees grow to the edge of the tide. One of these ancient trees is an oak. Up to about 100 years ago sailing ships of considerable size were built at Dornie, on the opposite side of the sea loch. It was considered that this oak, because of its shape, would be specially valuable in fashioning the keel of a new vessel to be built. The sum of £1 was offered to the proprietor of the ground but was refused. That was 100 years and more ago, and the oak must, therefore, be of great age. It is still alive, and has indeed the appearance of a very old tree. The ship for which this tree was intended was the *Donnan Castle,* a three-masted schooner of 300 tons which later traded with Baltic and north European ports. She was ultimately in collision with another ship off Lizard Point and sank far from her home sea loch.

A few hundred yards farther along the shore of the loch the road ends at Totaig, where there was formerly a public ferry across to Dornie. Here a shag was drying his wings on a skerry and a strong tidal river was entering Loch Duich.

The road abruptly ends but the path, rising gradually, leads along the shore to the remains of a splendid *broch*, Caisteal Grùgaig. This *broch* is built close to a hill burn which would have provided its occupants with water. In the greyness of a winter morning the Castle of Eilean Donnan across the strait could be seen. Could the stones of this castle speak, they might tell of centuries of clan warfare and of dark deeds.

It is said that many centuries ago the son of a Kintail chief received his first drink from the skull of a raven. Both the Celts and the Norse believed that the raven was a bird with occult powers, and this drinking rite enabled the infant to understand the language of birds. When he came to manhood he travelled to France. The King of France could get no sleep because of the music of the birds in the grounds of the royal residence. The young Highlander who could speak to birds in their own language, was asked if he could help. He held a conference with the birds and they obligingly agreed to make music beyond earshot of those in the palace. As a mark of his gratitude the King of France made him a present of a fully manned ship. In this vessel he journeyed to many lands, and at last returned to his sea loch. He was now wealthy and respected, and Alexander II, King of Scotland at this time, commissioned him to build the Castle of Eilean Donnan as a defence against raiding Norsemen.

The Castle of Eilean Donnan has withstood many sieges. In the year 1590 Donald Gorm MacDonald sailed with his war galleys from Skye hoping to take the castle, which was then lightly garrisoned. The defenders were said to have numbered no more than three and when their resistance had apparently ended Donald Gorm, showing himself rashly, was hit in the leg by an arrow. In his anger he tore out the arrow roughly by the shaft, almost severing an artery. He was carried to his war galley and taken to a low grassy isle, Glas Eilean, nearby and, here, in a rough shelter that was hastily built for him his followers attempted to stop the bleeding of the wound, but in vain.

The place where he died is still named Larach Tigh Mhic Dhomhnall which can be translated *Site of MacDonald's House*. We know that the Castle of Eilean Donnan was a fortress at the time of the first Jacobite rising in 1715 and at the Battle of Glenshiel in 1719 a force of Spaniards assisted at an abortive Jacobite rising, having been brought by sea and quartered in the Castle of Eilean Donnan. They were defeated by government forces and the castle was heavily bombarded by government war vessels. For nearly two centuries it remained a ruin, but was restored by Colonel MacRae-Gilstrap, whose ancestors were the constables of the castle.

HS-71

EIGG AND ITS MASSACRES

O f Hebridean islands Eigg is one of the most distinctive. It is recognised
from afar by its Scùir—a precipitous hill which rises gracefully from the
southern end of the island.

Looking across from Arisaig or the sands of Morar on a summer evening
one sees the Scùir of Eigg rising ethereal on the horizon, and from Sleat of
Skye, too, Eigg is often inspiring because of its deep spiritual blueness, and
from the northern coast of Mull it is one of the most distinctive of the isles.
Eilean Eige is the Gaelic name of the island, and it means *the Isle of the Notch*.
In Adamnan's *Life of Columba* (A.D. 700) it is written of as Egea Insula.

The patron saint of Eigg is Donnan; he is commemorated in Kildonan,
in Eigg, and probably also in Eilean Donnan in Kintail. Saint Donnan was
massacred on Eigg, whither he had gone to preach the religion of his master
Columba. With Donnan were slain his fifty-two followers. It has been suggested
that the murderers were Norsemen but the Eigg massacre took place before
the earliest Norse invasion and old records merely call the assailants "piraiti" or
pirates. There were roving bands of pirates in the Isles long before the Vikings
appeared. A curious tradition for this massacre said that Saint Donnan in some
way aroused the anger of a proud queen who hired unscrupulous men to
exterminate him and his band.

Their bones were found by Martin many centuries after. Martin, writing
about the year 1700, says,

> There is a church here in the east side of the isle, dedicated to Saint Donnan,
> whose anniversary they observe. About thirty yards from the church there is a
> sepulchral Urn under the ground. We found a flat thin stone covering the
> Urn. It was almost full of human bones, but no head among them, and they
> were fair and dry. I inquired of the natives what was become of the heads,
> and they could not tell, but one of them said, perhaps their heads had been
> cut off with a two-handed sword and taken away by the enemy.

Another and more recent massacre is still spoken of in the Isle of Eigg.
The MacLeods of Harris and the MacDonalds of Clan Ranald had long been

at enmity. The pretext for the crime known as the Massacre of the Cave of Eigg was the maltreatment by the men of Eigg of certain messengers who had been sent to them by the MacLeods. It was also said that one of the MacLeod chiefs had made himself unpopular on the island because of his amorous escapades and had been tied to a boat and set adrift on the Minch.

In revenge for these indignities a strong force of the MacLeods sailed from Skye to Eigg in their war galleys. It was the season of early spring—the most bitter time in the whole year in the Hebrides. A north wind blew mercilessly upon the green waters of the Minch beneath a hard blue sky. The Cuillin were deep in snow. Even Eigg was snowbound to the shore. From Rudha Thalasgeir on Eigg the approach of the galleys was observed and the alarm was given. There was fear in the hearts of the people when the news was brought to them for most of the men were absent from the island at the time. On the eastern shore of Eigg is a great cave. The entrance is partially hidden by a burn which flows in a small white waterfall from the moor above, and drops immediately over the cave's entrance. To this cave all except two of the island families hurried, the men assisting the small children and carrying the infants across the high ground. The two families who did not accompany the rest hid in another cave, farther along the coast.

The MacLeod galleys landed, the men with difficulty leaping ashore in the strong wind that sent the cold spray against the frozen rocks. A film of drifting snow lay above the island that bitter March day, for the north wind was blowing the powdery snow before it in clouds, and was piling up great drifts in the sheltered hollows. Almost as soon as they were made, the footprints of the fugitives to the cave were covered in by the drifting snow, and when the MacLeods searched the houses and found them empty, and saw no footmarks in the ground, they doubtless imagined that the population of Eigg had escaped them. They searched the island, satisfied themselves that no person remained on it, then embarked and set sail towards Skye.

The wind now became less violent and one of the men of Eigg left the cave and climbed to the high ground to see whether the coast was clear. His action brought disaster on the island. He saw the galleys departing, but they also saw him and at once put about. The friendly wind no longer drifted the snow and when the enemy landed they were able to follow the watcher's footmarks back to the cave. Here the whimpering of children and the barking of dogs told them all they wished to know. In the latter part of the sixteenth century there was little mercy shown to an enemy in the highlands. The entrance to the cave was narrow. To escape, and even to fight, was impossible, for a MacLeod claymore would have put a swift end to any person crawling laboriously from the cave's mouth.

A ruthless plan was decided on. The nearest houses were stripped of their thatch for kindlings and when the course of the burn had been altered so that it no longer flowed over the cave's mouth a great fire was lighted at the entrance and wet fuel was piled upon the flames.

Thick clouds of smoke rolled into the sky and into the cave. At the far end of this underground passage there is little air at any time and gradually the people within were overcome by the smoke. The cries, the moanings, and the shouts lessened. At long intervals came a gasping sob and when these too ceased the men of Skye embarked beneath the stars, leaving a smouldering fire at the entrance to what was now a cave of the dead.

Through the centuries that followed the whitening bones of the victims remained in the cave. It is not so long since they were gathered and reverently interred. They were found in family groups—father, mother and children mingling their dust in that dark recess. The two families (in some accounts only one family is mentioned) who were in hiding in another cave escaped the massacre. Thus in a few hours was the population of Eigg virtually wiped out. At the present day there are living on Eigg only one family who are original natives of the island; all the rest are settlers from neighbouring islands or the mainland.

Skene's *Celtic Scotland* has an account of the massacre. This report is believed to have been prepared for the use of James VI and must have been written before 1595, as James Stewart of Appin, who died in that year, is mentioned as being alive. It has never been settled beyond doubt whether this massacre was in revenge for a crime of equal turpitude, the massacre of the MacLeods in the church at Trumpan in Skye by the MacDonalds of Clan Ranald (Clan Ranald owned both Eigg and the Outer Hebridean island of South Uist). The MacLeods assert that the massacre of Trumpan preceded that of Eigg. The MacDonalds aver that their raid on Trumpan was in revenge for the Eigg massacre. Let us recall briefly the massacre at Trumpan and the Battle of the Spoiled Dyke which was fought the same day. One Sunday morning in summer Clan Ranald's galleys reached Trumpan on Vaternish of Skye and, surrounding the small church during the service, set fire to it and burned to death those within. MacLeod's clansmen cut off the raiders before they could reach their galleys, and the Battle of the Spoiled Dyke was fought. The MacLeods were being hard-pressed when the miraculous Fairy Flag was unfurled. One galley only escaped. The rest of the incendiaries were slain and the stones of a dyke were heaped above their bodies.

Eigg is now peaceful. Its most illustrious son of the present day is the Reverend Kenneth MacLeod who has perhaps done more than any man to rescue the old music of the Gael. Eigg is full of music. Even the sands of the seashore sing when one walks upon them. These Singing Sands lie, white and gleaming, on the western side of the island. Here is the broad Bay of Laig, where gannets fish among the breakers and at dusk the clan of the shearwaters fly inland from the darkening sea. Beside these white singing sands of Laig there is green *machair,* where many sweet-scented flowers blossom, and the crimson orchis blends with the yellow of the iris and trefoil.

Eigg is an isle of flowers. The scented dog rose blossoms on the shore and on the hills, while the sea cliffs at midsummer are white with *Dryas octopetala,* crimson with the cushion pink, and golden with roseroot. High on the slopes the bell heather flames, and the wild honeysuckle twines among the rocks. By day buzzard and raven sail above the cliffs of Eigg. At dusk the shear-waters speed in from the sea to their nesting burrows on the cliffs, and throughout the nights of spring and summer make wild music there. But as the glow of the lighthouse on Ardnamurchan pales and the outline of Rhum across the Sound becomes clear the shearwaters sink into slumber and the robin and mavis, taking their places as musicians, salute the approaching day.

H&BW-35

Loading sheep, Pabbay, near Barra Head.

9

Wildlife Notes

Seton Gordon was an all-round naturalist, whether studying seals on a remote Hebridean island or seagulls in London, a roundness which owes much to his growing up on Deeside with the Cairngorms at hand. He became friends with many of the best naturalists, the keepers, men who knew their wild world at all seasons, in every weather; an influence he frequently acknowledged. In this big world he could still stand fascinated by bees flying past a ferry or put music into a list of hill berries.

Importuning young ravens on their nest in the Outer Hebrides.

A baby grey seal less than two weeks old.

THE ATLANTIC SEAL

O ff the coast of Scotland and the Isles are found two species of seals, the grey or Atlantic seal and the common seal. Of the two the Atlantic seal is very much the larger and there was once shot a bull which weighed forty-nine stone.

The Atlantic seal is a lover of the open sea; the common seal frequents sea-lochs and the more sheltered waters of the ocean. In their habits the two seals differ widely. The common seal gives birth to its pup in early summer, and the infant seal is immediately at home in the water. The young grey seal, on the other hand, is born in autumn. It is dropped by its mother above the reach of an ordinary high tide and, unless alarmed, does not enter the sea until a month or six weeks old. Thus, during the first month of life, an Atlantic seal pup is helpless and falls an easy prey to an enemy. Officially the Atlantic seal is protected during the time she is rearing her young but many fishermen are unaware of the Grey Seals' Protection Act and are none too anxious to make themselves acquainted with it. For centuries the crofter-fishermen of the Isles have sailed every autumn when the weather was favourable to one isolated rocky island where a colony of Atlantic seals have their nursery. But the last time—a few years ago- a boat had a narrow escape from being swamped in the heavy sea that suddenly arose and since then the seal people have been unmolested.

More than two hundred years ago the annual battue of Atlantic seals took place, for Martin writes in 1703:

> On the Western Coast of this Island (North Uist) lyes the Rock Cousmil, about a quarter of a mile in circumference, still famous for the yearly fishing of Seals in the end of October. This rock belongs to the Farmers of the adjacent Lands; there is one who furnisheth a boat, to whom there is a particular share due on that account besides his proportion as Tenant; the Parish Minister hath his choice of all the young Seals and that which he takes is called Cullen Mory, that is the Virgin Mary's Seal. The Farmers always imbarque with a contrary wind, for their security against being driven away by the Ocean, and likewise to prevent them from being discovered by

the Seals, who are apt to smell the scent of them. When the Crew is quietly landed they surround the Passes and then the signal for the general attacque is given they beat them down with big staves. The Seals at this On-set make towards the sea with all speed and often force their passage over the stoutest assailants, who aim always at the Forehead of the Seals, giving them many blows before they be killed. The Natives told me that several of the biggest Seals lose their lives by endeavouring to save their Young ones whom they tumble before them towards the Sea. I was told also that 320 Seals, Young and Old, have been killed at one time in this Place."

Probably because of these attacks the Atlantic seal has abandoned 'Cousmil,' or Cousamul as it is to-day and now rears its young upon less accessible isles. The Atlantic surf guards these isles well from human trespassers.

I shall always remember my first visit to a crowded nursery of the Atlantic seal. For three weeks I had waited on a neighbouring inhabited island for fine weather.

My steamer for the mainland sailed and my chances of seeing the seals seemed hopeless. But that evening about midnight the wind shifted north-east with heavy squalls of hail and when at dawn next morning I looked out across the Atlantic the air was windless, the sky serene and clear, and the white-crested waves rolled slowly in on the low sandy shore. The swell was quickly subsiding and the boatmen were willing to make an attempt to reach the island of the grey seals.

It was November. From a deep blue sky the sun shone with almost summer heat. Westward, on the rim of ocean where Saint Kilda showed, a layer of white cumulus clouds seemed to tower from the blue waters. North and east were high hills that gleamed white with unbroken snow. Into the blue sunlit sea we sailed. Our course at first was through a maze of islands. It was necessary for us to pass between two of these islands by way of a tide-swept sound.

A crested wave would have been disastrous to our small craft, and when a great wave did curl over ahead of us right in our course, the boatmen spoke excitedly among themselves in Gaelic, and debated whether they should put about. Up the great flanks of the advancing wave we climbed giddily but fortunately for us no second wave broke until we had sailed beyond the danger zone and were steering west through deep waters that showed a very dark blue.

As we neared the island we lowered our sail lest the seals should see it and very cautiously approached the shore. We could see many Atlantic seals, both old and young, basking on the sun-warmed sand. Behind this pleasant shore the surf broke constantly, and in the calm air the spray hung above the rocks. It even mounted far up the hillside above and was suspended there as morning mist lies in some silent glen of a midsummer dawn. Suddenly from the sea around us thrust the great heads of the seal-folk and solemn, questioning eyes watched us as we made ready to land.

Upon a grassy slope above the beach a numerous company of barnacle geese stood. They gazed at us uncertainly for no boat had touched at the island since they had left their summer haunts in Greenland or Spitsbergen and it was not until some time after we had landed that they rose in a body and filled the air with musical calls as they complained to one another of our presence.

We went ashore some distance from the beach and then stalked the seals which dozed on the sandy shore. On seeing us, those seals nearest to the water hurried with shuffling gait into the sea but a number of the animals were too far from the water to make their escape and these eyed us doubtfully as they kept their ground. We came upon some of the colony lying on broken rocky ground which had hid our approach from them. These animals had no warning of our coming and eyed us with sudden alarm. Side by side two seals were lying beside a rock: one of them was black, the other a silvery grey. The skin of the silvery-grey seal hung loosely in folds; she seemed to be very old. For a moment they lay there, full of anxiety. Then, with deep moaning roars they charged us, and it was impossible to keep them back from the sea.

Over all the island Atlantic seals were lying. Some were of enormous size. As we approached them, all the mother seals except one left their youngsters and made for the sea. This one seal guarded her young with supreme devotion. She allowed me to approach to a distance of about ten feet; nearer than that she would not permit me to come and lunged towards me menacingly, opening her mouth wide and uttering hollow roars. From time to time her pup bleated like a lamb and then she turned anxiously towards it, her thoughts momentarily distracted from her own plight. The young seal lay in the shelter of a log of driftwood, its white silky coat stained grey with peat.

On a grassy flat was a small peaty tarn. In this tarn two huge seals were swimming. One of the seals, no doubt excited by our appearance, set upon the other, and a desperate struggle began. The black waters of the tarn were churned into foam as the seals sprang one upon the other and gripped each other with their teeth. Quickly the battle ended, and side by side the two huge seals raced (if such a word may be used to describe their laboured but astonishingly rapid progress) from the tarn to the sea.

In a large pool beside the tarn a number of grey seal pups were hiding, and with them one old mother seal. The pups, although not more than a month or six weeks old, were able to remain below the surface for long intervals. All over the island the old Atlantic seals were cautiously making their way to the sea from the nurseries. But the seal pups were too young to follow them.

In the air was a bleating as though many lambs were calling, and in this plaintive calling and the clamour of the barnacle geese as they passed often overhead was a wild musical harmony very pleasant to hear.

Some of the grey seal pups lay on their backs fast asleep in quaint attitudes. They were absurdly fat, and a number of them showed not double chins but quadruple and quintuple chins! So soundly did they slumber that it was possible to walk quietly up to them and photograph them without arousing them from their siestas! The pups were of different ages. Some of them were not more than a week old, and were clad in the long white silky fur that is worn only for the first week after birth. Their eyes were large and very dark brown. Other pups had grown their second coat—thick cream-coloured fur, rather short and curly; while the oldest of them had already assumed the third coat—dappled grey, and not unlike the adult seals' fur in colour. But although some of the pups were at least six weeks old, none of them showed any inclination to take to the sea, and it is said that the only thing that causes them to enter the Atlantic during the first two months of their lives is an intense frost.

It is believed by scientists that the grey seal was much more recently a land animal than the common seal; hence the terrestrial habits of the seal pups. Certainly when one remembers that the young common seal swims actively the first day of its life, the difference in their behaviour is striking.

Behind the pool rose dark rocks; beyond these lay the sun-kissed Atlantic plains. One after the other great waves hurled themselves ponderously upon the isle, shattering themselves in spray upon the grim barrier of rock. In the air was suspended a film of spray, dimming the middle view. No wilder or more magnificent scene can be pictured than that sunny November day from this island outpost where the Atlantic seals rear their young.

Across the short grass the mother seals had worn many paths as they had visited their pups to suckle them, and upon the grass lay the shed fur of the youngsters. I noticed that two of the pups had lost an eye—perhaps pecked out by grey crows—and that two baby seals lay dead.

Wherever one walked were young Atlantic seals. They must have numbered at least three hundred. Near the centre of the island a wee burn had its source, and flowed to the peaty tarn in a series of pools. In each peaty pool seal pups wallowed. Some of these youngsters at our approach submerged their heads in the peaty slime. They evidently believed, like the ostrich, that if they could no longer see us we could no longer see them. Others crowded and splashed as though they were giant salmon pressing up to their moorland spawning beds.

Again, after the lapse of a twelvemonth, we sailed out to the grey seals' nursery. On the calm waters were swimming many black guillemots and long-tailed ducks, and as we neared the isle a great northern diver flew swiftly ahead of us. As before, the barnacle geese fed on the grassy slopes and many grey seals dozed on the sandy beach. On a rock, fast asleep in the sun, lay an old bull seal. I stalked him with a camera, and succeeded in photographing him just before my nailed boots slipped on the rock and awoke the sleeper with a start. He seemed mildly surprised but not alarmed, and without undue haste dragged his great bulk to the sea.

As we neared the beach, the seals, just as they did before, scrambled to the water. Even on land they moved considerably faster than a man can walk but once in the sea they sped forward, the tail of each churning the shallows like the propeller of a lightly loaded steamer. Immediately they reached sufficiently deep water they dived swiftly.

After they had recovered from the excitement of that first mad rush for safety they swam cautiously inshore, and from time to time a crowd of dark heads eyed us.

Again I saw a fierce fight. Perhaps because we disturbed her one of the mother seals encroached upon the territory of another and thus the fight commenced. With deep moaning cries of rage the assailants struck at one another. Soon it was seen that one of the seals was severely bitten. Her thick neck streamed with blood, and during each breathing space in the fight she took the opportunity of rolling herself seaward very, very slowly. She did this in order, I think, that her antagonist should not realise her intentions of escaping. Suddenly the animals saw me standing a few yards from them and paused in their battle and the wounded seal quickly reached the sea and submerged her gory neck, tingeing the waters with red.

On the western side of the island a seal pup was lying fully sixty feet above the sea. The rocks dropped almost sheer to the Atlantic. Looking over the cliff, we saw the mother seal lying sound asleep on a rock near the water's edge. I set out to stalk her and, profiting by my experience with the old bull seal, removed my boots before starting. I reached the seal and stood looking at her lying three feet from me. After a time violent tremors ran through her body, as if in her sleep she sensed something. At last she awoke, stared up at me an instant in astonishment, then sprang in a swift dive to the friendly water a dozen feet below.

No one who has watched the Atlantic seals at close quarters can fail to be impressed by the intelligent expressions of the animals, and among the people of the isles these great seals have always been regarded as half human. It is said that the clan MacCodrum had affinity with the seals, and at the time of the annual seal battue in autumn an old woman of the clan was always seized by violent pains out of sympathy with her kinsfolk of the sea that were then being murdered at their surf-drenched island home. On one island the destruction of the seals continues and only the year before the grey seals had been attacked by a crew of crofter-fishermen who killed many helpless pups and sailed away with their craft deep loaded.

But one must in fairness remember that the destruction of the grey seals is not an act of senseless slaughter. The crofters and fishermen boil down the thick layer of fat which is present on every Atlantic seal. The oil thus obtained is excellent nourishment for cattle and is mixed with their winter feed. The skins of the seals are cured and are made into waistcoats and into sporrans worn with the kilt.

In the old days portions of the seals were eaten by the islesmen. The meat smelt so strongly that it was conveyed to the mouth on long sticks in order that the hands should not come in contact with it.

Amongst fishermen the seals are, to say the least of it, unpopular, and there is no doubt that they do kill salmon and sea-trout, besides cod and other sea fish. But the seals prey upon dog-fish also, and every fisherman knows that dog-fish are the riff-raff of the ocean, tearing the herring-nets, eating the baited hooks and making themselves thoroughly objectionable.

Atlantic seals haunt Skerryvore, an isolated rock on which a lighthouse stands west of the Island of Tiree. Sometimes of an evening the lightkeepers fish for big pollack from Skerryvore and I heard an amusing story of how a great seal one night seized the fly and threatened, before the line broke, to drag rod and angler into the water.

In the old days there lived in the Isle of Mull a hunter called Donnachda Donn, *Brown Duncan*. This hunter owned a famous musket, with which he killed three deer with one shot in Glen Clachaig. One day shortly before his death Duncan unfortunately shot at a mermaid which he mistook for a seal. The mermaid thereupon laid a spell upon hunter and musket, and when next Duncan fired his gun it burst, and Duncan did not long survive.

On the flood-tide we sailed away from the island of the seals. The breeze had freshened from the north-east and the sun was dipping westward, flooding the corries of the snowy hills to the north that stood out like mountains of the Arctic. In the sunset the many isles seemed to glow with the soft mystic light of the west, and over the waters was wafted the pleasant scent of peat fires as one by one the stars appeared and the Milky Way spread, like a shaft of the Merry Dancers, across the zenith.

T11-26

BAGPIPE MUSIC

There is a skerry named Sgeir nam Maol, much frequented by seals, in the Minch midway between Skye and Harris. One warm calm day we were fishing for lythe around this skerry. I had my bagpipes with me and knowing the seal's interest in music I landed on the rock and played for a time. It was interesting to watch the effect of the music of the *piob mhor* on the seals. They approached, full of curiosity, and one huge bull Atlantic seal swam in nearest of all. Almost aground, he swam slowly in shallow water only a few yards from where I was playing. The other seals rose half out of the sea as they looked at me and wondered at the unusual sound.

Red deer also are interested in pipe music. One night when I was playing outside a stalker's bothy a herd of stags approached me and performed a curious dance standing on their hind legs.

ITH-31

A trio of baby kestrels.

OTTERS AT PLAY

Otters are devoted mothers, and the young are full of fun. When I was fishing the Spey my gillie told me that one of the most interesting sights he had ever seen was a family of otters at play in a river backwater. The little fellows were sliding, one after another, down a steep clay bank into the water. Time after time they climbed the slope in order to have the excitement of a plunge into the clear depths. All the while the old otter was swimming lazily and happily in the pool. Then the observer made an incautious movement and a stick cracked faintly. The otter in alarm called to her family, and they at once disappeared.

ITH-31

ANYONE FOR FROGS' SPAWN?

Otters are fond of frogs' spawn, and will travel far for that delicacy. In search of it they cross snowy hill slopes and passes. I heard of a domestic cat which also had a fancy for frog spawn and although she did not go so far afield for it as the otters she spent most of her time searching the pools and bogs of the neighbourhood for embryonic tadpoles.

ITH-31

HILL FOX'S HEAVY LOAD

An observant shepherd in Knoydart told me of an experience he had while watching, through his telescope, a fox approaching a number of sheep and their lambs feeding in a grassy corrie. The season was June and the lambs were well grown. They were cropping the young grass at a little distance from their mothers. Although in full view of the fox, the ewes showed little alarm at its approach. The fox suddenly sprang on a lamb and quickly killed it.

It then attempted to carry off the victim but the lamb was too heavy. For a short time it seemed to think out the problem, then seized the lamb, and with a quick movement, threw it over its back, as a human workman might do a sack of coals. With the body of the lamb resting thus, the fox, still firmly holding its prey in its mouth set off.

(Scotsman. 19.3.60)

CAT AND MOUSE

The wild cat is the only British animal which no man has succeeded in taming. People who have kept wild cats in captivity tell me that they are quite untameable. One day an acquaintance of mine placed a mouse in his wild cat's cage, thinking that it would be appreciated. To his astonishment the cat uttered a shriek of terror and fled round and round the cage away from the mouse. But when he placed a small bird in the wild cat's cage it was seized and eaten at once.

ISNB-41

BLOOD–CURDLING YELLS

The head deerstalker of a West Highland forest was out one late summer day looking for a woodcock for the pot. He was crossing rocky ground on which there was some natural wood when he heard an unearthly yell followed almost at once by a second scream. Thinking the cries were human he hurried as fast as he could to a cliff less than 100 yards below him and when he was half-way saw a golden eagle rise from the ground, then dive earthward once more. Almost immediately two more blood-curdling yells shattered the silence, and when he had reached the edge of the cliff he saw below him a wild goat standing on her hind legs and bravely defending her little kid about two days old. The small creature had the intelligence to keep between its mother's hind legs when the eagle stooped and was thus protected from the fierce and determined attacks. The stalker watched the great eagle thrice swoop down upon the kid, then he showed himself and the eagle flew away.

HY-44

BEELINE TO SKYE

Bees are powerful fliers, and are rarely carried out to sea against their will. Twice of late I have seen bees at a considerable distance from land. On a warm sultry morning early in August I was crossing from Mallaig to Armadale in Skye on board the mail-boat *Plover*. When we were three miles from Skye a large humble-bee flew alongside of the ship. We were making ten knots at the time and the bee passed us at a speed I estimated at ten knots. That would make its actual speed twenty knots. This bee was apparently on passage from Knoydart on the mainland to the coast of Skye. There may be a regular flight-line of bees between these two districts and the bees of Knoydart may search for honey in Sleat, where the land is more fertile and a greater variety of honey-bearing flowers are to be found.

ITH-31

A TROUT DRIVE

One chilly afternoon in June, I watched a party of goosanders driving the trout of a loch in a systematic manner. There were eight goosanders: five drakes and three ducks. They were working in line up–wind when first I put the glass on them and after appearing on the surface for a few seconds the birds dived, one after another, leaving scarcely a ripple behind them. The goosanders fished the loch carefully from end to end then returned and went over it again. From time to time they swam at great speed through the water with much splashing and churning of spray. Apparently they sought to drive the trout ahead of them. During these drives the birds swam low and at times skimmed below the surface although they did not dive. The loch has many small trout in its peaty waters, and the bottom is strewn with fir roots and branches where the fish can shelter from their enemies.

ITH-31

Spying deer on Rannoch Moor.

SALMON RECORDS

By netting fish in the sea and returning them, marked, to the water again the Fishery Board for Scotland have brought interesting facts to light regarding the speed at which salmon travel. Of seven salmon marked in the sea off Loch Inchard in North West Sutherland two were taken the same season in the nets at the mouth of the Aberdeenshire Dee, and five were taken farther south, off the coast of Montrose. A grilse marked off Loch Laxford was caught by rod and line on the river Tay at Murthly, 290 miles away, the same season. Another salmon marked on the coast of North West Sutherland was recaptured a little later in the same season off Whitby in Yorkshire, while a fish marked at the same place was caught again off the Sognefjord in Norway.

Some of the fish which were recovered after being marked reveal the speed at which salmon travel. A fish marked off the East Sutherland coast and recaptured off the Forth seven days later averaged thirty-five miles a day, one of the salmon marked off the North West Sutherland coast and caught in the Forth averaged thirty-three miles a day. It is possible these fish had been cruising in the Forth before they were caught and the average may have been greater. These journeys however, are as nothing compared to the voyage of a salmon marked in Norway which covered 690 miles at an average of sixty-two miles a day. Another remarkable Norwegian record is a salmon which averaged thirty miles per day over the great distance of 1560 miles.

HY-44

MONSTERS IN DEEP LOCHS?

The Loch Ness Monster has attracted so much publicity that little attention has been paid to other Highland lochs which traditionally are the home of a creature of similar habits and appearance. Loch Morar, the deepest freshwater loch in Scotland—its depth exceeds 1,000 feet—has in its depths a creature which has been reported to me on more than one occasion. The name of this creature is Mhorag; its appearance was, in a less sophisticated age, believed to portend the death of a MacDonald of Morar, or of a Gillies.

I heard from the owner of a motor boat of the sudden appearance of the Beast of Loch Morar. The boat's owner was taking a party of visitors in his launch to the head of this long, dark loch, where I have seen a golden eagle sail like a gigantic shearwater across the path of a boat and where high hills rise steeply to the clouds. All at once a huge creature emerged, with much splashing and the throwing of spray, only a few yards from the boat.

The boat owner told me that, had he been alone, his story would not have been believed but all his passengers saw it and thus put it on record that a creature far larger than a seal had surfaced on Loch Morar. Long before there was a motor boat on Loch Morar the people of the district from time to time saw what seemed to be a boat towing two or three smaller boats at speed up the loch. It was supposed that this was the Mhorag and that the small boats on tow were in reality its humps showing above the water.

The Loch Ness Monster is more frequently reported than the Beast of Loch Morar but this is only natural as Loch Morar lies in a remote and sparsely populated area, with no main road along its shore.

Loch Shiel in the West Highlands also has its Beast, named Seilag by the local people. I have heard of no recent appearance of the Seilag but here again no road runs by the shore of this long and deep freshwater loch.

The 1857 *Memoirs* of the tool of Malmesbury has the following, when he was tenant of Achnacarry.

My stalker, John Stuart at Achnacarry, has seen it twice and both times at sunrise in summer, when there was not a ripple on the water. The creature was basking on the surface; he saw only the head and hind-quarters, proving that its back was hollow, which is not the shape of any fish, or of a seal. Its head resembled that of a horse. The Highlanders are very superstitious about this creature. They believe that there is never more than one in existence at the same time.

The theory that these creatures are landlocked sea animals is supported by the fact that Loch Ness, Loch Morar, and Loch Shiel are all so near sea level that they must at one time have been tidal lochs. Indeed it would seem possible that sea water may even now remain in their depths. A team of scientists from the Institute of Oceanography at the University of British Columbia in Canada has carried out observations in Powell Lake, some eighty miles north of Vancouver. This freshwater lake was once an inlet of the sea. The area of salt water begins at a depth below the surface of approximately 400 feet. The concentration of salt increases with depth; the salinity of the water at the bottom of the lake is half that of the sea water in the Strait of Georgia less than a mile away.

The scientists who made these observations think that the sea water now deep in Powell Lake was trapped somewhere between 7,300 and 12,250 years ago. It is not without interest that the depth of Powell Lake, namely 1,180 feet, is almost exactly the same as the deepest part of Loch Morar. The research work in Powell Lake was a result of reports by a Norwegian oceanographer, who found salt water at the bottom of two Norwegian lakes.

This scientific research raises the question: is there perhaps a deep-seated layer of salt water in one or more of the Scottish freshwater lochs where large, unknown creatures reputedly have their home? Until now, so far as I know, there has been no testing of the deep waters of our home inland lochs for an area of salinity and it would seem that this opens a fascinating field of future investigation.

Loch Ness certainly has never been known to have ice on it. In the words of an old manuscript, 'The lake never freezeth and if a lump of ice is cast into it, it soon after dissolveth'. The writer goes on to mention the possibility of a subterranean communication between Loch Ness and the sea and he certainly would have been thrilled by the discoveries in Powell Lake.

HS-71

The Malmesbury quote is from Highland Year *(1946) in which Seton Gordon discusses, the Loch Ness monster subject at length.*

DEER BEHAVING ODDLY

A TAME HIND

In one of the upper Deeside forests there is at present a hind showing the most complete absence of fear where mankind is concerned. The hind—a true wild beast of the forest—was gradually tamed by timely gifts of turnips and soon made herself quite at home near the bothy where a number of estate workmen were employed. At luncheon-time she would stand and call at the entrance of the hut and refused to become quiet until a share of bread had been doled out. Her calf on these occasions always remained behind at a respectful distance, apparently not sharing his mother's trust in her human friends. One day a workman, to test the trustfulness of the hind, held a slice of bread between his teeth and stood at the entrance of the bothy. The hind, without hesitation, walked up and calmly began to devour the morsel held out so temptingly towards her!

COH-12

RUTTING STAGS

In October the roar of the stags is heard in the forests and at this season of the year a couple of stags will occasionally fight to the death; an old watcher told me he had twice come across stags lying with their skulls split completely in two. The stronger animal has the advantage in these encounters and as a result these stags have a following of hinds two or three times as large as their weaker brethren. The roar of a stag is similar to the lowing of a cow, only it is a harsher call and pitched in a somewhat higher key. During autumn the stags lose their natural shyness and occasionally attack a man walking through a forest alone. Some seasons ago a cyclist had a narrow escape in this way. He was pushing his cycle along a road which traversed a deer forest when he suddenly became aware of a stag galloping towards him. The stag bore straight at him and, knocking him to the ground, pursued its way without even turning its head.

COH-12

A CUDDLING CALF

Once when sitting on a hill plateau I saw a hind arrive from the lower ground and cross the hill. I thought nothing more of this but half an hour later I imagined I felt a pressure against my side. I quickly dismissed this as being absurd, but when later I attempted to rise to my feet I found myself held fast by a considerable weight. Looking down, I saw a small red deer calf lying sound asleep on my mackintosh.

HS-71

A red deer calf in the Cairngorms; less than a week old.

BERRIES OF THE HILLS

Summer is gone. Already the high tops have received their second coating of autumn snow, and the birches and hill grasses show golden and brown against the dark hillsides. It is now that the berries of the hills are at their best. As yet they are untouched by the frosts and the tribe of the grouse and ptarmigan have not thinned their numbers so everywhere one may wander on the hills they are things to delight the eye by reason of their rich and delicate colouring.

Of them all perhaps the two best known species are the blaeberry, *Vaccinium myrtillus,* and the cranberry—or more properly the cowberry—*Vaccinium vitis idaea.* One frequently finds the two berries growing profusely together, and their season of ripening is nearly the same, though the blaeberry is rather the earlier of the two in forming its fruit. The blaeberry is one of the very few hill plants that is deciduous—that is, it sheds its leaves with the coming of each autumn. There is, to my way of thinking, no more delightful scent of the high hills than the aroma of countless blaeberry plants on a hot sunny day. The blaeberry, far more than the cranberry, is a true Alpine plant, and is found as high as between the 3,000-foot and 4,000-foot levels, though its fruit here is indifferent. The fruit of the blaeberry is of a dark blue colour, comparatively sweet to the taste, and the only berry with which it is likely to be confused is the crowberry, *Empetrum nigrum,* but whereas the leaves of the blaeberry are deciduous and delicate, those of the crowberry are heath-like and sturdy.

The cranberry—for it is always thus that the cowberry is named in Scotland—is a plant of the lower hills and pine forests rather than the high tops. In height it is considerably less than the blaeberry and retains its sturdy leaves throughout winter. Its flowers are borne in a cluster at the apex of the stem. They are usually white, but may sometimes be found of varying shades of pink. Almost alone amongst hill plants the cranberry may be found flowering during every month of the summer and even in late autumn when there is little or no chance of the berries coming to maturity. The fruit of the cranberry is of a dark red and one flower stem often bears quite a number of the berries, but the stem is sturdy and is quite able to carry the weight of the fruit.

The leaves of both blaeberry and cranberry frequently turn to a flaming red at the approach of autumn. I noticed in Rothiemurchus during a recent summer that shortly after producing their leaves the blaeberry plants were almost everywhere attacked by a species of caterpillar and their leaves rolled up into unsightly withered balls. The disastrous fire which swept Rothiemurchus Forest in June, 1920, was largely aided by this fact for the thick undergrowth of blaeberry plants, instead of offering a moist barrier to the flames, was almost as dry and inflammable as the heather itself.

A plant closely akin to the cranberry in its fruit is the bearberry, *Arctostaphylos uva-ursi*. Its berries are somewhat smaller than those of the former plant and of a slightly lighter red. The habit and appearance of the two plants are however entirely different, for the cranberry grows erect and sturdy, while the bearberry creeps prostrate over the hills. Although the two species may be found growing together, the bearberry is the more Alpine and is usually met with on the high ground—3,000 feet and over. It is probably owing to this fact that its habit is prostrate for it is thus better able to withstand the gales which so frequently sweep the high hills. The bearberry fruits late and its berries are frequently buried, while still at their best, beneath the first early winter snowfall. Frequently I have noticed, while on the high hills in winter with only a few inches of snow on the ground, that at almost every step I crushed some bearberries underfoot, their juice appearing through the snow and staining it red.

A plant little known on the hills is the great bilberry *Vaccinium uliginosum*. The stems, unlike those of the blaeberry (or bilberry as it is known in the south), are stout and woody and the leaves are more glaucous in colour than those of the common blaeberry. The great bilberry does not seem to be found so near the sea level as the common nor does it reach such great heights. Its berries too are smaller and of a more bitter taste. I have only exceptionally seen it bearing fruit on the Cairngorm Hills.

Perhaps of all the hill berries the crowberry, *Empetrum nigrum*, is the most alpine. It is extremely hardy and seems impervious to cold winds and frosts. The leaves are small and of a dark colour and are very zerophytic—that is, drought-withstanding. The flower is barely noticeable but the berries are of almost similar size to those of the blaeberry, only black and sour. The shoots of the crowberry are eaten in winter by the ptarmigan and probably the berries also.

The true cranberry, as distinct from the cowberry which, curiously enough, everywhere in Scotland usurps its name, is known to scientists as *V. oxycoccus*. It is comparatively rare and in its habit prostrate, resembling the bearberry rather than *V. vitis idaea*. Its berries are more transparent and inclined to yellow rather than red and it grows mainly on boggy ground.

A plant widely different from any of those mentioned above is the cloudberry—or avern (sometimes spelt avron)—*Rubus chamaemorus*. It is in its habits comparatively local but is usually found on or near boggy ground. I have seen it on the Cairngorms well over 3,000 feet up but here it is late in forming its flowers and its fruits rarely mature. A delicate plant, it withers quickly when plucked, and its fragile white blossom has a short life at the best. The fruit before ripening is of a reddish colour which, curiously enough, turns more to yellow—not to a darker red—as the berry becomes mature. When the plants grow in sufficient profusion—as in the Border district—the berries are gathered and make excellent jam but I have never heard of them being used for this purpose in the Highlands.

Such is a brief record of some of the better known berries of the hills. The levels they touch in this country are, of course, insignificant as compared with the Alps for, to take a single example, in the Maritime Alps the blaeberry certainly reaches an elevation of 9,000 feet, if not more.

WON-21

DUNKELD'S HISTORIC TREES

Overshadowing Dunkald cathedral, but just outside its grounds, stands one of the historic larches of Scotland. It is one of a number brought from the Tyrol in 1738 by Menzies of Culdares. These seedlings were considered to be so precious that they were reared at first as greenhouse plants and since they did not thrive under glass were thrown out on to a heap of refuse, where they revived and were then planted in various districts. Originally there were two great larches here but the finest of the two was, I believe, struck and killed by lightning during the early years of the twentieth century. Near the surviving larch grows a splendid oak, one of the finest I have seen in the Scottish Highlands.

At Dunkeld the Tay is crossed by a wide bridge, built in 1808 by the Duke of Atholl, its seven arches proudly spanning the broad river. Rather less than half a mile below the bridge on the south bank are two very old trees—an oak and a sycamore. Only when I stood beneath them I realised their great size and the majesty of their leafless branches as they slept their winter sleep on the January day of frost when I admired them. The spread of their naked branches was truly majestic, yet even in this Arctic winter's day, when the ground was iron-hard and ice floes slowly drifted down the Tay, the sycamore spoke of the coming of another spring—for its buds, tight-sealed against the frost, were fresh and green. The buds of the old oak besides it were small and brown, yet even they gave evidence of the young life that was hid deep within them. These two trees are believed to be 1,000 years old and to be a relic of the original Birnam wood of the time of MacBeth. They were veterans in the time of Dundee and Prince Charlie: they were perhaps saplings when the priory of Dunkeld was burnt by the Danes. It was a strange thought to think that the trees may have been vigorous saplings when MacDuff, Thane of Fife, fulfilled the prophecy made to MacBeth, the Scottish King, that he should reign until "Birnam wood do come to Dunsinane".

It has been suggested that the story of MacBeth was narrated to Shakespeare when he passed the district in 1601. He was then journeying with his company to perform comedies and stage-plays in Aberdeen.

On the river-bank this winter day a considerable company of mallard were resting, and in a long, placid pool of the river two goosanders, swimming low on the water like miniature submarines, were threading their way among other waterfowl gathered there. In a stream of the river, a dipper was diving repeatedly as it searched the stones on the river-bed for its food. Each time it reappeared on the surface it was carried a short distance down-stream. After some half a dozen dives it had reached the end of its beat, and then rose from the water and flew perhaps one hundred yards up the river, there to go through its diving programme once more. Despite the extreme frost and the freezing temperature of the Tay that dipper was the cheeriest bird I saw.

Away to the north-west, from either bank of the river, rose the two steep hills Craigie Barns and Craig Bhinnein. How trees were made to grow on these precipitous hill faces is a romance of comparatively modern times, given in *The Highland Tay* (Hugh MacMillan).

Originally these hills towered up to heaven bare and gaunt their sides too precipitous to admit of being planted in the usual way. But Mr. Napier, the famous engineer, while on a visit to the Duke of Atholl, suggested that the cannon in front of his host's residence might be loaded with tin canisters, filled with seeds of pine and spruce and larch, and then fired at the Craigs. This was done, when the canisters, striking the rocks, burst like shells, and dispersed the seeds in the cracks and ledges, where they grew, and in course of time formed the vast billows of forest which have now submerged the highest points of the scenery.

H&BC-48

THE DISRUPTIVE SKYE MIDGE

It is ironical that the pleasure of the finest August days in the Highlands—and especially in the Western Highlands and the Hebrides—should be impaired, or even entirely spoilt, by the onsets of the midge. Midges make their appearance early in some parts of the West Highlands. On May 30, 1944, they were active at Craignure, Mull though they had not then appeared in the north of Skye. In Sutherland I have known road reconstruction actually put a stop to by the attacks of midges. Some anglers in that midge-infested county wear special veils when fishing and certain gardeners in the Isle of Skye are provided with these veils by their employers.

This pest loves heathery lands but attacks the climber even on the bare rocky tops of the Cuillin, three thousand three hundred feet above the Atlantic. The midge prefers damp, calm weather, but is active even during cloudless August days, awaiting the lessening of the sun's power and appearing in myriads in the late afternoon to feast upon any luckless wanderer.

I recall August when the shade temperature in Glen Sligachan was in the eighties and the sun shone with tropical heat. The family and I were that day in Harta Corrie where the huge boulder, Clach a' Phuill, *the Stone of Blood,* commemorates a clan fight between the MacDonalds and the MacLeods. During the homeward walk in the early evening the sun was still high and, since we made our own wind current as we walked, no midge was felt. When we reached the road at Sligachan, where we had left the car, I was some distance behind the others. We were all weary after a long day on the hill and were looking forward to our tea which we had left in the open car. When I came in sight of the car I saw that the family, instead of sitting comfortably and enjoying this well-earned tea, were walking briskly up and down the road. At first I was at a loss to understand the reason for this apparent unnecessary exertion. When I reached the car things were even worse than I had imagined. It may be that the human scent pervading a car attracts the midge as carrion does a fox. Whatever be the reason it is certain that a stationary car *does* attract them. On this occasion the car was literally veiled in a thin mist—myriads upon myriads of midges dancing above the windscreen and hood, swarming upon bonnet and wings. I had time only to snatch a cup of tea and a scone before being set upon and was then glad to do my four miles an hour on the hard road while I quickly finished that afternoon meal.

HY-44

Early motoring in Sutherland, with his collie Dileas.

10

Islands of the Edge

St Kilda and Rockall are very much 'on the edge' and I wonder if anyone else has visited both. Seton Gordon wrote about islands all his life – he lived on Skye – and Stroma, Ailsa Craig, Arran, the Bass, the May, Mull, the Treshnish, Shiants, and the Small Isles are some regretfully omitted, as are English, Welsh and Irish islands, Iceland and Spitzbergen.

A St. Kilda family.

St. Kilda: the frantic scene of men and dogs on
launching a boat.

THE ISLANDS OF ST. KILDA

HIRTA

St. Kilda is now deserted. Two summers before its people left it Mr. John MacKenzie, MacLeod's factor, invited me to accompany him on his visit to the island and in the factor's house he and I spent the best part of an enjoyable and interesting week. St. Kilda lies some eighty miles into the Atlantic westward of Skye, and it was from the small Skye seaport of Uig that we sailed very early one June morning. The good ship *Dunara Castle* lay at the pier, a thin line of smoke trailing from her red funnel. At six o'clock we slipped our moorings and headed out into the Minch. The sea was calm.

Past the Ascrib Islands, past Rudha Vaternish, we steamed and saw the old ruined castle of Duntuilm near the north arm of Skye and the island group of Fladday Chuain. Almost before we realized it we had crossed the Minch and were passing through the intricate channel in the Sound of Harris. We saw Pabbay with its shapely hill where the MacLeods of old had their stronghold and, on the north shore of the Sound, the once thriving but now almost deserted settlement of Leverburgh.

The isles of the Sound of Harris seemed delightful this June morning: green machair, white sands, and dark heathery slopes surrounded by the deep blue of the ocean, while above all was the blue sky in which white clouds idly drifted. Before we were abreast of Shillay (most outlying of the islands that stand at the entrance to the Sound of Harris) we began to feel a long northerly swell and this swell rocked the *Dunara Castle* gently during the last fifty miles of her passage. When we had passed Shillay we saw the cone of St. Kilda rise faintly on the horizon, and a little later the peak of its neighbouring island Boreray appeared. In the intense light the Atlantic sparkled and gleamed. It was good to be alive.

In our wake sea-gulls followed and off Hasker fulmars joined us. A pair of Arctic skuas for a time circled gracefully about the steamer and when we were abreast of Hasker a single oyster-catcher passed us, flying towards the Harris coast a full dozen miles away. The oyster-catcher is rarely seen far from land and I wondered what had sent him on that overseas flight. The origin of the name St. Kilda is strange. There is a well on the island known as Tobar Childa. The original name was simply Kelda, a Norse word meaning a *well*. The Celtic people, being ignorant of this, added the Gaelic word for a well to the name, so that it became Tobar Childa or Tobar Kelda. The Dutch were active fishers in the western seas in the seventeenth century, and a Dutch map-maker of that period was responsible for the addition of the word Saint to the Norse word for the well. Thus arose the ghost-name St. Kilda.

Four miles north of Hirta is Boreray with a cliff over 1200 feet high on its northern face. Near Boreray are two great rock-stacks—Stac an Armuinn and Stac Lii. Here thousands of gannets nest and the captain of the *Dunara Castle* courteously altered his course so that we should sail close to the stacks and see the birds. We approached the smooth grim faces of the rocks and a great flock of gannets launched themselves into the keen northerly breeze. The birds flew out to meet us and sailed in circles and spirals a full five hundred feet above our decks. Each bird as it swung round and faced the sun was suddenly illuminated so that it seemed as though many lamps were flashing from the blue deeps of the sky. We rounded Stac an Armuinn (said to commemorate a knight of Lochlann) and steered south, gently lifted on the long swell which followed us. We passed Stac Lii and here also gannets were crowded so densely that they appeared at a distance like barnacles clustering on a rock at low tide. We later learned that a boat from St. Kilda had gathered a rich harvest of eggs from this stack the week previous to our arrival. The portion of each man was one hundred eggs, and there were twelve men on this egg-raiding expedition. It will be interesting to see whether the gannet increases now that the eggs are robbed no longer. The St. Kildans said that a gannet lays another egg nineteen days after her first egg is robbed.

We noticed a small colony of gannets on Stac Lii resting on a sloping face of rock rather below, and distinct from, the nesting colony. Those birds, we were told, were the old-age pensioners. They were no longer able to rear families and so were outcasts from the busy throng above them. Amongst the flying gannets were a number of dark-plumed immature birds. These would not nest for several years.

On our voyage from Harris we had seen flights of gannets pass, all steering for St. Kilda. It was delightful to watch them glide and drift rather than fly above the ocean. They flew in single file, following one another closely, and now and again they rose a short distance into the air from their usual flying station only a few inches above the Atlantic. As they slanted upward each bird carefully followed the leader and the sun flashed on rhythmically moved white wings. They may have climbed on some faint current of air rising from the surface of the Atlantic. After flying at a little height for perhaps a minute they planed down to the ocean's surface again, progressing with no effort at a speed of forty miles an hour.

We reached Hirta, and passing close to the rocky point where Coll Ciotach, Lord of the Isles, is said to have landed, then sailed into a quiet bay where sunlit waters showed pale green above the submerged sand. The shore sloped gently to the bay. In a crescent the houses of the village stood a short distance from the shore. Beside the houses were the smallest of fields of potatoes and oats, fresh and green in the strong June sunlight. In the bay a Belgian trawler from Ostend was at anchor.

It was Sunday morning. The village was deserted. We dropped anchor. After a time the congregation could be seen to leave the small church at the conclusion of the service and walk towards the village. The women had scarlet shawls covering their heads and these bright red shawls contrasted in a pleasing manner with the green of the young grass. That Sunday morning scene remains a vivid memory: the vital air, the intense blue of the sea, the brilliant sunlight, the atmosphere of rest and peace—all these were memorable.

Rising from the village to a height of 1400 feet were the stone-strewn slopes of Conachair. Along the ridge of that hill graceful fulmar petrels soared, and from time to time one of the birds glided across Village Bay. To the south, and almost joined to the main island, rose the Dùn, *the Fortress*. Here, it is narrated, the Fir Bolgs, an early race of half-mythical beings, lived. Beside the Dùn towered the grim headland of Ruaival, the scene of early sacrifices. So clear was the day that, even from sea level, the hills of Harris could be seen. A boat was now launched at the island slip and men rowed out to the steamer to welcome popular John MacKenzie, the factor. Much conversation in animated Gaelic and much hand-shaking followed and we were rowed ashore, where we were greeted by some of the older people to whom English was an unknown tongue. The islesmen were strong and deeply bronzed, keen of eye and lithe of limb. The women, with smiling faces framed in their scarlet shawls, made a pleasing picture as they stood in a little group by themselves.

Late that afternoon I climbed the hill of Conachair. The lower slopes were strewn with the St. Kildan's substitute for peat. The peat moss is perhaps a mile from the village. No horses were kept on the island and in order to save themselves trouble the people actually destroyed some of their best grazing for the sake of fuel easily gathered. They pared off the grass in thin divots or turfs, turned them over, and left the grass to be dried by sun and wind. When the turfs were dry they were collected into small stone shelters known as *cleits*. The people of St. Kilda were thus depriving themselves annually of a proportion of their best pasture, for the grass did not again grow on the bare strips of earth or stone that were exposed. This lazy habit has been commented on, often forcibly, by visitors to the island.

I climbed a grassy slope where rock-pipits twittered and wheaters called and when I reached the ridge near the hill-top found that I was suddenly looking over the greatest precipice in Britain. Twelve hundred feet and more beneath me the Atlantic swell broke about the foot of the precipice. Seals thrust grey faces through the surf here and gannets were diving beneath the blue waters. Many fulmar petrels nest on the giddy ledges. Beings of grace and vitality, they soared on the north breeze that carried a rising current of air above the top of the cliff.

From the hill-top that evening was a view such as the west alone can give. Westward, sun and shade alternated on the lonely Atlantic plains that stretched away towards the setting sun. North-east rose the Flannan Isles. They were so clear that the lighthouse could be distinguished. Behind them was Lewis and all the other Outer Hebrides. The eye rested in turn upon Harris, North Uist, Benbecula, South Uist, and Heaval of distant Barra. Hasker seemed close at hand. The lighthouse upon the Monach Isles rose needle-like. A telescope revealed the houses of Baleshare of North Uist and buildings on the low shore of Benbecula. On the far horizon rose the Cuillin hills of Skye, almost one hundred miles distant. Even at that great distance each member of the range was clear cut. I could recognize Sgùrr nan Gillean with its slender conical peak, Bruach na Frithe, Sgùrr na Banachdich, Sgùrr Alasdair, and Gars-bheinn. When I spoke to the St. Kildans that night some of the old people said they had seen the Cuillin hills but it was only at long intervals that they were visible.

Where I stood at the summit of Conachair the north wind blew chill as though it had come straight from distant ice-fields but on the sheltered slope the sun was warm, and I sat awhile looking across the rugged coast of Hirta to the neighbouring island of Soay. Fourteen hundred feet beneath me the houses of the village clustered. In the bay the *Dunara Castle* lay at anchor, a thin wisp of smoke trailing from her funnel. Some miles out to sea, away beyond the gliding fulmars, a small motor yacht was approaching and that evening she dropped anchor in the bay. She was owned by a native of St. Kilda whose affairs had prospered in Glasgow. None but a native would, I think, have ventured on the long passage from the Outer Hebrides in a craft of her size.

That evening at the service in the small village church there was thankfulness in more than one heart at the safe arrival of the fragile craft. As I sat in the church I looked through the window on to the deep blue of the sea, and could hear the hollow suck of the waves on the shore and the deep music of the unresting swell upon outpost cliffs. These blended in harmony with the cadences of Gaelic psalms sung fervently by an earnest and simple congregation. Half an hour after midnight, with the ending of the Day of Rest, the unloading of the *Dunara* began.

IOW-33

BORERAY

The June sun was shining brilliantly on the blue waters of Village Bay. Slowly the north wind drifted the turf smoke from the houses seaward. There was an air of excitement abroad for an expedition had been planned to the neighbouring island of Boreray.

On St. Kilda the dogs appeared to outnumber the population. They were certainly more in evidence than their owners on any day of stir. This morning the barking of the dogs was deafening. They fought and yelped on the jetty as the islesmen prepared a boat for launching. Suddenly two dogs engaged in a desperate struggle and as the fighting animals refused to be separated, despite the heavy blows rained upon them by their respective owners, they were picked up and hurled in deadly embrace into the sea.

They swam ashore quietly enough. The launching of a boat on St. Kilda was invariably accompanied by shouting, gesticulating, and arguing on the part of the crew. The volume of Gaelic that was poured forth was tremendous. There was little or no discipline and as each man had his own ideas of what should be done pandemonium was let loose until the boat had been run down the steep stone slip and was actually afloat.

Lest we should be caught by some sudden storm and be obliged to remain prisoners on Boreray, each man had brought with him a tin in which were a loaf and some provisions. The helm was fitted and with oars dipping rhythmically we moved through calm waters, past Rudha an Uisge, where a stream of clear water drops to the sea in a thin waterfall, its source a giddy ledge bright with sea-thrift and scurvy grass.

Life was an uncertain thing on St. Kilda. We passed the place where, a short time previously, a young man slipped while carrying his catch of fish up the face of the rock. His companions who had been fishing on the rocks near him saw the man fall. They hurried to the village for help, but the boat which put out was a hundred yards from the spot when the fisherman disappeared for the last time beneath the waves. In Martin's day the men of St. Kilda were noted swimmers, but latterly this art was lost.

Near the Point of Coll we passed Mìne Stac, a high rock separated from the main island of Hirta by a narrow but deep channel. I heard then the tradition that there was at one time a narrow pathway of rock joining Mìne Stac to the main island. During the wanderings of the defeated Spanish Armada one of the war vessels, drifting helplessly before a furious storm, was forced by wind and tide through this narrow channel. Her mast caught the rocky bridge, which was broken off by the impact. The rock fell upon the deck of the Spanish vessel, driving her to the bottom like a stone.

Close to the great precipices of Conachair we passed. The surf roared and thundered. Our boat was lifted like a cork on the irresistible swells that were advancing from the northern ocean. When we judged the tide to be favourable we left these cliffs and steered on Boreray, *the Isle of the Fortress,* which towered from the Atlantic four miles to the north. The sea was green, untroubled by any wind. About us fulmar petrels sailed. Puffins, guillemots, and solans peopled the waters. Every few minutes the rowers called for a burst. "Ho ro," they cried in unison, and their strong oars made music which blended with the swish of the water at the bow. What a setting the scene would have made for an *iorram* or old Gaelic rowing song! The crew were questioned. It was found that Finlay MacQueen had in earlier days sung an *iorram.* In vain John MacKenzie and his brother boatmen persuaded him to try his voice. His islesfolk coaxed him and teased him, but to no purpose, and so the boat was urged forward without music, but with periodic shouts of "Ho ro; ho ro," so that the well-tried timbers of the old craft strained and protested at each vigorous stroke of the oars. Four miles of open ocean in a heavy boat is a wearisome pull.

In the preceding summer, nine months previous to our visit, the St. Kildans had made their last visit to Boreray. They had gone to the island for sheep, and one of their dogs on that occasion fell over the cliff and was left for dead. But now, miracle of miracles, the missing dog was seen on the upper slopes of the island. The sheep, it was remarked, fed fearlessly beside him. From the boat the dog's owner called to the animal. The dog, almost a thousand feet above, howled dismally in reply.

The tide was low. The rocks rising from the sea were almost sheer and were coated with slippery seaweed. I am convinced that a landing on this inhospitable island would have been impossible to any man but a St. Kildan. The order was passed, "Boots off." Each man then removed his boots and drew on a thick pair of socks over the pair he was already wearing. All was now ready for a landing and as the boat was lifted on a wave the most agile member of the crew made a spring, poised himself for a moment on the rock while he regained his balance then, cat-like, climbed quickly up to a broad ledge. He carried a rope with him, and with one end of the rope to aid them the crew one after another sprang ashore, the veteran Finlay MacQueen landing with the grace of a young athlete.

The rocks, one hundred feet above the tide, gave place to a grassy slope where thousands of puffins were nesting. The previous season the St. Kildans had watched a walrus with her young on the coast of Boreray, and there were interesting tales told to-day about the behaviour of those wanderers from the Arctic. The dog joined us as we climbed the grassy slope and soon showed us how he had been living of late. A puffin appeared at the mouth of its burrow. Before it had time to take wing the dog rushed upon it. Seizing the luckless bird it shook it violently then dropped it dying on the grass. But the dog could not have lived on puffins during the winter months and its friendly feeling for the sheep showed that it had left them alone. It was therefore remarkable that it had survived the hard times of winter. Amongst the puffin colony small and delicate fork-tailed petrels were nesting. The St. Kildans ruthlessly dragged them from their burrows. When released the petrels flew down to the sea with curious swerving flight.

On the steep grassy slope of Boreray are a few primitive dwellings. These were used when the St. Kildans visited the island to clip sheep (or rather to cut the wool with a knife, for they did not possess shears). But on one occasion at least the dwellings served as more than a temporary lodging. This was in the year 1727 when smallpox broke out on the main island a day or two after a party of men had been landed on Boreray to cut the wool. Since there was no crew on the main island able to man a boat to relieve them they remained on Boreray all winter in exile, and it was not until the factor's boat approached the island the next summer that they were seen and rescued. It was then found that no single man, woman or child had survived on the main island; all had succumbed to the plague of smallpox.

It is narrated that a fairy once appeared to a man on Boreray and asked him his wish. The man said he would be glad of a cow. The fairy told him that if he went outside his door he would find a cow there and that he could fearlessly take her for she would be his. The night was dark and stormy, and the man was tired and sleepy. He therefore remained comfortably in his bed. On stepping outside the bothy in the morning he saw footmarks of a cow in the snow which covered the ground, but no more tangible traces of the fairy cow were ever found.

On Boreray are the remains of a very ancient dwelling known as Tigh Stallar. Here according to St. Kilda tradition a hermit named Stallar lived by himself for many years. The stones for this dwelling were, it was said, taken across from the Dùn of Hirta.

Boreray, like Hirta, is an island of precipices. It was startling to climb twelve hundred feet of grassy slope and on reaching the hill-top to find oneself looking over a great cliff to the ocean far beneath. Gannets were nesting almost to the top of this precipice. I calculated that the highest of the nesting birds were 1050 feet above the Atlantic, and I imagine that this is easily a record height for nesting gannets in Britain. Fulmars nested even higher. Some of these birds were brooding their eggs within a few feet of the hill-top, 1245 feet above the sea. I could see many gannets clustered on Stac an Armuinn far beneath me, and many more sailing on strong white wings through the sun-lit air. To the west rose Stac Lii. The air was clear above the great seascape that was spread out before me. Some miles to the north a small whaler steered west from the Harris whaling station. The Outer Hebrides were distinct, and I saw the Cuillin of Skye.

The day was far advanced when we returned to our boat, disturbing a purple sandpiper asleep beside the tide. Against wind and tide we rowed round the island to Stac an Armuinn. The St. Kildans lift their oars high. They adopt this style of rowing because the heavy swells would submerge the oars between the strokes unless they were raised high. After a heavy pull we rounded Boreray and saw Stac an Armuinn rise sheer above us. An endless procession of gannets were arriving or leaving the stack. Thousands more wheeled gracefully against the sinking sun. Stac an Armuinn is sheer. As we passed immediately below it the impression given was of tremendous strength and utter inaccessibility—for on its rock face seaward is no ledge on which the most skilled rock climber could find a foothold.

Stac an Armuinn is the *Rock of the Knight* or *Hero*. A St. Kildan was once asked whether those on the island were never in fear of being attacked. His answer was that there could be no cause for fear since on Hirta they had two redoubtable guardians. They had, said the old man, "An Torc fo'n iar, agus an t-Armann fo'n ear" (*The Boar to the west and the Knight to the east*). The Boar is a rock rising from the sea a short distance from the south-west shore of Hirta.

After leaving Stac an Armuinn we had magnificent views of the north-west cliffs of Boreray. They rose, with the soft light of the sinking sun full upon them, from the green depths of the sea, strangely beautiful, mysterious, and full of colour. They reminded me strongly of parts of the coastline of distant Spitsbergen when seen under the light of the midnight sun. Soon we were past Boreray, and now rowed beneath Stac Lii, also with its thriving gannet population. Hoisting our brown sail we had a fair wind and soon crossed to Hirta, Many fulmars again kept us company, and we heard of a strange fulmar petrel of black plumage which had formerly haunted this passage. The June sun had sunk behind the cliffs as we entered Village Bay. The wind was freshening.

The sky showed windy streamers of cloud. The moon was dim and hazy. It was well for us that we had chosen that day for Boreray for next morning a south-east gale brought in heavy seas and rough weather.

SOAY

It was my good fortune to spend a day on Soay also. Even in the times of the Norsemen Soay must have been noted for its pasture, for Soay (*Saudha-ey*) is Norwegian for *Sheep* Island, and to-day the Soay sheep remain, although the people have gone from Hirta. Soay rises close to Hirta, on its north-west side, a high rocky island, and has been from time immemorial the home of a race of brown-fleeced sheep, agile and sure-footed, that feed on the grassy ledges of the dizzy thousand-feet precipices where neither man nor dog is able to follow them.

Who has not heard of the celebrated four-horned sheep of St. Kilda? The remarkable thing is that these sheep exist in the imagination only. A freak four-horned sheep from Uist was, I believe, the originator of the legend of the St. Kilda four-horned sheep, but in reality they possess two horns only, and their distinction lies in their small size and brown fleeces.

With the usual stir we launched our boat on Village Bay on a clear sunny morning. We reached the mouth of the bay, and found the tide and a freshening breeze against us. The motor yacht which had crossed from Harris the previous evening offered us a tow as he passed and we accepted the offer. In the shelter of the land we made good progress but before we reached the Atlantic the wind had increased and a choppy sea was rising. Almost before we were aware of it a dangerous situation had arisen. Our boat was heavy, and she was also overloaded. We were being towed too fast and those on board the yacht did not realize our plight. The old boat began to bump in the trough of the waves in an alarming manner. She felt as if she were striking upon rocks. Her timbers creaked and strained. She shipped seas fore and aft. Our crew shouted to those on board the yacht to slow down her engines but in the wind and noise of the seas they failed to hear and, shaken and half-blinded with spray, we were dragged forward helplessly. Our crew were divided in council. Some wished to cut the towing rope; others laughed and shouted with excitement like children at the novelty of their experience. Our difficulty was soon solved. When passing through a narrow channel, where the tidal stream flowed fast and the surf leaped upon the smooth cliffs of Hirta perilously near us, the rope parted under the strain and at once we began to drift on to the rocks. The oars were seized and with no loss of time we rowed back into the channel and completed our voyage in a slower and less adventurous manner.

As we reached the calm water beneath the cliffs of Soay a landing seemed impossible. No more inhospitable coast could be imagined. Our boat was rowed in beneath a narrow rocky peninsula. The men removed their boots and, while one member of the crew kept the boat off the rocks with a boathook, the most skilled rock climber leaped ashore and the other men followed in turn. The procedure was similar to that at the landing on Boreray. The dogs also landed. That leap from the boat on to the slippery rock-face was a testing thing, even for them, but once they had reached the dry rock their paws gave them good foothold. At the close of the day they were filled with dismay at the descent and howled dismally.

When it came to my turn to make the leap a rope was passed round beneath my arms and I was dragged ignominiously up the smooth seaweed-covered rocks so quickly that I had no chance of finding any foothold during the ascent. We stood together on the cliff ledge and then set about climbing what seemed to be a hundred feet of sheer cliff. Mr. John Matheson (who was making a survey of the islands), his assistant Mr. Cockburn and I were all roped during this hundred feet of formidable climbing. Above each of us was a St. Kildan, who took the strain during the worst yards of the climb.

We scaled that cliff and found ourselves on a steep boulder-strewn slope tenanted by innumerable sea-fowl. Puffins in great numbers were present. A rifle shot was fired from the yacht beneath us. Immediately puffins flew out from the island in such numbers as to darken the air. It seemed as though a cloud had passed over the face of the sun. They reminded me of the midges which swarm in the glens of an August evening and so high were these puffins flying above us that many of them appeared no larger than midges. Little auks fly thus about their nesting cliffs in the Arctic but they keep up a continuous whistling, and puffins fly always in silence. Through the dense ranks of anxious puffins fulmar petrels gracefully steered their way, gliding, banking, and wheeling.

At one time the women of Hirta were landed on Soay each summer. They spent some weeks on the island snaring sea-fowl and lived in wee, primitive houses. The woman in charge of the expedition was known as the Queen of St. Kilda. When I landed on the island this custom had long fallen into disuse but there was still a Queen of St. Kilda. This old lady told me that at the age of twelve she had caught twelve score of puffins during a summer's outing on Soay. Puffins were eaten with relish on St. Kilda up to the last. The puffin season on Soay began with a curious rite. The first puffin caught was plucked, all except tail and wings. It was then liberated in sorry plight. Unless this were done the people believed that bad fortune would follow.

It was on Soay that I heard the tale of Dugan and Fearchar Mór. These two men, who inhabited Hirta in the dim past, were of great strength and courage. So daring were they that they sailed for sheep to the distant Flannan Islands and thought nothing of crossing in their small boat to the Outer Hebrides. But they were so avaricious that they decided to kill all the rest of the people in order that they might seize their flocks and lands. One Sunday when the people were at church they set fire to the building and supposed that all on the island had perished. But unknown to them, one old woman had escaped. This crone hid herself in a cave that was pointed out to me not far from the village. At nights she would leave the cave and search for what little food she could find, living always under the dread of discovery. Next summer, when the factor's boat from Skye sailed into Village Bay, Dugan and Fearchar went down to the shore to relate a tale of disaster that had wiped off the entire population except themselves. Then to their astonishment they saw the old woman appear. They attempted to kill her but she eluded them and denounced their crimes. The miscreants were seized. Fearchar was landed on barren Stac an Armuinn where he had gannets as his companions. There is no water on that rock and as death was inevitable Fearchar sprang into the sea and swam after the retreating boat hoping that those on board would have pity on him. They refused to take him on board and he was drowned. Dugan was taken to Soay. Here he lived and died alone and the ruins of his house, marked on the map as *Tigh Dugan*, were pointed out to me. Another version of the tale is that Dugan and Fearchar were both landed on Soay without the means of making a fire. It was thought that they could not long survive without the means of cooking their food or warming themselves. But as the men were leaving them Dugan was overheard to ask Fearchar if he had the flint and tinder safe, and only then was it decided to take Fearchar over to the barren solitudes of Stac an Armuinn.

This curious old tale I heard on Soay where the sun shone brightly and the sea-thrift blossomed pink on the ledges. Here and there small brown sheep were feeding and tufts of their brown wool lay on the ground. Where the contours of the grassy slopes were broken by small cliffs fulmars were brooding their smooth, shiny white eggs. Near the top of Soay are the remains of what is known as the Altar. Its history is obscure, but it is in a good state of preservation.

Soay, according to the latest survey, rises to a height of 1225 feet above the Atlantic. At the summit of the island the great wood rush (*Luzula sylvatica*) grows plentifully, and from its shelter a pair of snipe fluttered. Their anxious behaviour showed that they had a family in hiding near.

As from Boreray and Conachair, the view was over a wide seascape. Where the clouds were reflected in the Atlantic the blue of the ocean gave place to pools of palest pink. Across the sea, Boreray seemed to float in air. Haze lay upon the Outer Hebrides. On narrow ledges far down the thousand-foot precipices sheep were feeding. It seemed impossible that they could return to safety up those grim cliffs.

Far out to sea I watched the birth of a swift-travelling storm. The clouds grew, became inky-black, and were driven in toward Soay by the wind. The wind freshened, and white waves formed on the sea. Quickly the rain cloud bore down upon Soay. The wind grew bitterly cold and of a penetrating dampness. I saw Boreray encircled by a belt of clouds, and then the mists pressed in upon Soay. Across the hill-top they passed at the speed of an express train and I stood in a chill grey land, with sea, sky, and islands invisible. Rain, sleet, and hail harried, the stunted grasses. Ghostly fulmars swept past as though they were the winged spirits of the storm. But, as quickly as it had come, the squall passed away to leeward and I could see the ragged clouds lying on Conachair and the main storm drifting east towards the distant peaks of Uist. The wind dropped. The summer sun again shone out upon the blue ocean, but the warmth of summer had gone from the air, and when that night the moon rose and shone upon the waters of Village Bay, Hirta was an isle shivering in the breath of the north wind that swept down upon her from the chill waters of northern seas.

IOW-33

St. Kilda was always looked for from Hebridean summits thereafter and there are scattered references, such as this note of 1950.

One of the earliest records of raids on St Kilda is in the year 1615. In a letter from Sir Rory More MacLeod to Lord Binning, MacLeod complains that Colla Ciotach MacDonald had sailed over to Hirta and had there slain 'all the bestiall of the ylle, both cowes, and horses and sheep, and took away all the spoolyee of the yle, onlie reserved the lyves of the enhabitants thereof'. Martin Martin, in his *Voyage to St Kilda,* which he undertook in the year 1698, gives a good description of the island and its birds at this time. He, like other early writers, refers to the great auk or gare-fowl, a flightless sea bird not unlike a gigantic razorbill, now extinct. Sir George MacKenzie. writing about the same time, puts it on record that the gare-fowl is 'bigger than any Goose and hath Eggs as big almost as those of the Ostrich. Among the other Commodities which they export out of the Island, this is none of the meanest, they take the fat of these fowls that frequent the Island, and stuff the stomack of this fowl with it, which they preserve by hanging it near the Chimney, where it is dryed with the smoke and they sell it to their neighbours on the Continent as Remedy for aches and pains.'

The birds of the St Kilda group of islands meant much to the inhabitants, who ate the eggs and young of the gannet and used the oil obtained from the fulmar for their lamps. They ate fulmar and puffin. It is probable that there is now an annual increase of many thousands in the birds of St Kilda, for in one season it was calculated that 79,000 puffins were snared there for food.

At the time of my stay on Hirta [1928] the people of the island still wove the St Kilda tweed, and this was given to the factor as rent. Even after the people left the island, some of them returned each summer to work at weaving the St Kilda tweed. Then came the Second World War, when St Kilda 'went off the map', and steamers no longer visit.

And now, for the first time since the Norse occupation, Hirta is uninhabited. The old people were reluctant to leave, but the young felt that their island was too remote, and since they could not be induced to remain, the old folk, being unable to carry on without them, left also.

Will this remote isle again be populated? I do not think this is likely, for the thread of continuity is broken; new times and customs have arisen, and a lonely life on Hirta would not appeal to the present generation.

AH-50

St. Kilda was evacuated in 1930

ROCKALL, THE LONELY ISLAND

Rockall is perhaps the most remote and lonely of all European islands. It is the highest peak of a great mountain range now deeply engulfed by the Atlantic, thrusting itself above the waters which ceaselessly vex and buffet it, for its summit is only seventy feet above the sea. Rockall is 289 miles west of Ardnamurchan Point, the most westerly headland on the Scottish mainland. The nearest land to Rockall is St Kilda, 191 miles away. A hazardous landing on Rockall by helicopter was made some years ago when the rock was formally annexed to Britain and the Union Jack hoisted but the last expedition to make a landing unaided by aircraft was under the leadership of the intrepid French scientist and inventor, Jean Charcot, who visited Rockall in his vessel the *Pourquoi Pas?* in the summer of 1921, but did not climb to the summit. Pieces of the rare mineral Rockallite were chiselled from the rock and brought back on that occasion. Charcot wrote of Rockall, after mentioning that it is the summit of a mountain several thousand feet high, that 'its dazzling crown of snow has been replaced by a covering of guano'.

One of the earliest accounts of any landing on Rockall was written by Captain Basil Hall of H.M.S. *Endymion* in the summer of 1810. He actually pursued Rockall in his vessel, thinking that the rock was a ship with white sails aloft and dark sails below. The boat's crew of the *Endymion* seem to have been engrossed in the character of the rock rather than its birds. Nothing indeed was known of the bird population, and rumours arose that here was the breeding place of the mysterious great shearwater, which is now known to be a wide wanderer and to nest beyond the Equator on the Tristan da Cunha group in the South Atlantic.

That Rockall, rising at so great a distance from the nearest land, can be a hazard to shipping was proved when the Norwegian liner *Norge* struck the reef near the rock and foundered with the loss of six hundred lives. There are two reefs off Rockall and these are a greater danger to ships than the rock itself for they are awash in the trough of the seas and scarcely show. One of them, Hasslewood Rock, is a small detached rock, covered at half tide, 1½ cables north-east of Rockall. Helen's Reef lies 1¾ miles east by south of Rockall: at low spring tide this reef has been seen in the trough of the waves, a deadly menace to a ship driven off course. From time to time suggestions have been made that a lighthouse should be erected on Rockall and now that the day of the helicopter has arrived this might be possible but the relief of the lighthouse in winter would be a serious problem.

By ship, Rockall is many miles' steaming from the coast of either Scotland or Ireland but air transport has brought it relatively near. A friend and I made a memorable journey by flying boat from Portree Bay in Skye to Rockall by way of St Kilda and back between breakfast and tea. That morning was misty and rainy and it looked as if the expedition might not materialize but as we arrived at the shore of Portree Bay the weather was clearing and the Sunderland was seen circling low above the sea. As we approached her she lay high in the water and was so large and steady that we might have been boarding a ship. We taxied back towards the island of Raasay, then turned and moved faster and faster into the wind before being airborne. The houses of Portree seemed to race towards us alarmingly and then we were up and away and a new country appeared beneath us.

It was exciting to approach at speed a high cliff where a pair of golden eagles had their eyrie but the eagles, if they were at home, did not fly out to do battle with the giant intruder as others had attacked a smaller plane over Ben Wyvis some years ago.

Ten minutes after leaving the north-west coast of Skye we had crossed the Minch and were flying above St Clement's Church at Rodil in Harris, where is the old burial place of the MacLeods of Harris and Dunvegan. Above the Sound of Harris we saw the beauty of white sand submerged beneath green sea water and watched gannets making their way laboriously towards their nesting ledges on the stacks of St Kilda, fifty miles ahead of us and as yet hidden in ocean haze. When Boreray of St Kilda did appear it rose, twenty miles distant, dead ahead. Four miles to the north was Hirta, the main island of the group.

Until the people left St Kilda ten years before the beginning of the Second World War, Hirta had been inhabited continuously since before its Norse occupation, which ended after the Battle of Largs, fought between the Norwegians and the Scots in the year 1263. We approached Boreray. The midsummer morning sun shone on the high grassy slopes, fresh and green after a night of rain. On either side of Boreray rose a great stack, dark but white-topped because of the thousands of gannets which clustered there, nesting so close together that the brooding birds touched. On the greater stack, Stac Lee, gannets were nesting in thousands. There were exciting moments as we approached and the great birds rose in alarm. They swarmed on white black-tipped wings about their rock as the bees of a hive might do when suddenly disturbed. One or two of the gannets, right ahead of us and in our track, seemed doomed: they saved themselves by hurling themselves seawards out of our path, and escaping, as it seemed, by inches only. It was a revelation to one who had studied these ocean birds for many years to realize the speed of which they are capable.

The deserted houses of Hirta, were seen for a few brief seconds rising at the foot of the grassy slopes of Conachair, a hill which falls away to the north-west in a sheer cliff of one thousand-three hundred feet. On the neighbouring island of Soay the precipices seemed still more formidable. Here is perhaps the greatest puffin colony in Britain. One of the puffins saved itself from destruction by a headlong dive from our aerial path.

From Soay our course was set for Rockall, 191 miles west-south-west into the Atlantic. For the first sixty miles of that flight we could see gannets far below us flighting west to distant fishing grounds: approximately sixty miles west of St Kilda a large flock of these birds were seen diving for the large and fat herring which frequent the Atlantic far from our coasts. During our ocean flight the sky was clear and blue, with white clouds of cumulus. On the horizon ahead of us towered a sheet of cumulo-nimbus cloud; as we entered it the light ebbed to twilight, and heavy rain, beating on the aircraft, almost drowned the roar of the Rolls-Royce engines. Soon we were through and once more in sunlight and now we suddenly saw on the distant sea what seemed to be a battleship steaming towards us and throwing the water from her bows in clouds of spray. A shower hid the supposed vessel but when we had flown past the rain we saw that this was no battleship, but was our objective—Rockall. After flying over the great precipices of the St Kilda island group we unconsciously expected to see an isle of comparable grandeur, and this tiny islet rising from a vast expanse of ocean was so unexpected that it was the more impressive. At a short distance from Rockall spray broke white over the Hasslewood Rock, itself invisible.

The aerial impression of Rockall is of a round haystack, slightly tilted to one side. The top of the stack is tied with a wip of white straw and the last dozen feet of steep slope white as though a shower of snow had passed. The gannet stacks on Boreray of St Kilda were that morning pure white as from a considerable snowfall but the covering on Rockall resembled the powdering from a single snow shower.

The reason for our flight was to determine, if possible, whether guillemots lay their eggs on Rockall. There had been a report that a trawler had trawled up a guillemot's egg near the rock. The day of the flight was Midsummer Day, June 24, and the guillemot broods its large pyriform egg during the month of June. On our first run over Rockall a flock of kittiwakes which had been resting—not nesting—on the rock flew nervously in a small white cloud out over the sunlit sea. In the lee of Rockall the sea was green and translucent in the swirl of the tide; a graceful fountain of spray was thrown upon the rock as a ponderous wave broke at its base. In less time than it takes to tell we had passed over the rock and saw startled guillemots rise from a broad, whitened ledge just below the top of the cone. The birds flew quickly out to sea. It was necessary to fly beyond Rockall before making another run over the isle and we saw more guillemots on the water. Altogether we made nine runs over Rockall and satisfied ourselves that no birds except guillemots were breeding here. During our first run, at least, seventy guillemots crowded that broad white ledge just below the summit. After our ninth run, all but six of the guillemots had flown. These six birds which sat doggedly and tightly were, from their characteristic attitudes, almost certainly brooding eggs. The seas sweep over the very top of Rockall during a severe winter storm. In June this happens rarely but I am sure that, for the guillemots of Rockall, the brooding season is always one of danger and that young leave the rock only in a June when there is fair weather over the Atlantic.

We were indeed fortunate to make the flight when we did: two days later a severe south-west gale almost certainly swept the eggs of those six birds into the sea. My friend James Fisher flew over Rockall just five weeks after our visit. He told me that the Atlantic was exceptionally calm but there was no trace of any young bird on the water although there were four adult birds on the rock and ten on the water. This little colony of guillemots nearly two hundred miles from the nearest land may yet one day be more carefully investigated. The main difficulty will be to find a day in June when the sea is sufficiently calm to enable a landing. There is no creek nor harbour and the sides of the rock are almost sheer and the Atlantic swell, even in calm weather, is almost always an insuperable barrier. Ornithological expeditions have sailed out to Rockall but have been defeated by the heavy swell. Until now (1963) no ornithologist has stood on that white, broad ledge of Rockall and handled an egg which, when it is found, will excite almost as much interest as the egg of a great auk.

HD-63

The shark's tooth of Rockall – taken during a flight from Skye in June 1944.

On the same flight Seton Gordon had this view of the St. Kilda stacks:
Stac Lee, Stac an Armin and Boreray.

II

Stories to Tell

If, in 'The Unrestful Past' (Section 8) I tried to keep to stories with some acknowledged historical reality, here the stories have crossed the boundary into myth and legend. This is a good representation of Highland folklore, stories which Seton Gordon was hearing, reading about, recording and, happily for us, retelling: animal or birds stories, the Fingalian legends, and all the various types of tale which appear in every country's lore and of which Scotland has a store to treasure.

Landing on the Shiants, looking to Eilean Mhuire.

Kelp burning in South Uist, c. 1920.

THE RAVEN, BIRD OF LEGENDS

The raven, if old writers be credited, was once a bird of the whiteness of snow. Ovid narrates how it was that the raven acquired his dark plumage. Apollo loved the nymph Coronis and believed that she loved him. But the raven which was his trusted messenger flew up to him one day and croaked that Coronis had given her love to another. Apollo then, darkly jealous, shot a far-reaching arrow into the bosom of his beloved. That deed done, he repented, and attempted by all his healing arts to prevent her spirit from taking flight from her sorely wounded body. When his efforts were unavailing he turned upon the raven and cursed it, saying that its plumage, and the plumage of its successors, should for ever remain black.

Even before that fateful day Apollo had been having trouble with his raven. The god one day sent it to a spring to fetch water in a bowl, to be used at a festival to Jupiter. But the raven saw a fig tree sheltering the well, and on the fig tree were splendid figs, not yet fully ripe. The raven could not resist waiting until the fruit had ripened, and knowing full well that its master's anger would be incurred, thought of a subterfuge: after waiting a considerable time, it ate the figs, then killed a snake and returned to Apollo with the snake and the bowl filled with water. Before Apollo could speak the raven poured out a tale of woe, and told how it had killed the snake, which had been guarding the well, only after a prolonged struggle. Ovid records that a memorial of this event may be seen in the heavens, where the raven, the snake and the bowl have ever since remained close together: the constellation which holds them was long ago named Corvus or Raven.

Philanthus, when besieged in a town of Rhodes, may have forgotten that ravens at one time had snowy plumage. He consulted an oracle as to his chance of success, if he continued to resist, and was told that the town could not be taken until ravens were white. The commander of the investing force, receiving news of this prophecy through his spies, had a number of ravens trapped and gypsum rubbed thickly on their wings and breasts. These ravens when liberated flew over the besieged town and Philanthus, believing that all was lost, thereupon surrendered with his force. White ravens do indeed occur. They have been recorded from the Hebrides, from Iceland, and from the Faroe Islands, but are very rare.

In the reign of Tiberius, narrates Pliny the Elder, a pair of ravens nested in a high niche of the temple of Castor and Pollux in the Forum. When the brood were learning to fly one of them entered a Cobbler's shop in the city. This raven in time learnt to speak and was in the habit of flying each morning to the rostra, on which it would perch and greet with the words 'Good morning', first the Emperor, then his heirs, and afterwards anyone who passed near. That raven was the pet of all Rome, and when it was killed, perhaps through jealousy, by a cobbler who worked near its owner, the citizens stormed the shop and killed the guilty man. The account of what followed is told in that scholarly work, *Bird Life and Bird Lore,* by R. Bosworth Smith:

> A public funeral was given to the raven; its body was laid upon a costly bier which was borne aloft on the shoulders of two Nubians, ebony black as their burden. A trumpeter marched before, and persons bearing wreaths and floral offerings of every description, while an unnumbered crowd of mourners followed after, till the solemn procession reached a lofty funeral pyre, which had been constructed on the Appian Way, two miles from the city; and then and there, in a level spot of ground called Rediculum, on the 28th of March, in the consulship of Servilius and Cestius, the ashes of the favourite were laid to rest among the magnates of the great Valerian or Cornelian families.

From earliest times the raven has been portrayed in verse and rhyme. In the poem 'The Twa Corbies' the poet hears two ravens conversing:

> As I was walking all alane
> I heard two corbies making a mane;
> The ane unto the t'other say,
> 'Where sail we gang and dine to-day?'

> 'In behint yon auld fail dyke
> I wot there lies a new slain Knight;
> And naebody kens that he lies there,
> But his hawk, his hound, and his lady fair.

> 'His hound is to the hunting gane
> His hawk to fetch the wild fowl hame,
> His lady's ta'en another mate
> So we may make our dinner sweet.

'Ye'll sit on his white hause-bane,
And I'll pick oot his bonny blue een;
Wi' ae lock of his gowden hair
We'll theek our nest when it grows bare.

'Mony a one for him makes mane,
But nane sail ken where he is gane;
O'er his white banes, when they are bare,
The wind sail blaw for evermair.'

In Norse mythology the raven is sacred to Odin, God of War; he who is commemorated in our Odinsday or Wednesday. One of the titles borne by Odin was Ravens God. Odin owned two trusty ravens, named Hugen and Munen (*Mind* and *Memory*) which each evening returned to him with news which they had received throughout the world. The Norsemen on their voyages of discovery carried with them ravens because of this bird's faculty of sensing land at a great distance. The great sea rover Flokki on a voyage of discovery from the Faeroes took with him three ravens which had been consecrated to the gods. For some time he sailed northwest and when beyond sight of land liberated the first raven. That bird, after circling awhile overhead, returned toward the Faeroes. For a space of a day and a night Flokki still kept his course and then he loosed the second raven, which for long flew above him, then returned to the galley, showing those who watched that land was far distant. But Flokki, undismayed, still sailed on toward the north-west and when at length he liberated the third raven the hearts of the Norsemen lifted, for that raven flew ahead of them and by following the course it had taken Iceland was discovered.

The Norse banner was woven in the form of a raven. Before entering battle the warriors paid special attention to the appearance of the standard. If it was blown out in the breeze, so that the raven appeared to shake its wings exultingly, the omen was good but if the banner drooped, so that the bird appeared listless, defeat was likely. Sometimes the raven-banner was woven under spells so powerful that it brought victory in the fight, but death to him who carried it.

In one version of the 'Passing of Arthur' the king did not die, but was changed into the shape of a raven, and will one day reassume human form and claim his rights.

ISNB-41

THE SWORD TEMPERED

Diarmid and Fionn and all the Feinne ran after the Fairy Blacksmith but he was taking ten yards at every stride. It was not easy to keep him in sight. Through time the Fairy Blacksmith reached the Fairy Smithy. He entered it and closed the door. Diarmid was the first after him, and he managed to open the smithy door and get inside. Diarmid asked the Fairy Blacksmith for a sword. The blacksmith said he would give him one. There were many smiths working at the sword. Every smith had four hands. While forging the sword they sang a refrain.

The sword was finished; it was given to Diarmid. The Fairy Blacksmith told Diarmid that there was one way only to temper the sword and that was by running it through the body of the first person who entered the door of the smithy. The Fairy Blacksmith's mother appeared at the door. Diarmid said to the Fairy Blacksmith (for he was anxious about his own brothers, in case they might come in), 'Now will you temper the sword?' The Fairy Blacksmith did not break his word. He ran his mother through and the sword was tempered. Diarmid gave the sword to Fionn, his father. It was ever afterwards known as the Magic Sword of Fionn, or Fingal.

COS-29

OSCAR AND THE SWORD OF FIONN

Long ago a giant had his home beside the grassy shore of the bay at Uig and the ruins of his fort are still visible. He was Ciuthach, a man of terrible aspect who, it is said, ruled the district with a rod of iron. This was in the time of the Fèinne or Fingalians and the oppressed people sent a message to Fionn, the chief of that renowned warrior band, to come to their help. The Fèinne arrived, and drew themselves up in battle array before the giant's *dùn*. Ciuthach (pronunced *Kew-ach*) treated the Fèinne with contempt and did not appear. The Fèinne then laid siege to the *dùn* and Oscar, tired of waiting, received permission from his chief to go on a hunting expedition. Rashly, as it turned out, Oscar took with him Fionn's magic sword Mac an Luinn. In those days no warrior deigned to carry his weapon, but only to wield it, and Oscar was no exception; he took with him his *gille*, or lad, to carry the sword.

They made their way towards the north of the island and on the moors of Barvas, cold high moors open to the breath of the north wind, they met a man who had a sword with a goodly sheath. The sheath on Mac An Luinn was, from much usage, worn and unsightly in appearance. When night fell, Oscar and the hunter sat beside the bright fire of peats and wood: they exchanged experiences, and, no doubt influenced by good food and good drink, became friendly towards one another, so that in the end Oscar gave the stranger his magic sword in the poor scabbard in exchange for the stranger's sword (which later was found to be poor and rusty) in the fine scabbard. Oscar's *gillie* saw the transaction with dismay.

While his master and the stranger slept he arose, drew Mac an Luinn from its scabbard, and sheathed it in the fine scabbard of the stranger's sword.

In the morning they heard the shrill note of a whistle coming afar across the moors to the south. Oscar knew the whistle came from Fionn. He said then: "Fights is on foot, and need is of men; Wind blows from host, but it is sad without Mac an Luinn."

As they hurried south across the moor, they heard the whistle a second time, clear and shrill. Oscar repeated what he had said when first he had heard it. The lad said then, "What if you had Mac an Luinn? "Oscar replied," I would take on me the third part of the battle."

They went on and at the swift sea stream of Loch Roag again they heard the whistle. Oscar said as he had said before, and the lad again put the same question to him. "I would take on two-thirds of the battle," Oscar replied.

They quickened their pace, and at Lag na Clibhe again came the shrill, long note of the whistle. Again Oscar said as he had said before, and again the lad put his question. Said Oscar then with enthusiasm and excitedly, vehemently, "I would fight the battle alone." Then the lad said joyfully, "You have it, and it was not yourself that won it for you."

Oscar drew the sword from the sheath, to see if it was indeed Mac an Luinn he had. To make doubly sure he swept the head off the lad—the deed of all the deeds he ever did that he was most sorry for. He hurried on alone, and when he came to the bay at Uig, he saw the Fèinne beaten to their knees, and Fionn in hard straits keeping Ciuthach off him. Rushing in to the fight with a shout, Oscar swept the head off the Ciuthach with one blow of his magic sword. The rock where the giant was killed is to be seen across the bay from his *dùn*: it is grass-covered and easy to climb.

AH-50

A fin whale on the slab at the Bunavoneodair station on Harris.

BEINN NA CAILLICHE

Overlooking Broadford and rising steeply from the blue waters of the sea is the shapely hill that is known as Beinn na Cailliche. The cairn which marks its summit is so huge that it is conspicuous even at a distance. A Princess of Norway, so it is said, is buried here: she may have been the same proud ruler who dwelt in Caisteal Maol, at Kyleakin and, by means of a chain stretched across the Sound, levied toll upon all ships that passed by.

When the Princess lay grievously ill and knew in her heart that few earthly hours remained to her she asked that when she died her body might be carried up to the very summit of Beinn na Cailliche and be buried full in the track of the Black Wind that sweeps, pure, cold, and vital, across from the shores of Lochlin, hundreds of leagues beneath the pale northern horizon

She passed and with sadness in their hearts her people carried her up the steep stony slopes of Beinn na Cailliche, perhaps beneath the strong rays of a midsummer sun, perhaps on a day when the winter wind surged in upon them with stinging hail on its breath and a wild army of ragged mists. On the hill-top they buried the Princess and with her, so is said, a casket of gold and they raised over her the great cairn of granite which still marks the site where her earthly remains rest 2400 feet above the sea that sparkles below.

Her burying-place is a lonely one. In summer a few sheep pasture this high and the ptarmigan's white wing at times casts a shadow on her cairn where the delicate parsley fern grows. Upon the cairn the golden eagle perches on calm days of sunshine and on silent, swift feet the hill fox passes and perhaps curls in slumber at the back of the wind behind the grey heap of stones that was piled here by strong, rough hands on a day that has long since gone.

COS-29

THE SEAL WOMAN

Ròn Mór is the Atlantic seal, that huge creature which in the folk-lore of the isles has human qualities. It is traditionally believed that these seals are the children of the king of Lochlann (Norway) beneath a spell. Their step-mother, jealous of their beauty, spent seven years and seven days perfecting herself in the Black Art. She then changed the children into seal form, so that they should be neither fish nor beast for ever, and that 'their sea-longing should be for land and their land-longing for sea, so long as wave beats upon shore'. But thrice in each year, in order that their sorrow should remain undimmed, they were compelled for a brief space to regain their human form. It is said that a man of North Uist walking along the western shore of that isle, on reaching the entrance to a lonely rock-bound cove, saw a number of seals casting aside their furry coats and bathing in human form. Unobserved, he picked up one of the discarded coverings and carried it to his home. The owner, too late, saw him make off with her coat. She was obliged to follow him, and when she reached his house he gave her human clothing and married her. Years afterwards, one of her children discovered the seal's coat, and brought it to her mother. She at once threw it about her and entering the sea dived below the surface, having sung a sad, strange song.

ISNB-41

A GREAT BATTLE

There was once a calf born upon one of the Hebrides which, being recognized by an old woman as a young water bull, was, according to her instructions, placed in a byre by itself for seven years and fed on the milk of three cows. One day a girl herding cattle sat by the shore of a loch. To her came a strange yet comely youth, who asked her if she would "faisg" his hair. She agreed to do him this service, so he laid his head upon her knee and she commenced to arrange his locks. But soon, to her dismay, she found growing amongst the man's hair a quantity of *liobhagach an locha,* a certain slimy weed found in lochs. Although terrified the girl continued her task without showing her fear, and when the stranger fell asleep with his head on her knee she untied her apron strings and slid the apron to the ground without awakening the sleeper.

But, as she hurried homeward, she glanced behind her and her worst suspicions were confirmed when she saw him whom she had befriended pursuing her in the likeness of a horse (the water horse, *each uisge,* assumed human form at will). He had nearly reached her when out sprang from his shed the water bull. He rushed against the water horse and so desperately did they fight that they entered the sea still struggling. But next day the body of the faithful water bull was cast up by the waves, all torn and disfigured by his supernatural enemy. It was said he still lived and was brought food by the lover of the girl he had befriended, and perhaps may be alive to this day.

HM-23

THE PIPERS' CAVES

The legend of the piper and the monster I have heard in Mull *and* in Skye. In the Isle of Mull the scene of the fight is MacKinnon's Cave, a deep cave on the south shore of Loch nan Ceall (on the maps wrongly as Loch na Keal), beyond Gribun, at an unfrequented part of the shore. Loch nan Ceall is the most beautiful sea loch in the Isle of Mull, and in its waters the Grand Fleet under Jellicoe remained for more than a week during the first year of the Great War when enemy mines and submarines caused great anxiety to the Commander-in-Chief.

In Skye the site of the conflict between piper and monster is Uamh an Oir, *the Cave of Gold*, on the northwest coast about three miles south-west of Duntuilm, and accessible from the land only during low spring tides.

In their essentials, the two versions of the legend agree. The piper, as he pipes, is attacked in the gloomy recesses of the cave by a supernatural monster. So long as he continues to play, the monster is powerless to injure him, but when at last exhaustion compels him to cease his music he is attacked and slain.

Both caves in which the fight is said to have taken place are in very lonely districts. MacKinnon's Cave, in Mull, is guarded by the great Gribun rocks, where peregrine falcon and buzzard have their home, and in sight of the saintly isle, Inchkenneth, where the Atlantic swell thunders white when the shore elsewhere is calm. MacKinnon's Cave is a very deep one. Its entrance is a little way above high-tide mark, and even on a bright summer morning no daylight penetrates into the gloomy recesses of the cave.

One winter's afternoon, when on coast patrol during the early months of the Great War, I took the head-light of my car—a powerful acetylene lamp—by boat to the entrance of the cave. Here the lamp was lit and the Admiralty Coast Watcher on whose beat the cave was, guided me to its inmost recesses.

The floor of the cave slopes gradually upward. At the entrance the air is fresh and the roof high, but farther in, the roof becomes lower and the air heavy and stagnant.

The tradition of the island is that a certain man, named MacKinnon of the Whelks, was in the habit of frequenting the cave in order to fast and humble himself. He fed on the shellfish of the shore, hence his title 'of the Whelks.' This MacKinnon was a piper, and one day as he was playing a *port* (tune) on his *plob mbór* he was attacked in the cave by the monster. Those who knew the language of his pipes realized that the piper was in sore distress, and in the lament they could understand the words: "Oh that I had the three hands, two for the pipe and one for the claymore." The monster's attacks became more fierce: the piper felt the clouds of death approach him and his music became confused and hesitating. Then at last the pipe was silent, and those who listened without knew that MacKinnon of the Whelks had met his death.

In Skye the piper of the legend was a MacDonald. Uamh an Oir, the place of the fight, is believed to have penetrated far inland at one time. MacDonald, when first he was heard playing on his pipe, was near the sea, at the cave's entrance. The music receded farther and farther into the cave, then became plaintive and appealing, and told as clearly as spoken words could have told, that MacDonald was attacked and in dire extremity. Here again the cry was the same: "Oh that I had the three hands, two for the pipe and one for the claymore," MacDonald's friends could hear the music of the pipes rising faintly from the earth until the piper had reached a point more than a mile inland from the entrance of the cave. The pipes then wailed and were silent and never again was the piper seen by mortal eyes. But his dog later rushed in terror from the cave and not one hair remained on its body, for the monster's breath had burnt its coat as though it had passed through a fire. Where the piper was last heard is near where the post-office of Kilmuir now stands.

Even in summer the sea is rarely quiet at the mouth of the Cave of Gold, and in winter when the north wind sweeps across the Minch and the hills of Harris are deeply snow-clad, the long swell from the northern ocean rushes into Uamh an Oir and thunders through its narrow entrance; as each wave recedes it draws back the rounded stones with a deep, muffled roar.

One warm summer day when I was at the Cave of Gold a mirage appeared in the west. Hills came to life and changed their shape, as perhaps they did on the day when MacDonald fought with the monster. I could fancy that the ghostly pipe sounded again from the cave as I explored the cool, damp rocks at the mouth of the cave and saw rock-pigeons dart from their shadowy ledges and red sea-anemones, with tentacles outspread, sway in the ebb and flow of the small waves.

I have mentioned two caves of the Western Isles which have this strange legend of the Piper and the Monster, but the legend is wide-spread and I have heard it on Islay, and on Rathlin off the north Irish coast.

The legend is believed to have an inner and occult meaning, more easily understood in the years of the distant past when faith was simpler and perhaps stronger.

AWP-37

THE CARLINS OF BEINN A' BHRIC

ist hid Beinn a' Bhric an hour before midnight; grey mist which
advanced, ghostly from the west and almost touched Loch Oisein,
murmurous with small waves. During the twilight of this short midsummer
night in Inverness-shire the face of nature was transformed and when at
sunrise I looked upon Loch Oisein the sky was unclouded and the loch lay as
if beneath a spell, its waters blue, silent and windless. Beyond and west of the
loch rose Beinn a' Bhric, clear, smiling and welcoming. Long ago the people of
Onich, on the shore of salt Loch Linnhe near North Ballachulish, had their
summer shielings on Beinn a' Bhric and each May made the long journey
with their stock. The remains of these communal shielings are still visible.

When I lived in the Isle of Mull nearly fifty years ago the Cailleach or
Carlin of Beinn a' Bhric used to be spoken of with respect, even with awe.
Near Ardura, where our home was at that time, is a small almost circular
lochan or tarn, which was supposed to have no bottom. It used to be said that
when the Cailleach of Beinn a' Bhric visited Mull to see her neighbour the
Cailleach Dotag, she forded the Sound of Mull with the water reaching no
higher than her knees, but when she crossed Crun Lochan (as the small tarn is
named) the water reached to her thighs. Her home was on Beinn a' Bhric
where her seat (*suidhe*) and her chair are still pointed out. Beinn a' Bhric rises
from Corrour station, itself the highest point of the West Highland railway, a
bold hill just under three thousand feet in height and standing near the
boundary between Rannoch and Brae Lochaber. It is in sight of Loch Oisein
or Ossian, named after the Celtic bard, and deep Loch Treig, the home of a
trout of fabulous age.

When we climbed Beinn a' Bhric the sun was still warm but the heather
was past its best. It is a pleasant, deer-haunted hill and the slope is easy. On a
broad ridge, two thousand, four hundred feet above the sea, is a granite rock:
Cathair na Caillich, *the Carlin's Chair*, and it is said that whoever sits on the
chair and makes a wish, that wish will be granted.

Higher up the hill than the Carlin's Chair is Tobar na Caillich, *the Carlin's
Well*. At this well three formidable witches once assembled in order to destroy
the Spanish Armada by conjuring up a tempest. The witches' names were the

Cailleach of Beinn a' Bhric, the Cailleach Dotag, and the Cailleach Bheur. This ritual was practised by mortals in more recent times for there is a strong Hebridean tradition that Iain Garbh MacLeod of Raasay met his death by drowning in a storm conjured up by spells practised by his sister.

The procedure in this particular type of spell was to launch on the clear surface of a well or spring a small object sufficiently light to float. Incantations were then chanted and the water gradually became agitated. The incantations continued with more and more fervour and excitement until the magic waves filled and sank the floating object. If the rite was under skilled control the actual vessel of the enemy would founder at that very moment, wherever it might be.

There were other uncanny happenings on Beinn a' Bhric. One of the summits of the hill bears the name Leum Uilleam, *William's Leap*, who was said to have made a leap of almost a mile here. William was a famous hunter of the red deer and much of his success he owed to a gift which Cailleach Beinn a' Bhric bestowed on him. When the Cailleach asked William what gift he would like to receive in order that his deer hunting might be helped he did not, as might have been expected, crave the cloak of invisibility, but said that many a time he had failed to slay his quarry because the stag or hind had got his wind at the critical moment.

William therefore asked the witch for the gift to be without scent and this, being granted him, he was able to slay many stags in future years.

From the high ground of the hill this quiet autumn day Loch Ba and its birch-covered isle, where the sea eagle long ago nested, were visible. Nearer at hand was Loch a' Chlaimh, *Loch of the Sword*, where Cameron of Lochiel and the Earl of Atholl met to determine their boundaries.

The hill silence was broken by the deep croaking voices of at least a score of ravens which sailed high in the blue sky overhead. Deerstalkers had recently been on the hill and the ravens had scented, or had seen the gralloch. A pair of golden eagles crossed above us and ptarmigan rose from a rocky spur on their white wings. To the east lay Loch Oisein and I remembered the unusual tragedy that had been enacted here a few years ago. Two stags had been fighting fiercely and in their head-on charges their antlers had become locked. All their efforts to disengage themselves failed and in the end they were seen to plunge, interlocked, beneath the waters of Loch Oisein.

HD-63

THE TAILOR OF LOCH AWE

Near the lower reaches of Loch Awe is the old chapel of Kilneuair, in Gaelic Cill an Iubhair, *the Church of the Yew*. The stones for this chapel were dressed in a quarry close to Killevin of Loch Fyne, and if we believe the narrative of the parish minister in the new *Statistical Account,* "on a particular day appointed the people attended in such numbers as to form one close rank from Killevin to Kilneuair, a distance of twelve miles, and each stone as raised at the quarry was handed from one man to another along the whole rank until it was fixed by the last of them in its place in the building."

There is a curious old story told of this chapel. A ghost was said to haunt the place and a daring tailor ventured to bet that he would make a pair of trews within its walls during the midnight hours. Carrying a torch, he arrived at the ruin and set about his task as boldly as possible but he had not sewn long when a hollow voice directed his attention to a hand of gigantic size rising from one of the graves within the chapel.

He then heard the words "Do you see this great hoary hand, tailor?" The tailor valiantly made answer, "I see that, and I will sew this." A skelton head then appeared from the grave and the voice, again speaking in blood-curdling tones, said, "Do you see this large grey head, tailor?" Less boldly the tailor this time made answer, "I see that and will sew this." The conversation proceeded on the same lines as each fresh member of the skeleton's anatomy appeared. At last the whole skeleton stood immense before him and the poor tailor fled in terror. He was only just in time, for even as he dashed from the chapel a huge bony hand was stretched out to seize him, and failing to grab the tailor left its impression on the wall. If the truth of this story be doubted the ghostly hand-mark remains to this day on the chapel wall for all to see. (A similar tale is told of a tailor of Beauly.)

H&BW-35

THE MACCRIMMONS' GIFT

Agreat piping championship was to be held at Dunvegan. A young herd boy was anxious to hear all the fine playing but his master would not allow him to go for he said that his work was to herd cattle and not to listen to piping. The boy, sad at heart, was lying on the hill grass with the summer sun warm upon him and the scent of the wild thyme in his nostrils when a beautiful fairy appeared to him. She said, "Have you your pipes with you, lad?" He said that he had and that if he had his way of it he would be down at Dunvegan listening to all the fine playing. The fairy said to him, "I will give you the choice of three gifts. Which will you have—the gift of sailing, so that your boat of spotted yew will cut a slender oaten straw, so fine your steering of her; or the might of battle, so that when you fight the ravens of the Dun will be satiated with blood; or the gift of piping, so that your music will bring the birds from the trees and give peace to wounded men and pain-worn women?" The lad looked shyly up at the fairy. She was beautiful with a wild beauty. Her eyes were large. In them he saw sorrow and the light of the spiritual world. She looked at him kindly but (he thought) a little sadly, and stood silent awaiting his reply. Her dress was "the pure colour of the green sea where it lies over white sand." The lad said, "Give me the gift of piping." She gave him a fairy chanter and the gift of piping, then faded from his view.

Picking up his pipes the lad hurried down to Dunvegan. The piping there was in full swing. Renowned players from every district of the Highlands were contesting in *ceòl mór*. MacLeod was angry when the herd boy arrived against his orders and, as a punishment, insisted that he should play a tune before them all (knowing that he was but an indifferent player) so that he might be disgraced. The lad stood out with his pipes. He tuned his drones. The great players around him smiled to think that the boy was to compete against them. But as he played the talking and the ridicule were gradually stilled, and all listened eagerly. The lad was carried away by his tune. His music was such as had never before been heard, even at Dunvegan, and, as he finished amid breathless silence, all were agreed that the unknown herd boy had gained Buaidh na Pìobaireachd, the Championship of Piping.

The lad became the first MacCrimmon.

The fairy had told the boy that he and his heirs must always reverence the fairy chanter, and if ever anything were said by its owner against it she would at once recall her gift.

Centuries after that MacLeod and his kinsman, MacLeod of Raasay, were returning to Skye from Applecross in the Dunvegan galley. MacCrimmon was with them, and after a time MacLeod said to him, "Seid suas" ("Blow up"). MacCrimmon blew up his pipe. He sat on the prow, the piper's seat, and the sea was so rough that he could not keep his fingers on the chanter. At last, in anger, he threw down his pipe and began to abuse the chanter. Scarcely had he finished speaking when the chanter wrenched itself from the drones and leaped overboard into the waves.

COS-29

HOW THE PLAGUE CAME TO CALLART

Centuries ago a foreign sailing vessel with plague on board sailed on the flood-tide through the narrows of Ballachulish and anchored below the old house of Callart. Her crew were perhaps in ignorance of the dread cargo they carried; at all events some of them climbed the small hill to the house and, asking to see the *Bean an Tigbe,* (Lady of the house), displayed to her and to the members of her household the brightly coloured shawls and other articles from foreign lands which they wished to sell.

Their friendly voices and good-humoured bargaining were overheard by the beautiful daughter of the house, Mairi of Callart, who was locked in her room. Her father had married a second time and her step-mother was jealous of her beauty and her popularity. Mairi was so impulsive and warm-hearted that she gave freely to all who were destitute, and it was because of some act of (in her step-mother's opinion) unnecessary generosity that she had been sent to her room in disgrace and had been locked in. Mairi was used to this sort of treatment, and when no one came near her that night nor the following morning she did not worry, but she was surprised that she could hear no sound of voices in the house the following day. There was an unexpected silence broken only by the sighing of the wind in the birches and none came to her door either to release her or to bring her food. The next day also there was silence and she remained a prisoner. On the third morning, when her anxiety had become acute and she was suffering greatly from hunger she heard footsteps approaching the house. She looked out of her window and saw a man standing beneath her with a lighted torch in his hand. They were equally astonished to see one another and at once Mairi called out to him that she had been for days a prisoner, and was delighted that she would now be released- His reply filled her heart with icy dread. "All in the House of Callart," he said, "are dead of plague and I have come to set fire to the house and those who lie dead within it."

Desperately Mairi of Callart cast about in her mind for some means to soften the man's heart, but in vain. In those days a plague-infested house was so greatly feared that none who had been in contact with the disease were permitted to mix with their fellows. Mairi explained to the man that she had neither seen nor been in contact with those who had brought the plague to the house nor those who had, unknown to her, died of it.

When she realized that the torch-bearer dared not release her she implored him at least to have a message sent to her lover, Campbell of Inverawe, and faithfully promised that if she were permitted to leave the house she would remain by herself in a cave in the hillside until her lover should arrive.

The man at first refused but at last agreed to do this and helped Mairi of Callart to leave the stricken house by the roof in order that she might not expose herself to infection. She retired, as she had promised, to the cave, the house was burnt to the ground and a message was sent secretly to Campbell of Inverawe who without delay launched his galley on the dark waters of Loch Etive and, borne west with the ebb on the full stream of Lora, made his way with sail and oars up Loch Linnhe to Ballachulish. He approached the Callart shore after dark, landed unknown to the inhabitants of the place and, making his way at daybreak to the cave where his beloved was in hiding, brought to her a change of clothing, lest her own garments might be infected. Happily she accompanied him to the shore and returned with him in his galley to Inverawe to marry him.

For centuries the burnt ruin of the old house of Callart was undisturbed for it was believed that the germs of plague were unaffected by the passing of the years and might remain active to the deadly hurt of him who should dig in the place. But there came a time when a Campbell of Monzie married a Cameron of Callart and he, unheeding his wife's entreaties, gave orders that the ground should be opened here and that the jewellery and other objects of value which had been buried in the burning of the house should be searched for. For two days the work proceeded but on the third morning Campbell of Monzie gave unexpected orders that the work should be stopped and that the earth and stones already removed should be replaced. It is said that in the night he had a vision, warning him not to proceed with the enterprise. Be this as it may, the ruins of the old house of Callart have since that day remained undisturbed.

This story I heard in the more modern house of Callart when, after a day of rain and storm and snow-squalls, the sky cleared at sunset and a young moon shone silvery in the heavens high above Glen Coe. The spirit of the past seemed to return as I listened to the tale, simply and arrestingly told, and clearly in the mind rose the vision of that plague-haunted ship, and of the old house disappearing in flames while a girl crouched, numbed with grief, in a bare cave on a lonely hill.

AWP-37

12

The Isle of Skye

For half of Seton Gordon's long life home was in the north of Skye so, unsurprisingly, he wrote extensively about this most famous of all Hebridean islands, including the early (1929) 'The Charm of Skye', but, as with the Cairngorms, Skye appeared in many articles and chapters in many books. Perhaps it is time for Skye to make more of one of its distinguished residents!

In the Cuillin, Skye: Am Basteir, Sgurr nan Gillean (behind) and Sgurr a' Fiónn Choire.

The Gordons' home at Duntulm, Skye (viewed on the return flight from Rockall, 1944).

SKYE

Skye—Eilean a Cheò, the Wingéd Isle (call her by any of her names of beauty)—at all seasons has a charm which draws those who love her again and again to her mystic shores.

In spring, while in the mainland glens frost and snow linger, a yellow carpet of daffodils is unrolled below the trees of Sleat and beneath the wood of Tallisker where Johnson and Boswell stayed awhile. In May, primroses scent the sea air, for they blossom on each sunny terrace of the great ocean cliffs. Wild hyacinths follow the primroses, and soon after them come the yellow flag and the wild rose. Beside the tide flowers the sea thrift, and the last of the sea thrift has not faded when the first of the bell heather appears on dry, sunny banks. In August, the moors are purple with heather bloom, and now the days are shortening. No longer does the Minch at midnight lie pale in a grey twilight. No longer does the afterglow burn throughout the night in the northern horizon, but the sky in the north is lighted with the pale green shafts of the Northern Lights that tremble and quiver and shoot out at vast speed across the night sky.

In October may come halcyon days when the hills of Harris are lifted in a mirage above the earth, when the spires of the Cuillin are clear-cut and a blue haze cloaks their slopes. Late in October, when sounding winds foretell of the approach of winter, the clan of the wild geese fly down from the Arctic and people the lesser isles of Skye until summer comes again. Upon lonely sea-girt islets they stand in great companies upon the rocks at the water's edge, or eagerly crop the short grass which they share with the sheep. In winter storms the deep-toned calls of the wild swans may be heard as they cross between Skye and the Outer Isles.

But the winter is short, and in late January the sun, shining warmly on sheltered banks, awakens the first primrose and the golden flower of Saint Bride of the Kindly Fires.

The Isle of Skye (1930s booklet)

A STORM AT RUADH HUNISH

All through the April night a north-east gale had blown with violence and in the morning came blizzards, sweeping harshly across the protesting land already soaked with rain. In the Minch a wild sea was running and from vast waves the eager wind was lifting the combs in spindrift. There was but one vessel to be seen abroad upon the Minch and she was a trawler running south before the gale. Beneath the old castle of Duntuilm the waves leaped in spray; three miles out to sea huge combers hurled themselves upon the lonely rock of Iasgair, completely enveloping it. Overhead a gaggle of grey geese passed; swaying, gliding, dipping and climbing as the gusts struck them, they strove with the rugged nor'easter and made progress until they reached the crest of a hill, where the wind caught them and hurled them like leaves high into the heavens so that they cried in alarm one to another.

For a time I walked in shelter on a south-facing slope where primroses were flowering, then heard the roar of the gale among the rocks as I approached the narrow pass which leads down through the cliff to Hunish, most northerly promontory of Skye. Hunish, an old Norse place-name, said to mean *Bear's Point*, rises on an average rather more than fifty feet above the sea. In length it approaches a quarter of a mile; in breadth it is some four hundred yards.

So tremendous were the seas that they leaped high against the basaltic rocks. Their crests were lifted still higher by the wind, rose above the cliff-top, and in sheets of grey spray drifted across and drenched the whole promontory. The grass slopes ran sea-water. A strong milky stream flowed in cascades past budding plants of rose-root and cushion pink. Very curious did that burn appear, by reason of its colour: it had its source in no clear spring but in the ocean, and was now flowing back to join the successors of the waves which had hurled it out of its element far over the inundated land. Everywhere the peat-hags and bogs ran sea-water. Behind a knoll the herring-gull population of the promontory sheltered, crouching motionless and low, heads facing the wind. When disturbed they flew a few yards then, fearful of the might of the storm, settled again hurriedly. At the edge of the cliff the strength of the wind was so great that I could not stand erect but was obliged to creep humbly on all fours, feeling the earth tremble as the mighty waves dealt smashing blows against the unyielding rocks. Out to sea was an expanse of wild, storm-vexed waters. Each wave as it advanced was awe-inspiring in its might but now and again came giants which towered above their fellows and broke in overfalls while still far from the promontory. These waves leaped mightily upon the rocks, engulfed them then leisurely mounted high above them and in a drenching shower of almost solid water invaded the land.

At the end of the promontory there was slight shelter and it was possible to crouch behind friendly rocks and watch the titanic contest between wind, wave and tide. Waves so great are rarely seen in the Minch, even in winter, and in April so violent a storm is remarkable. Some of the waves moved past the end of the promontory without breaking, making their way towards Vaternish and South Uist; sometimes a sea broke far out with shuddering violence and the Minch herself appeared stunned by the impact.

Fighting their way into the storm, gannets beat up towards the north. They usually flew singly but sometimes in small parties. Their speed was perhaps ten miles an hour; they glided for shelter into each trough between the seas, they rose above each crested wave; they flew only a few inches above the surface of the water and skilfully advanced against the storm. These solans were perhaps on their spring migration to the nesting stacks of Sùla Sgeir, near North Rona, or Sule Skerry, west of Orkney. Some of the birds appeared weary as though even they, tireless fliers though they be, had found this stern battle with the gale a tax on their endurance. Once, in the midst of a flight of gannets, a small flock of kittiwakes were seen battling their path into the storm and advancing with surprising ease on erratic, fluttering wings.

I had momentary glimpses of the snowy hills of Harris and Lewis appearing phantom-like beyond the Minch, and of a huge wave that completely enveloped Bord Cruinn, the *Round Table* of Fladday Chuain. Then a racing snow-squall moving fast over the Minch hid hill, sea and sky and mingled its eddying flakes with the sea spray that beat relentlessly upon this storm-vexed cape of northern Skye.

That storm was long in passing, and for long evidences remained of its might. The well on Fladday, in the centre of the island, gave salt and not fresh water for three weeks, so that the lobster-fishers could not use it. Each grain was washed away from a shore of firm sand at Kilmuir and did not return for more than two years.

AWP-37

WATERFALLS IN STORM

Boswell, in the narrative of his wanderings in Skye with Samuel Johnson, tells us that at Tallisker he "looked at no less than fifteen different waterfalls near the house in the space of about a quarter of an hour." In a winter storm these waterfalls are a wonderful feature of this stern coast. Above the north shore of Tallisker Bay a considerable stream of water falls in a gleaming cascade to the sea, a full five hundred feet below. On this day of southerly storm the strength of the wind was such that the falling water was caught on the arms of the gale and swept back over the hill slope above the cliff in a cloud of grey spray. Now and again, as between the squalls the gale lessened in violence, the waterfall reached the sea. But even then the wind-torn spray, harried relentlessly, swayed, now this way now that, like some living protesting thing. From time to time the low winter sun shone out from behind the flying wrack, and then a splendid rainbow hung, halo-like, above the fall. Lesser waterfalls in the vicinity offered no resistance to the gale. They were swept upwards and backwards with such ease that they gave the illusion of chimneys smoking furiously in a strong wind.

COS-29

LOCH CORUISK: MOONSET AND SUNRISE

"For rarely human eye has known
A scene so stern as that dread lake
With its dark ledge of barren stone."
SCOTT.

Loch Coruisk, *Loch of the Corrie of Waters,* is renowned as a loch of unusual beauty, not only in Scotland but throughout the world. It is a long loch, lying in the heart of the Black Cuillin, in a magnificent setting. Sir Walter Scott immortalised it in 'The Lord of the Isles,' and on a rock near the loch chiselled out his initials. Many writers have praised the beauty of Loch Coruisk, many artists have painted it, but few have seen it beneath the midnight sky. In the silent, windless watches of the night Loch Coruisk casts a spell that is graven deep in the memory, for by moonlight it has more affinity with the world of dreams and visions than even the ocean at sunset or the Isles lying asleep beneath the pale fingers of Aurora.

By sea the approach to Loch Coruisk is easy. Loch Scavaig, *the Dark* or *Shadowy Loch,* gives good anchorage, and from the shore of Loch Scavaig to Loch Coruisk is a distance of only a few hundred yards. But by land Coruisk is not so accessible. One must traverse (on foot or on a hill pony) the weary miles of Glen Sligachan or, from Glen Brittle, cross the heart of the Black Cuillin.

The passes of the Cuillin are arduous—almost as testing as the peaks themselves—and in the crossing from Glen Brittle to Loch Coruisk the climber must make his way up the steep and rocky Coire a' Ghrunnda, cross its pass and descend to the silent shore of Loch Coruisk by the desperately *rough* Garbh Choire.

On a warm, windless day of May I crossed the Cuillin from Glen Brittle to Loch Coruisk. The sky was overcast. The peaks were dark, clear, and full of silence.

On the hills of the Scottish mainland in May one hears the love song of the curlew, the mournful pipe of the *feadag* or golden plover, and, on the last wind-swept slopes, the croaking of the white-winged ptarmigan. But May in the Cuillin of Skye is a time of intense silence. There is scarcely a ptarmigan on all the range; no curlew sings here. Save for the delicate young growth of the alpine plants and the increasing warmth of the sun there is nothing to show that spring is come.

Of all the high corries of the Cuillin, Coire a' Ghrunnda is the most sunny. It leans toward the south-west, and the spring sunshine lingers here late in the day. Immense slabs of rock, smooth-worn by the glaciers of a past age, form a vast sun trap. In niches of the rock small shrubs of juniper grow, and in May the roseroot puts forth pale rose-coloured buds.

A blue hare and a few meadow pipits were all the life I saw in Coire a' Ghrunnda this May day but unexpectedly, at a height of 1700 feet, I passed the nest of a wren. Domed, compactly built, and newly finished, it was placed in a cranny of a great boulder.

Like an oasis in the desert, Loch Coire a' Ghrunnda refreshes the eye of the climber after his toil up the steep rocks and scree of the lower part of the corrie. It is a delightful loch of clear waters, lying in a rocky cradle 2400 feet above the ocean seen far beneath. From the loch a steep ascent over boulders brings the climber to the *bealach,* or hill pass.

It was evening when I stood on the pass at the head of Coire a' Ghrunnda. Forty miles westward the cloud canopy ended, and Barra showed in orange light. The lighting was so unusual that Maol Domhnaich, a rocky island some miles to the east of Barra and usually indistinguishable from it at a distance, was startlingly clear. It rose from the sea, entirely altering the appearance of the Isle of Saint Barr, so that I looked upon it at first doubting whence it had come.

Loch Coruisk, 2700 feet beneath me, was already in twilight and the Garbh Choire a place of gloom. Upon the cone of Blaven, across Loch Scavaig, was a luminous veil of transparent blue until the rays of the setting sun, blood-red, crept over it like some spiritual fire. Here and there, high in the heavens, faint showers hung.

The walk down the Garbh Choire seemed unending. Everywhere were enormous boulders, piled in confusion. It is indeed *the Rough Corrie,* and to descend it is a toil and a weariness but at length I had passed beyond the scene of desolation and lifelessness and was walking towards Loch Coruisk, over heather and sea thrift, beside a small burn of clear water.

A herd of deer crossed beneath me; on the horizon a stag was seen standing, sharply defined, against the last of the sunset. Beside Loch Coruisk my friend and I made our evening meal. The loch was calm and dark, and as the twilight deepened it became each moment more mysterious.

From Coruisk the Cuillin are magnificent, but never more so than in the last of the sunset that precedes the night. For a time the turrets of Bidein stood out against the afterglow; when that light had gone the hills were faint and intangible until the coming of the moon. The air was warm. There was no dew. Our camp fire flickered, glowed, became dim, in turn. Blue aromatic smoke from dried rowan wood rose like incense into the night air. A gull drifted ghost-like across Loch Coruisk. Above us towered Sgurr nan Eag, steel-grey with dripping flanks from the melting snows.

At ten o'clock the sky cleared. A star shone out. Little flurries of wind crossed Loch Coruisk. Dileas, our faithful collie dog, slept. Upon a faint north-west breeze thin mackerel clouds drifted past, high over head. Southward the sky commenced to glow. We knew that where we rested the rising moon would be hidden from us. We therefore walked south beside the sleeping loch until we had reached the Atlantic at Loch Scavaig. There, in deep heather, we lay awhile, with the murmur of the river in our ears, and the peace and stillness of the night all about us.

Orange, full-orbed, and majestic, the moon climbed above the sea. Bars of cloud floated in her course but soon she had mounted above them and shone serenely upon a silent, sleeping world of unusual beauty.

On the horizon lay the distant Isle of Eigg, pale and etherealised. It was there that Saint Donnan was martyred by the island Picts in 617, together with his fifty-two companions. There were pools of golden light where the moon shone upon the transient ripples of Loch Scavaig. Much dark water separated these pools for the moon showed her reflected light only where the loch was rippled and for the most part it was glassy.

There was no swell on the shore. The tide was low, and from time to time, on a faint cold air, drifted the tang of seaweed, healthful and vital.

Slowly the moon climbed and now the great snowfield upon Sgurr a' Ghreadaidh glowed faintly with reflected light. Gars-Bheinn, rising almost sheer from Loch Scavaig, towered gigantically into the night. The heather was warm and dry. One slept for a few minutes and, awaking, saw that the moon had moved perceptibly. Before the dawn first showed pale in the eastern sky the light of the moon was dimmed by thin clouds floating at a great height and the margins of the clouds were gilded by her rays.

The air became colder. The light strengthened. The gulls upon a grassy isle of Loch Coruisk bestirred themselves. They rose on white wings, drifted out over the loch, alighted on the water and bathed. I admired them for that early morning icy bath.

For long the sunrise tarried. The heavens again were cloud-free. The sky, clear and blue, was permeated with the freshness of dawn. At last a pale rose flush burned upon the black rock walls of Sgurr a' Ghreadaidh and we knew that the sun fire had touched the high tops of the Cuillin. Imperceptibly though surely the power of the sun-flood increased. In the high corries the snow began to sparkle; the snowfields glistened like diamonds in their dark setting.

In the corrie at the head of Loch Coruisk a thin haze hung. The previous night also it had been there. It appeared as though faint blue smoke, inconceivably delicate, permeated the atmosphere. Can it have been the magic mist in which the nymph of Loch Coruisk conceals herself—that nymph "who comes there only when she knows that someone is present who will love her"? Beside the loch, in the silence of the night, she sings and weaves beautifully, but never a word must one say to her.

It was long before the sun shone in the deep corrie of Loch Coruisk. Indeed, each moment the air became colder, and the breath of frost was near. The sea-gulls clamoured above their isle. They swooped upon a merganser duck who was passing by at her fishing and compelled her to dive hurriedly with much splashing. Above the black deeps a pair of courting sandpipers circled.

Now it could be seen that small trees grew on the farther shore of the loch. They were birches and rowans. The delightful green of their young foliage contrasted strongly with the dark brown of the heather and the black, merciless, rock walls above them.

At last the sun reached us, and full morning was come to the Loch of the Corrie of Waters.

Miles of arduous climbing and rough walking lay between us and our base in Glen Brittle. The sun was warm as we retraced our steps up the rock-strewn and painfully steep Garbh Choire but a north wind was piling billowy clouds upon Garbh-Bheinn and the air was keen. Far up the Garbh Choire we passed a single hind. She was in a wild and rocky part of the corrie and could go no farther because her escape was shut off by a precipice. When she saw us she crept behind a rock and lay down out of our sight.

A golden eagle sailed magnificently above the ridge of Sgurr Dubh. In hot pursuit of him flew a raven, making angry dives at the eagle, who was indifferent to his smaller adversary and disappeared from view beyond the hill-top. A few minutes later the raven's furious croaking could be heard. Perhaps the eagle had perched upon some rock and the raven was mobbing him there.

It was after midday when the narrow *bealach* between the Garbh Choire and Coire a' Ghrunnda was reached. On the instant a glorious view south-west and south opened out. The sunshine was brilliant, the sky almost cloudless. The Black Wind from the north was rushing across the Atlantic. Upon the island of Soay white waves were breaking but between Soay and Rhum was a plain of calm water.

Four hundred feet below us the blue waters of Loch Coire a' Ghrunnda sparkled. Thousands of insects had hatched from the loch. Above sheltered slopes they danced in the air; on the wind they were herded protestingly in clouds.

The wind increased. In the shelter of a rock we boiled our tea on a fire of white juniper wood. On Loch Coire a' Ghrunnda were white-crested waves; across the loch the wind swept in eager gusts. That night, before sunset, the north wind down in Glen Brittle bore winter on its breath. It scattered the cherry blossom like snow and silenced the liquid notes of the cuckoo and the song of the merle. Thus winter followed close upon the heels of summer on the spires and glens of the Black Cuillin.

COS-29

Seton Gordon (holding a stoat) and a keeper friend at an eagles' eyrie.

THE OLD BUTTER KEG

It was a hot July day in the year 931. There were rumours in Trotternish of Skye that Norse galleys were shortly to bear down upon the island and a keen watch was kept northward over the seas towards Lochlann. In those remote days there were thick woods in Skye, and out of a tree-trunk a man of Trotternish had skilfully fashioned a keg or small barrel. This his good wife had filled with butter and the Skyeman carried it on his back to a neighbouring peat moss. Here he dug a hole and buried the keg so that the butter might be preserved by the peat and might lie without harm in a place of safety should Norse raiders ravage the land.

Not many days after this the sails of a Viking fleet were seen moving south through the Minch. The sea was calm and in the bay of Kilmaluag the Northmen landed. In the fight that followed many of the islesmen were slain and among them was he who had buried the butter keg.

Centuries passed. Skye became a Norse island, prosperous and contented. The maidens of the island took strong fair-haired Norsemen as their husbands. The Viking tongue displaced the Gaelic. Later came days of distress and grief. The Earl of Ross, crossing over from the mainland, brought fire and sword to Skye, whose people sent a cry for help over the sea to Norway and called for vengeance for their murdered bairns. Haco, the wise and kindly King of Norway, was old and was disinclined to sail the seas on warlike expeditions yet he considered that it was his duty to help his people in distant Skye. In the summer of 1263 therefore he sailed with a strong fleet for the Hebrides.

How King Haco fared on that expedition can be read in the extraordinarily interesting contemporary *Haco Saga,* of which more than one English translation have been published. The fleet met with one misfortune after another and that autumn we can imagine the surviving galleys limping north towards Norway through October mist and storm.

A few years after this expedition Skye was ceded by Norway to Scotland but the Norse place-names remain to the present day and the Norse element remains in the population. All these centuries the peat had been forming above the butter keg at the rate of an inch in eighty years.

Came the early virile years of the seventeenth century when we are told in an old account that the minister of Kilmuir in Trotternish walked to church of a Sunday with his claymore at his side and his servant behind him carrying his bow and arrows as a strong defence against evil men. Came the rising of 1715 when Sir Donald of the War led his men across the hills to the Braes of Mar where the standard of the Jacobite cause was raised. Came the stirring days of the '45 when Prince Charles Edward, a homeless wanderer after Culloden with a price of thirty thousand pounds on his head, was "ate of flies at Mugstot" beside the Minch. Came the soul-destroying Disarming Act making it a grave offence to wear the kilt or to play on the bagpipe. Finally came the dark days of the Great War, when the men of the Island served in many lands and on many stormy seas.

All this time the butter keg was being covered more deeply by the growing peat and seemed likely to remain buried for all time, when one May day in the year 1931 two brothers, cutting peats on the moss, felt the peat spade strike something strange and hard. Carefully they removed the surrounding peat and (not without difficulty) hoisted the barrel to the surface of the moss. They removed the lid, and saw the butter that had been churned that summer's day one thousand years ago. The butter during the long centuries had changed its composition. It had now the colour of the inside of a coco-nut, and a smell that was curious but not unpleasant. At first the butter was not recognized and the substance was believed to be tallow, but when a sample was sent to an expert at the University of Aberdeen it was pronounced to be stearine—what butter becomes after having been buried in a preservative like peat for many centuries.

The old butter keg is well preserved and shows the careful craftsmanship of an age when wolves roamed in Skye and osprey and sea eagle plunged beneath the green waters of the Minch in quest of silvery prey. It is now in the keeping of the University of Aberdeen, which has had many associations with the Western Isles during the long centuries of Scottish history.

IOW-33

A RESCUE ON THE TALLISKER CLIFFS

Donald Cameron was with his two sheep dogs about three miles south of Tallisker. At the edge of the high sea cliff a large fox sprang from the heather ahead of him. His dogs gave instant chase, and all three disappeared over the cliff. Looking over the edge the shepherd could see nothing; from a distant rock he could see the fox lying lifeless at the cliff foot, and his favourite dog, still alive, lying on a ledge about half way down the rock, which at this place is a full five hundred feet high. The rescue of the dog appeared hopeless but repeated attempts were made by Mr. Wood, Customs Officer, Portree and a lad of under eighteen, John MacDonald, from Tallisker.

The district is one of the most remote and storm-swept in Skye. The first attempt at rescue was abandoned because the rope was not sufficiently long; at the second attempt the gale was so violent that it was impossible to stand at the top of the cliff. At the third attempt the epic rescue was successful. It was a day of bitter cold and the waves were leaping on the rocks five hundred feet below as the two rescuers, taking with them ropes and a pickaxe, worked their way down the cliff until they reached a narrow ledge about eighteen inches wide. They traversed this ledge for a considerable distance, hoping that it would lead them to a point above where the dog was lying. But the ledge petered out, and still they were not above the dog. They climbed back to the top of the cliff and again descended with a piton and more rope. With the pickaxe, working under conditions of great danger, the rotten rock falling about and upon them, they extended the ledge for a distance of some twelve feet. At last they were above the dog. Mr. Wood, an experienced rock climber, drove the piton into the rock and descended on a rope (John MacDonald steadying him with a second rope) to the ledge between thirty and forty feet beneath them where the dog was lying. Mr. Wood tied two ropes to the dog, which had now been eight days on the ledge and was very weak, and climbed back to the ledge. The two men after a rest then hauled the dog up to them and now began the perilous traverse of the ledge and the climb to the cliff top with the added burden of the dog. But at last safe ground was reached and that evening, long after dark, the dog's master was overjoyed to see his faithful friend and companion with great excitement enter the door of his house.

HY-44

THE BLACK WIND

From the East blows the Purple Wind,
From the South the White,
From the North the Black,
From the West the Pale.
Sencbus Mor.

To the old Celtic seers each wind was known by its own mystical colour. These colours were not woven out of human fancies; they had an occult, inner meaning. Not to the Celts alone was the north wind black. The Romans also saw that it was dark. To them it was *aquilo*. From *aquilo* come the words *aquilus, dark coloured*, and *aquila, the eagle*, literally *the dark coloured bird*.

The mystical dreamers of the Celts perceived also that white was the spiritual colour of the south wind. Here the Greeks were in harmony with them, for it is recorded that they sacrificed a white lamb to the white (south) wind.

As I pen these lines the black wind's eldest son, White Feet, is treading the Hebrid Sea from Tiumpan Head and Rudha Stoer south to Skye and beyond that isle. Before him he herds fast-moving snow showers—white columns that constantly change shape as they speed towards the south. So delicate, so ethereal are these drifting showers that one can imagine the *Fir Gorma* are sweeping the dust from the tireless waves on which they play of a moonlight night between Lewis and the Bespelled Isles. Some of these showers are white, others are creamy. One of them is grey; it might well be thin smoke from some passing steamship ploughing the foam-tipped seas.

Little more than an hour ago I stood upon the snowy crown above the Quirang and saw, in the clear air northward, the white heights above Rudha Stoer and the Summer Isles rise dark against a glistening background. Southward, across Skye, MacLeod's Tables were draped in white; over each was spread a snowy cloth. Black storm clouds hid the Cuillin. The north wind must have made stern music to-day among their precipices, and from their harried spires the powdery snow must have been swept far into icy space.

As I stood above the Quirang, at a height of fifteen hundred feet above the eager waters of the Minch, a flock of snow-buntings crossed the hill-slope below me. It was curious how lustreless their white wings appeared against that snowy expanse. The flock alighted, fed restlessly for a few moments upon the seeds of the long hill grasses that thrust trembling heads above the snow, then continued their flight.

At that time the air was clear and sunny but now, as I write, soft drifting snowflakes are veiling from my window the sunlight that quickens the emerald waters of the Minch. In the bay beside the castle a small herring-drifter lies at anchor, her masts and deck grey with powdered snow. Gradually the ground is whitened to the very edge of the tide and rhythmically the white waves advance to greet the new-fallen snows.

These snows that come while autumn lingers with us have an unusual beauty. Beside the strong tides of the Atlantic they do not lie long. They are here to-day and gone to-morrow but the memory of their virgin purity lingers after their passing.

A day of fierce storm on the black wind I recall. A tumbling glass had prepared the men of Skye for heavy weather, but the morning had dawned with the lightest of airs drifting across the sea and at sunrise fragments of rainbows had been lighted low above the water's surface. Two hours before midday the wind freshened, veered from west through north-west to north, and in half an hour was blowing with gale force. The sky was leaden; all distant view was hidden by rain and clouds of flying spindrift. Each succeeding wave was greater than the last. Pale green walls of water advanced eagerly to the dark rocks. As they neared the cliff they appeared to pause and to crouch for their spring, then leaped upon the black walls that had withstood these white-maned horses of Manannan for so many ages.

Late that afternoon, when the flood-tide had fought its way foot by foot against the storm and at length was at the full, the spray from the great waves passed in an almost continuous cloud across Rudha Hunish. Over the grassy slopes the spray drifted in dense grey showers, lashing the grasses so that they became withered as at midwinter. Towards sunset a rift appeared in the racing clouds, and above the tossing waves a splendid rainbow was lighted.

What I then saw was in harmony with the spirit of the storm. A peregrine falcon shot out from his giddy perch upon the topmost pinnacle of the high rock above Rudha Hunish. His thin and pointed wings were bent back so that they almost touched his flanks. For a moment, outlined against the clouds, he hung suspended, then swerved and flew a short distance down wind. As I wondered that he had left his perch I saw a gaggle of grey geese making their way laboriously northward in the teeth of the gale. Grimly the falcon awaited their coming. The geese did not see him until he descended like a thunderbolt in their midst. I expected to see one of the geese fall but because he had noticed me below him or because he had misjudged the strength of the gale, the peregrine missed his quarry and the geese, calling loudly and excitedly, scattered at once. Against that wind even the peregrine could not hope to overtake them, and, returning sullenly to his dark perch, he faced the squall of hail that now rushed on the black wind across the headland.

The geese and a few solans were the only birds abroad on this day of storm. A pigeon was standing upon a narrow ledge of rock. It feared to move, for had it attempted to fly it must have been swept away like a leaf.

At dusk a curious frothy smell hung above the narrow gulleys. Here the waves flowed in with milky-white overfalls. Many stems of laminarian seaweed had been torn from their moorings by the huge seas and now lay piled upon the rounded, slippery pebbles. Each wave as it leaped high over the rocks threw fronds and stems of sea-weed far into the air.

At high-tide I looked from a little hill across the tumbling surf. From the headland I had been driven by the great and increasing waves that threw their spray high above my head and caused Dileas my collie to shiver with fear. The tide was now so high that each sea battered the headland and sheets of spray drifted like mist across the boggy land where in fine weather snipe have their home. Some of the greater waves broke with a force that called to mind the explosions from the floating mines with which the seas were strewn during the Great War. Manannan himself, god of the ocean, could scarce have urged his chariot across those waves which the black wind was driving in confused, sullen ranks southward.

The morning following the storm broke calm. Gone were the great waves; there remained only a gentle swell that broke in long, white combers below the cliffs. The autumn sun shone brightly upon the blue sea, above which an unending procession of migrating sea-birds were flighting south. The feathered travellers were mainly kittiwake gulls and guillemots and the low sun lit up their plumage as they passed.

But it is not always that the black wind brings rain and impetuous seas to the Isle of Mist. More often it is the bearer of fine weather—of clear air and rare visibility. It is usually on nights of north wind that the aurora is seen. The weather-wise were accustomed to watch closely the appearance of the aurora or northern lights. When reddish rays appeared and gave place to others of darker hue it was believed that bad weather, which would last for some time, was approaching.

One night of early winter the aurora on the black wind was unusually impressive. With the coming of darkness a wide arc of green, ghostly light stretched across the northern horizon, dimming the stars and the bright flashes of the Scalpay light across the Minch. From this luminous band of palest green, narrow streamers of light leaped into space as though giant searchlights were sweeping the northern sky. Later in the evening the character of the display changed. The glow was scarcely so bright; the streamers were gone, but luminous pools, calling to mind mackerel clouds that presage rain, lay upon the sky from the northern horizon to the zenith. They flickered, died away, then reappeared to pursue one another madly like gigantic wills-o'-the-wisp across the infinite space of the heavens. Momentarily the merry dancers shone behind the old castle of Duntulm so that its jagged walls rose up black as night. Then the mysterious revellers hastened to another part of the heavens, and the castle showed no longer.

At midnight I looked across the Minch from my window. From a rift in the mist a flood of aurora light streamed down upon the sea, as through passing clouds a wide beam of sunshine may be seen sometimes to pour earthward. That great ray was arrestingly beautiful when seen through the lonely darkness of a winter's night. It was as if the searchlight of some great airship were trained upon the sleeping waters, troubled by a bitter and increasing wind.

Another day of the black wind I recall. In Skye the sun shone brightly but over Harris a great cloud, dark and ominous, floated throughout the day. Backwards and forwards this cloud drifted idly and from it torrential rain descended. The Minch was pale green and Fladda, with purple bloom upon it, was outlined against the storm.

On the far northern horizon white streaks of snow fell seaward and when a shaft of sunlight shone diagonally upon these lines of snow the Cross of Saint Andrew was suddenly formed, as it appeared to Achaius, King of Scots, and Hungus, King of Picts, on the eve of their great battle with Athelstan of England. At the base of the cross a fragment of rainbow burned mistily upon seas that were oppressed by the vast cloud canopy that hung above them. West and north the sky was so dark that it was a relief to look southward; in that direction magnificent cumulus clouds towered into the blue of the sky.

At this time the black wind persisted day after day. It brought sometimes snow and storm, sometimes sunshine and clear weather. Daily the snowy covering upon the Black Cuillin thickened and one afternoon, when the storm clouds of the morning lifted, the white spires of the Cuillin rose, like some polar range, against the blue of the autumn sky. The beauty of these needle-like peaks was startling. The hills were in shadow but on the ridges the low sun shone. On these ridges the snow was white; the snowy corries, deep in shade, were a dark blue-grey.

At last, after many weeks, the reign of the black wind ended. One day, early in November, his brother the white wind sped eagerly northward. The morning of his coming had been cloudless and before dawn Mars had awakened me by his ruddy light as he steered west high above the dark waters of the sleeping Minch. By noon the sky was grey and lowering and the south wind momently increased in strength. Early that afternoon the Cuillin were the abode of the storm spirit. The white wind from the south was lifting the snow that had been driven by the black wind to the southern slopes, and now hurled it high into the air toward the north whence it had come. Each peak was enveloped in a cloud of fine, drifting snow. Upon Sgurr nan Gillean the driven snow was rising to a height of several hundred feet above the hill-top. Against the leaden sky that cloud of furiously whirling snow was a ghostly and arresting spectacle; that day no climber who had ventured upon the Cuillin could have remained alive for long on the high tops.

Thus the white wind for a time replaced the black, but even in June the north wind may return to whiten the spires of the Cuillin, and since its birthplace is amid polar wastes, its breath, even at midsummer, is chill across western sea-lochs and lonely Highland glens.

COS-29

A Hebridean croft well supplied with haystacks.

THE OCEAN WAY HOME TO SKYE

There is another approach to Skye, the Ocean Way—the Blue Way it might have been named on the summer day when I made the passage on board the good ship *Dunara Castle,* a vessel of venerable age. I joined her at Tiree, but the traveller can board the vessel, or another of her line, at Glasgow or at Greenock and sail leisurely northward, rounding the Mull of Cantyre and calling first at Islay. Thence the passage is under the shadow of Jura to the island of Colonsay, from which place the ship crosses to Iona before touching at Bunessan in the Ross of Mull and then steering west to Tiree. After unloading a considerable cargo at Tiree the ship steers north, along the rocky shore of Coll, then beneath the high, majestic hills of Rum, and approaches the great Cuillin range at Elgol in Skye.

On that summer day when we neared Elgol and sounded a long blast on our high-pitched siren, a small rowing-boat came out to meet us (there is no pier at Elgol). The boat was rowed by two men, who conversed heatedly in Gaelic with one of the steamer's crew while the total cargo for Elgol—one sack of flour—was dropped into the boat. We crossed from Elgol to Soay, a couple of miles distant over the sea, leaving the noble cone of Blaven in deep shade. Again we were met by a small boat, into which we unloaded two small drums of oil. At neither Elgol nor Soay did any passenger leave or board.

We now steered through the Sound of Soay, a narrow sound calling to mind a Norwegian fjord, for the Black Cuillin rose almost sheer above us, with mighty rocks and gloomy corries. On the ocean shore of the sound the breeze swayed the birches of the North Harbour of Soay. We passed the entrance to Loch Brittle, down which white-crested waves were racing, and watched a deeply laden motor-boat making heavy weather into them. The wind increased as we steamed northward along the high, rock-bound coast of Skye. Here was a grim, stern land, of recent rock avalanches and landslides, and of gloomy sea caves rarely visited by man, for no house was visible until we were abreast of an opening in that wall of rock and saw, amid its sheltering trees, the old house of Talisker, where Johnson and Boswell stayed on their Hebridean journey.

We reached at length the entrance to Loch Bracadale, where King Haco's fleet long ago anchored, and now saw those dark pillars of rock, MacLeod's Maidens, rise from the sea, and near them the low island of Wiay on which flax was at one time grown. We anchored in the loch after making a call at the tweed-making township of Portnalong, and very early the next morning continued the voyage to Dunvegan, steaming into Loch Dunvegan as the July sun broke through the clouds after a night of rain and thunder.

Ahead of us the castle of Dunvegan rose strong and stately above the trees which surround it. A tempting offer to remain for breakfast at the castle was refused because the *Dunara Castle,* having fed her passengers often and well, had provided breakfast at an early hour. Dara, my old collie, was thankful of that visit to the castle, for she had had a disturbed night on board ship, and now slept soundly on the thick carpet of the castle dining-room.

My voyage home was now almost completed, for I was to disembark at Uig, the next port of call. We steamed slowly out of Loch Dunvegan and rounded Vaternish Point, the sea cheerful with birds of ocean, to enter the broad mouth of Loch Snisort. Off Vaternish Point the tidal stream was heavy and the temperature of the air dropped suddenly as though we were approaching ice. Puffins, razorbills and fulmars were fishing in that ocean river, and a party of solans passed us. They flew low above the sea, in close formation, and from their course I had little doubt that they were from Sùla Sgeir, returning to their ocean rock far below the horizon northward.

When we had passed the Ascrib Islands and were well into the loch, the air once more became warm, and in Uig Bay the sun was bright and the scent of clover and other flowers was in the air. At Uig I left the ship and the friends I had made on this pleasant sea passage. I walked home, a distance of seven miles, finding on the moor that scarce [Pale] butterwort, *Pinguicula lusitanica.* I reached my house at Upper Duntuilm just as the first of the hay was being put up and thus was able to finish the voyage and the walk with hard work in the hayfield. I had arrived in Skye by the old way, the Sea Way, and had avoided all trains, ferries and buses.

AH-50

'At the potatoes'; Spring planting in North Skye.

The family haystack at Duntulm, Skye.

13

Bird Notes

These mostly short pieces show Seton Gordon's constant fascination concerning anything to do with birds. Keepers, friends, readers all constantly wrote with observations and speculations like these. How delighted he would be to see the millions who follow his enthusiasm today.

Seton Gordon's mentor Richard Keaton taking a photograph; in an album of 1906.

Storm petrel with its fluffy chick (see Section 5).

A PIPIT'S LIFE

The meadow-pipit is victimised more than any bird by the cuckoo, and probably the reason for this is that the latter is often plentiful on the moors where, except for the moor linnet, there are few birds for the marauder to victimise. It has been proved that the cuckoo does not invariably lay her egg actually in the nest of her victim, as in one instance a meadow-pipit's nest was found under a rock in such a position that a cuckoo could not possibly have entered the hollow, but must have deposited the egg outside and then placed it in the nest by means of her bill. Probably this is more often the case than is generally supposed, as cuckoos have been shot while carrying eggs. An extraordinary thing when the size of the bird is taken into consideration is the smallness of the cuckoo's egg. When laid in a meadow-pipit's nest it can scarcely be distinguished from the eggs of the rightful owner so alike are they in size and markings. The meadow-pipit is an interesting bird. It's call-note is an oft-repeated "zizick, zizick," or "sphink, sphink," while the male has a song very like his near relative, the tree-pipit. Flying to a good height, he descends precipitately to the ground, uttering his song the while, but the notes he uses on his ascent are different from those uttered during the downward flight.

The first brood are able to look after themselves by the month of June, when the majority of the parent birds start housekeeping afresh, and I have seen newly hatched young as late as the middle of July. The birds are very anxious when any danger threatens their young, and fly restlessly around the intruder with their bills full of food, calling incessantly. It is rather interesting to notice that their having food in their mouths in no way interferes with their call-notes. The birds feed their young principally on insects, daddy-long-legs being a very favourite morsel. Even as late as August an occasional meadow-pipit will be seen collecting food for her brood, but by this month the majority of the birds have finished their nesting cares. Until late October, or even November, however, they linger at the nesting haunts, as if they would, were there a sufficient supply of food, prefer to remain on the uplands.

On a certain occasion I came upon a meadow-pipit's nest containing four lawful eggs and one cuckoo's egg. I half thought of taking the one laid by the cuckoo but in the end left it to be hatched out. A fortnight or so later, when the young cuckoo was only a day or two old, I found that even then he had thrown out the rightful occupants of the nest which were lying stark and stiff within an inch or two of their dwelling while the ugly, black little villain was in sole possession and even at that early period of his life strongly resented my taking him up to look at him—opening his bill wide with rage.

As the cuckoo is so very young when it evicts the other occupants of the nest, it is probably due to instinct and not to premeditated wickedness that it treats its fellow-nestlings so callously; but perhaps the strangest thing of all is the indifference of the parent birds to the fate of their offspring for they will not make the slightest attempt to replace their young in the nest once they have been thrown out but will devote their whole attention to the alien while their own chicks slowly perish outside. This at first sight seems to be a terrible state of affairs but if the foster parents had their own brood to feed as well as the cuckoo the food they provided would not be sufficient for all, as it takes them all their time to feed the cuckoo alone when he is nearly ready for leaving the nest. But why, it may be asked, do not the cuckoos still rear their broods themselves, as their foreign relatives do, and as they themselves undoubtedly did at one time? To this question I fear there can be no satisfactory answer. Sometimes, however, the cuckoo lays her egg in the wrong nest, for instances are on record of an egg being deposited in a carrion crow's nest and, when the young birds were hatched out, the cuckoo was killed and thrown out of the nest.

COH-12

THE BULLFINCH

ost bird photographers set about photographing their bird either with
the help of a hide, or by approaching their sitter with extreme wariness.
I believe I was exceptional in that I photographed my first bird by taming her
until she was fearless as a household pet and indeed bolder than many pets. I
worked hard and patiently but the delight of having a truly wild bird fly off her
nest and settle on one's hand is worth the hours spent in establishing a contact.

In the grounds of my father's house on Deeside a pair of bullfinches nested
most seasons. The bullfinch is often a tame bird at the nest and one summer I
found a nest which I visited frequently. This bird became so fearless that she
allowed me to stroke her on the nest. She would fly from her nest, alight on
my hand, and take hemp seed from it, shelling each seed carefully. She would
then fly back to the nest and feed her family on the seed. At last she became so
tame that she would take a hemp seed held between my lips! She seemed to
realize that too much hemp seed would be bad for her brood, for after taking
perhaps a dozen seeds from me she would fly off and search for birch catkins,
on which the young were chiefly fed.

The behaviour of the young bullfinches during my visits was interesting.
If I arrived at the nest when their mother was absent, the fledgelings showed
signs of alarm and crouched in the nest: when the mother bird returned and
fed from my hand, or even from my lips, confidence returned to them and
they sat up and watched the proceedings with interest.

One summer a pair of bullfinches nesting in our grounds had their nest
blown down, and I found the young birds scattered on the ground and already
cold and stiff. They were set before the kitchen fire, and when they revived I
placed them in the nest. I remember that I set the nest on a small table on the
balcony of the house, for I feared that the birds would again fall to the ground
if I replaced it in the tree. I still recall my anxiety lest the bullfinch might not
discover, nor recognize, her family in their new surroundings and my delight
when her soft whistle came gradually nearer and at last she flew on to the
balcony and fed her young.

30Y-36

HERON AND BLACKBIRD

In the grounds of Viewfield, near Portree, a small heronry has been giving much interest. Several young herons from a late brood this year have become unusually tame and frequent the lawn. One of the young herons was standing in moody reflection on one foot on the lawn. A hen blackbird hunting for worms, and engrossed in her search, fed nearer and nearer to the heron. The thin, long-legged bird suddenly became rigid and alert. With incredible swiftness it shot out its long neck, seized the unfortunate blackbird and, more wonderful still, swallowed it, feathers and all, at a gulp.

(Typescript NLS)

Statesman and ornithologist Lord Grey at Falladon, with tame mandarin ducks.

AN ISLAND TRAGEDY

One sunny winter day when the air was of that soft clearness so characteristic of the Isles, I sailed across the Sound of Harris and passed close to
the resting-place of the green cormorants. The birds had breakfasted, and
crowded together on the flat top of their rock. So close did they press one
upon the other that each inch of the rock was occupied. With solemn gaze the
great black-plumaged company watched the passing of the boat. It was then
that an old fisherman in the boat recalled the tragedy of the rock of the green
cormorants.

Many years ago a great frost gripped the Isles. In the Outer Hebrides
frost is usually a fleeting thing, but that winter the temperature was so low that
the wild swans were frozen upon the lochs and even the Atlantic had an icy
margin.

Day after day, in the clear sunny weather, the green cormorants could be
seen fishing in the Sound, and at dusk winging their way to their lonely rock
amid the sleepless seas. At length came a night when the frost was so numbing
that the crofters at their peat fires could find little warmth; when the springs
were bound with black ice and above the Atlantic a layer of frozen mist hung.

Next day the fishermen of the Sound of Harris, as they lifted their creels,
remarked upon the absence of green cormorants from the sea. The waters
were so calm that the birds should certainly have been visible since the other
winter visitors to the Sound were there as usual. Long-tailed drakes, with
tail-feathers jauntily curled, were riding buoyantly on the lazy swell, or else
were diving with a flick of the wings to their feeding-ground upon the ocean
bed, and great northern divers were beside them. But of the *scarbh* or green
cormorant there was no sign. Day succeeded day, and always the shags were
absent from their accustomed fishing-grounds. Then one morning—since
the weather remained calm and settled—a boat sailed out to the remote
resting-place of the green cormorants in order to set lobster creels about it.

As they neared the rock the boat's crew began to be aware of a tragedy so
weird as to be almost unbelievable. The rock indeed was peopled with its birds
as usual but as the craft sailed close in the bird company remained motionless; it
was as though they were be-spelled. As they looked more closely the fishermen

began to note something unusual in the attitude of many of the birds, and to wonder what had befallen the dark-plumaged clan. Only on landing upon the rock itself was the full extent of the tragedy realised.

Straight from their last fishing the birds must have flown to the rock one evening of intense frost. Their feet when they arrived had been damp and as they slept the frost bound them with iron clasp. One can picture the scene next morning. The cormorants on awakening discovered to their dismay that they were unable to fly to their fishing-grounds, and from the rock must have come a wild chorus of harsh, terrified cries that drifted unheeded across the lonely sea. Day after day the frost continued, and the green cormorants became gradually weaker. One by one they sank exhausted, and the sleep of death overtook them until the very last of that great assembly left its imprisoned body and flew swiftly in the spirit to the unseen isles beyond the ocean horizon where is, one likes to imagine, the spiritual world of the sea-birds.

Soon the grey crows, the ravens, and the great black-backed gulls gathered about this rock of the dead. Followed days of feasting, so that when spring at length was come all that remained upon the isle were many bleached bones many bedraggled feathers, and mummified feet long since liberated from their imprisonment.

This is the story of the tragedy of the green cormorants as I heard it when sailing across a sunlit sea. For years after the event the shag population on these seas was small, but now the feathered fishermen are as plentiful as ever upon their smooth wave-worn rock.

T11-26

THE HOOLIGAN

The great skuas of Noss seem to spend most of their time acting the hooligan. During the two hours which I watched at this comparatively new colony the skuas were continuously attacking passing gannets and forcing them to disgorge the herring they were carrying home for the family. The outraged expression on the gannet's face was comical but it was unable to shake off its assailant and was forced to disgorge its herring, which was caught by the tyrant skua in mid-air.

One of these attacks was highly spectacular. A gannet, flying past at its best speed, was overtaken by a great skua, which actually alighted on the back of the flying solan and, maintaining its poise like a skilled horseman, by digs at the gannet's head and neck compelled the terrified bird to deliver up its herring. A few minutes later I came across a great skua murdering a kittiwake, eating into the back of the victim's neck as a stoat might behave with a rabbit. Even when the motor boat in which I was a passenger approached it, the skua was reluctant to leave its dying victim.

WBB-38

AN INLAND GANNET

The gannet or solan, being a true bird of ocean, has a strong aversion to land, except to its own nesting rock, and it will sometimes add many miles to its journey from fishing banks to its nest in order to avoid flying above even a short area of land. I was to observe a remarkable exception to this rule on July 14, 1952. A companion and I were travelling by car on the hill road which then crossed the hill from Cluanaidh, at the head of Glen Moriston, to Tomdoun. We were at an elevation of a thousand feet above the sea when, looking down upon Loch Cluanaidh, we saw a solan climbing on narrow black-tipped wings. It was making its way west and it was necessary for it to reach a considerable elevation in order to cross the hills in that direction. It was a mature bird and had it not been so unmistakable I should have doubted my eyes. It may have taken in error its course up Loch Ness and then, having discovered that its navigation was faulty, had flown west high above Loch Cluanaidh. The summer day was fine and clear, and there was no mist to account for its unusual course, far from the sea.

HD-63

A STRANGE CHOICE OF NEST SITE

Major W. H. Hunt, who was engineering the new road through Glencoe to the south some years ago, has given me the details of the strange nesting place of a pair of wagtails. The scene was the main quarry from which the road metalling and stone for the bridges was obtained, near the county boundary between Perth and Argyll, 1,000 feet above sea level. In this qarry was a pandemonium of noise—the gun-like hammering of the drills, periodic earth-shaking detonations when the rock was blasted, a stone-crusher constantly at work, and trolleys being run frequently backwards and forwards over the small railway tracks, produced a deafening and jarring chorus. Despite this the wagtails decided upon that quarry as their nesting place and unfortunately chose a part where the rock had to be blasted before the eggs hatched. Shortly before the detonation charge was fired in the rock the workmen carefully lifted the nest from its place in the quarry-side, set it down in the centre of the quarry, and built around it a small splinter-proof shelter between two of the railway tracks. The wagtails found the nest in its new site—or they may have watched it being placed there—survived that blasting and many others, hatched their eggs and reared their brood.

HY-44

A SHEARWATER IN THE CHIMNEY

Another wanderer was the shearwater which one day came down the chimney of a house near a West Highland sea loch. The occupants were from home at the time and when they returned my friend's wife heard a scratching noise under the piano late in the evening, and a Manx shearwater in an exhausted state was found. The right wing and right leg of the bird appeared to be injured and it was unable to fly. The visitor was placed in a box of hay near an electric radiator that night and next morning seemed better. After resting for two days the captive was livelier on the third morning and bit my friend's hand.

By inducing it to repeat the biting, means were found of feeding the bird, for when it gripped the human hand its bill was half open and food could be inserted into it. This was a slow process, and a painful one for the owner of the hand! Diet consisted of small pieces of herring, brown trout and mussels. Latterly it was found that small pieces of raw beef did the bird most good. After its meal the shearwater was dropped into a butt of water, where it swam and cleaned itself. It loved the warmth of a coat or jersey and found pleasure in burrowing down the sleeve, chirping and chortling with satisfaction.

When the invalid had recovered it was carried to the shore and placed in a small sandy pool as the tide was coming in. The shearwater swam round, then tried a flight, which was successful, and after an elaborate toilet and apparently a feed amongst the seaweed, was last seen farther out on the loch.

HY-44

A FIRESIDE GUILLEMOT

A correspondent who tamed a guillemot and cured it of its oily state, tells me that although the bird is now tame it will never of its own accord enter the water, and has lost all desire for a seafaring life. Its great joy is to sit on a cushion in front of the fire, slowly turning round, so that all its surface may in turn receive the grateful heat. My correspondent's terrier is permitted by the guillemot to use the cushion only after it has itself finished with it, for the bird has established a complete mastery over the dog.

ISNB-41

AN UNLUCKY PARTRIDGE

When I was a boy I saw a partridge meet its death in a remarkable way. It was an autumn afternoon, with a strong south wind blowing, and a covey of partridges flew at express speed down wind over the road along which I was cycling. One of the birds struck a telegraph wire: the head dropped at my feet, but the body, because of its weight and momentum, continued perhaps twenty or thirty yards in the air before thudding to earth.

WBB-38

A PTARMIGAN SWIMMER

Young ptarmigan have to be tough to survive on the high hills. One stormy day I remember seeing a young ptarmigan blown into a lochan by a fierce gust as it tried to fly across the water. I imagined that this was the end of the young bird's career, but my sympathy was wasted. Without hesitation the youngster swam 100 yards straight to the shore, landed, shook itself and disappeared in the shelter of a stony slope.

HS-71

Golden eagle chicks in their nest, an unusual threesome,
though one has died or been killed.

AN EAGLE DEFEAT

Two men were crossing the wild and uninhabited country beside Cape Wrath one winter day. They saw a golden eagle alight on the moor ahead of them and then rise into the air. The great bird mounted upward until it was a tiny speck in the heavens. Then a remarkable thing happened. The eagle began to fall with a staggering corkscrew descent, its great wings swaying listlessly as the air currents caught them. Down fell the bird, and at each thousand feet its momentum increased till it crashed to earth. They ran up and saw to their astonishment a stoat emerge from beneath the eagle and hurry away. They lifted up the eagle. On its throat was a great wound. The eagle had swooped down upon the stoat and had carried it off. The stoat in desperation had buried its sharp teeth in the eagle's throat. The eagle had climbed higher and higher hoping to rid itself of its small assailant but had gradually weakened from loss of blood and fallen, unconscious or dead, to the ground.

ITH-31

EAGLETS MOVED?

I was talking recently to a stalker about eagles removing their eaglets from the eyrie. He then narrated to me the following. His father, an experienced stalker and naturalist, was close to an eyrie one day when he saw the eagle fly off over his head carrying some object in its talons. Beneath the eyrie lay a dead eaglet. It had no doubt been killed for it is not unusual for one eaglet to kill the other during their early weeks in the nest. The stalker climbed to the eyrie and found it empty. He was in the neighbourhood a week later and when he looked into the eyrie was astonished to see there an eaglet, alive and flourishing. He reached the conclusion that the parent eagle had removed her remaining eaglet when she saw him approach, and had subsequently returned with it.

Another informant told me he had had an experience of the same sort. He had an eagle's eyrie under observation one spring and he was certain that no eggs had been laid in it, yet at the beginning of June two thriving eaglets appeared in the nest. He was convinced that they had been carried there from another eyrie.

ITH-31

294

AN EAGLE AMPUTATION

One cold day of spring a friend and I were on the hills in Badenoch. As we walked along a rocky ridge my friend (as he told me afterwards) felt that he must turn aside and look over the edge of the rocks. Immediately below he then saw a golden eagle, hanging head-downward over the cliff, its foot held in a strong trap which was secured to the top of the rock. We pulled up the eagle. It was light as the proverbial feather for it must have been suspended there for days without food and in the track of a bitter north east wind. The foot was almost severed and we amputated it. The eagle then got away from us and began to flop its way toward the precipice. My friend shouted to me to catch it before it was dashed to death but I was too late. The eagle reached the edge of the cliff—and then a wonderful thing happened. The bird, feeling the up-rising wind current, opened its broad wings. In a second he was rising vertically, higher and higher, on wings held motionless. The swift transition, it might almost be said, from death to life, was a thing never to be forgotten. When the eagle had reached a height of perhaps a thousand feet above us his mate came out of the rocks, I think from her nest, and rose to meet him. Together they soared awhile, then disappeared from our sight.

GE-55

THE TYRANNY OF THE TERNS

The tern is a bird with which I am very familiar, and I have had ample proofs of its overbearing conduct towards its neighbours. I remember once, while photographing a colony of common terns, seeing a luckless rook attempt to fly through the colony. He had only progressed a few yards, however, when he was beaten down and fell to the ground. The terns apparently had some idea of chivalry, as when the bird was on the ground they refrained from attacking him; but directly he attempted to fly off, the whole colony were after him instantaneously, and this time, so far as I could make out, the luckless bird fell to the ground in sheer terror and there remained.

Having discovered a twite's nest, I placed my handkerchief on the ground to mark the spot and then returned to where I had left my camera, a few hundred yards away. I soon became aware of a great commotion among the terns, all of which assembled above the inoffensive handkerchief, evidently under the impression that it was an enemy of some sort. After shrieking and swooping down on the handkerchief for some time, they at last began to realise that it was quite harmless, and gradually gave up their fierce attacks. A kestrel sailing by was mercilessly mobbed, and a stray cuckoo had a very bad time of it, the terns seemingly mistaking it for a hawk and mobbing it furiously. It is to the credit of the terns that they are quite devoid of fear, and will attack even the peregrine falcon should he come near the nesting grounds. I have also seen them in hot pursuit of grouse and curlew.

The black-headed gull is the only bird which is not afraid of their attacks, for I know of a small colony of these birds which nest on the fringe of a colony of some 2,000 terns and make periodical raids on the eggs of these latter. Seizing its opportunity, a gull will dash into the nesting ground of the terns, and securing an egg of one of the latter birds, will fly off at top speed with a screaming mob of sea swallows in hot pursuit.

The gull carries the egg in an ingenious manner, sticking his bill into it, and absconding with it thus impaled. Terns are very easily excited, and often, when a young tern is making strenuous efforts to fly, but is unable to succeed, the whole colony appear on the scene, and, hovering a few feet below the struggling bird, keep up an incessant shrieking, as though uttering words of advice to the youngster.

COH-12

Feeding a refugee golden eagle chick.

A SWALLOW'S SPECULATION

Towards the end of May, when I was at Langwell, on the coast of Caithness, I happened to notice large numbers of swallows, apparently on migration. Now the interesting thing about those birds was that they were all flying *south,* and not north, as might have been expected at that season of the year. Is it possible that swallows, and perhaps other summer visitors also, travel to the north-east counties of Scotland by way of the western seaboard? I have reason for believing that terns do this—that they fly north to Cape Wrath, then east through the Pentland Firth, and pass southward along the coast of Caithness to their nesting haunts on the east coast.

ITH-31

THE MISTLETOE SONGSTER

The *mistle thrush* or storm cock, known by early writers as the mistletoe thrush from the belief that the young were fed only on the berries of the mistletoe, is a lover of full daylight. It was believed that the seeds of the mistletoe, held sacred by the Druids, were transplanted from one tree to another by the mistle thrush. This thrush, the largest of our song birds, is found throughout the British Isles. His song is loud and wild, a single phrase repeated again and again. The mistle thrush's song has a quality of impatience, and of defiance; the pauses between the phrases are abrupt, and after a brief silence the song falls again suddenly on the ear, in its full power. There is a stately measure in the music of the song thrush; the blackbird's flute-like song flows easily, like some moorland stream; the song of the storm cock is a song of strength, a challenge to all the world.

WBB-38

CHRIST'S BIRDS

S aint Bride's servant was the oyster-catcher, and it is in February that *Gille Bride,* as the oyster-catcher is named in Gaelic lore, arrives on the banks of Tay and Dee, Spey and Don, where it nests. In the Isles there is a tradition that Christ was once resting at ebb tide beside a seaweed-covered rock. Over a ridge appeared His enemies, seeking for Him. A pair of oyster-catchers then flew up. Swiftly they covered Christ with seaweed which they carried in their red bills, and when His enemies arrived they saw two oyster-catchers standing beside the tide, but no trace of Him whom they sought. Because of this service the oyster-catcher was honoured and when it flies there is seen on its under plumage the form of a cross.

The crossbill, too, befriended Christ. When Jesus was crucified and in agony, a wandering crossbill flew to the cross and with its bill tore desperately at the great nails. Its bill was wounded and disfigured and as it flew sorrowfully away, Christ said, "Because of your love which has brought you to Me this day you and your descendants shall henceforth bear a sign that shall tell the tribes of the air and of the earth and of the sea that you have come to My aid in My hours of pain."

And so the crossbill's beak is twisted to this day, and the blood of the Saviour remains on its breast.

ITH-31

The landing on Soay, St.Kilda, 1928.

14

A Vanished World

Seton Gordon seldom wrote directly about his family or close friends, respecting their privacy, but now and then we catch cameos of the very different world they lived in. Syd Scroggie and friends on their first Cairngorms visit found, on returning to a dilapidated Corrour bothy, that Seton Gordon had left his visiting card! Seton Gordon wrote always from first-hand experience; words, like his camera, focused on what was out there. Here then are a few rare personal glimpses: revealing, poignant, wry, sometimes sad, but ultimately triumphant.

An early 20th century express, from a 1906 Seton Gordon album of trains.

The tidal 'airdrome' of Traigh Mhor, Barra; still used today.

FIRST ATTEMPTS AT PHOTOGRAPHY

In the early months of the year 1903 when I was seventeen years of age, my parents presented me with a half-plate Thornton Pickard Ruby camera with Dallmeyer lens and at once I began photographing birds' nests.

For a year or two previous to this I had attempted with little success to photograph the nests and eggs of some ground-nesting birds but now, well equipped, I was more successful. I divided my spare time and holidays between photographing birds and travelling with my camera on the foot-plate of the engine of the Deeside express and photographing scenes on the line from the view-point of the engine driver.

Two incidents I remember clearly about this time. I was on the engine (James Hay, a great friend of mine, being the driver) steaming up the Dee Valley one lovely summer evening at dusk. We were travelling between Park and Crathes, where the line is much overshadowed by woods, and on rounding a sharp corner, to our consternation we saw, low down, right ahead of us, and apparently very close, what appeared to be a gigantic flaming object. While we stood, rooted with horror, we realized, I suppose in a fraction of a second, that the flaming object was the Hunter's moon, full-orbed and immense, climbing slowly above the horizon.

The second incident I recall was my unsuccessful efforts to pull up the express at the platform of Aboyne station. I had a certain knowledge of railway engines and on occasions was permitted to drive. There is a considerable down-gradient into Aboyne from the east and the Westinghouse brakes on the engine were not working too well that day. I applied the brakes in good time but despite all my efforts the train slightly over-ran the platform and stopped with the first two coaches beyond it, and from the cab of the engine I watched with some anxiety the staid businessmen of Aberdeen jumping down from their compartments on to the line.

James Willox was another driver I came to know. He was a fast but careful driver and picked up speed more quickly and stopped more gently than the other drivers. I remember being on the foot-plate with him on one occasion when we attempted a record run from Crathes to Holborn Street station at Aberdeen and my excitement was great when we travelled the distance of thirteen and three quarter miles from start to stop in thirteen and a quarter minutes. Although that was thirty years ago I do not expect this record has been beaten for the old Great North of Scotland engines were very fast when the load they were drawing was not too heavy.

In natural history at first I contented myself with photographing nests and eggs and did not attempt to photograph the owners of the nests. This was in the very early days of bird photography when even the nests of some British birds had never been photographed and the bird photographer was satisfied with modest results.

My first illustrated article I wrote for *Country Life* and the illustrations were either nests or nesting sites—there were no birds shown. I was then working quite alone and when I began to photograph birds I used to rely on my skill, such as it was, in stalking them. This I now see could never have led to great success but there are certain birds which are close sitters and these I did succeed in photographing. The ptarmigan, red grouse, bullfinch, and curlew were among the birds I photographed by stalking. To photograph on the nest a bird so wary and unapproachable as the curlew was a considerable feat, and I might have added another shy bird to my list. It came about in this way.

When I was a boy I frequently climbed the hill of Morven (almost three thousand feet) near my home on Deeside. This hill was greatly beloved of birds. Besides a large resident population of red grouse, many migrants arrived in late spring on its grassy upper slopes. Curlew, lapwing, lark, ptarmigan and golden plover all nested near one another on the south slopes of Morven. Golden plover were plentiful, and one day when I was wandering on the upper slopes, which were in thick cloud, I almost walked upon a golden plover sitting on her nest. The golden plover is usually a very light sitter yet this bird allowed me to stand only a few feet from her without attempting to leave her eggs. Almost always I carried my camera with me but on this day, perhaps because the light was bad, I had left it at home. Judge then my disappointment as I looked longingly down on the beautiful variegated plumage of the plover, as she sat breathing quietly at my feet.

The next day I returned—a sixteen mile ride on my pedal-bicycle and a long climb with my half plate camera on my back. I knew all the time that it was a forlorn hope. Sure enough, when I reached the plover's nest I found that the bird had already left it and was calling with her alarm note some distance away. I have never, before or since, seen a golden plover sit so closely.

Another experience which made a deep impression on my youthful mind was a covey of ptarmigan one winter's afternoon flying up the shadowed north slopes of Morven and catching the setting sun as they passed over the summit. They were, in an instant, snow-white birds no longer but flushed with a delicate purple glow very beautiful to see.

At the time of which I write there were very few bird photographers. I believe that R. B. Lodge was the first man to photograph birds; his results, and the patience and ingenuity he showed, were remarkable, but to my mind the most outstanding of those early pioneers was Richard Kearton. His books inspired me to take up bird photography and his photographs of the birds and their nests were a continual delight. I am sure that Richard Kearton's simple, direct prose and beautiful photographs brought to many a love of nature which has been to them a treasure without price throughout their lives.

One year I had found a pair of dotterel with their young. On that occasion I was alone and a short time after I had found the dotterel with their young I saw three people approaching me. They waved excitedly and hurried across. They were appalled by the loneliness of the hill! They confessed that the solitary hill plateau (although the day was sunny and warm and most pleasant on the high ground) alarmed them. They were unable to understand how I could walk there alone, and they had come to me to ease their loneliness.

On looking through old photographs I realize that the cameras used by the early bird photographers were in some respects equal in the quality of their work to the cameras of the present day but their lenses were slower and the telephoto lens was in its infancy. Lightness is a great advantage when one has to carry a camera long distances over rough or boggy ground and the tendency now is to perfect the miniature cameras rather than to improve the larger and heavier ones.

Some nature photographers frequently change their cameras but during the thirty-two years I have photographed birds I have had only two cameras— the Thomton Pickard outfit and, during the last fifteen years, a Una Sinclair camera with a Ross telecentric lens. This camera, which has given me some very fine results, has the distinction of having been partly submerged by the ice-cold waters of the Greenland Sea when I left it below high-tide mark on the shore of a fjord in northern Spitsbergen—but it is none the worse for this unpleasant experience!

During the thirty years of my work as a nature photographer I have seen a remarkable increase in the number of photographers of wild life. But the modern enthusiasts as a rule lack the patience of the early school of nature photographers. Some want to do a great deal in a short time. A complete stranger may write to me and tell me that he has planned during the coming season (these letters generally reach me in early spring) to photograph all the rarer birds in the highlands: will I, therefore, tell him how to set about it and exactly where to find these rare birds and their nests.

I published my first book on birds before I went up to Oxford, but until I met my wife (that was at Oxford's Vincent's Club ball in 1913) I had never used a hide but had done all my photography by stalking the birds. But even when successful the results were not so happy as if a hide had been used for the sitters crouched timidly on their eggs, alarmed by the man and the Cyclops eye of the camera.

30Y-36

Castlebay, Barra. Fishing boats with Kisimul Castle.

A HEBRIDEAN CAMP

June in the Outer Isles is a month without darkness. For perhaps two hours around midnight a soft twilight lies over the land and the winding lochs but not until the beginning of August does true darkness come.

The Outer Hebrides is a country of innumerable lochs, sea-lochs and freshwater lochs, the latter so numerous that they form a maze out of which it is hard to find one's way. Beside one of these lochs my wife and I pitched our tent early in June, amongst young green heather and the tender fronds of the bracken. We were close beside the main road of the island yet there was no house to be seen and the eye rested on a great expanse of moorland with many lochs and a range of hills bounding the horizon east and west.

The bird-life of the Outer Isles is distinctive. Here one sees birds little known on the mainland and as we sometimes lay awake in our tent at midnight we heard the curious far-carrying cries of red-throated divers flying across to the sea to their early morning fishing or through the open flap of our tent could see other divers winging their way eastward in the rosy flush of the dawn to their small freshwater nesting lochans.

Alas, not for many nights did that tent-flap remain open! We pitched our camp when the weather was cold and unusually wet. But the day after our arrival summer came suddenly to the Isles and during our two weeks' camp we had uninterrupted warmth and sunlight. How delightful was the unaccustomed warmth! Yet it brought with it a terrible pest—the Highland midge. At first these small insects appeared singly then in twos and threes and finally, as the heat became almost tropical, they increased to incredible swarms that rendered life a burden. At night they danced in dense clouds around our tent. Through the closed flaps, through tiny openings, they forced their way. Inside the tent they eagerly sought out their long-suffering prey so that we were able to snatch brief intervals of sleep only by covering our heads with a towel and warily fashioning a small tunnel for a meagre supply of fresh air. Sunrises passed us unheeded; sunset of each day found us tightly enclosed in our tent, to which clouds of blood-thirsty insects eagerly and persistently sought admittance. In addition to the midges the heather swarmed with small ticks which burrowed into our persons and added to our discomfort.

One morning, when the sea mist lay close upon the hills and gave promise of a day of great heat, we were driven from the tent at five o'clock by the insupportable attacks of myriads of midges. These attacks were so fierce that it was impossible to dress within the tent; outside we found an eager, compact host awaiting us, and a few moments later any onlooker might have seen two apparently demented figures running backwards and forwards over the moor while they hastily clothed themselves !

It was impossible to prepare breakfast; in desperation we rowed far out into the loch and with our boat lying idly on the windless waters we fried our kippers, so thickly coated with midge corpses that they were scarcely recognisable. Our one cause for thankfulness was that the Outer Hebridean midge was decidedly smaller and less poisonous than his relative of Skye and the mainland.

Each day of our camping we used to pray for a breeze; with joy we beheld far up the loch the slight ruffling of the glassy waters which showed the approach of a current of air that would cause the midge world to take refuge in the grass and heather.

T11-26

CHARACTERS

The Highland deerstalker had a strong personality, a keen sense of humour, was of a fine integrity and most loyal in friendship. English was with him an acquired language and he spoke it sometimes quaintly and often forcibly. I remember that after a cold sunless season a stalker was telling me of the weather in his glen. He said, "At times it would appear as though the sun were to gain the *masterpiece,* but then the wind would get *up,* the mist would come *down,* and the atmosphere would become most ungenial."

Two old worthies of this kind one Saturday evening boarded a local train and entered my compartment. They had both had a good dram, and before long a discussion started as to the wing-spread of the golden eagle. I ventured to agree with the opinion of one as against the other. He in the minority looked at me rather doubtfully and although he plainly thought I did not know what I was talking about he was too polite to say so. But his friend, who I had seen eyeing the label on my luggage, said to him quietly, 'Do ye know who yon is?' 'No, indeed' came the answer. 'Well', said the first in triumph, 'yon is Seton Gordon!' This remark was rather a score, for his convivial companion, remarking 'A'm din' (I'm done) and ceased to argue.

A grand man was Sandy MacDonald who for many years was stalker on the Derry beat of Mar Forest. When we lived at Aviemore Sandy walked through the Lairig Ghru to visit us. He had never seen the sea and took the train to Inverness to look at it.

I recall crossing the Lairig one September day with my friend, Major Hay of the Forty-Second Highlanders. Major Hay was six feet eleven in height, the tallest man in the Army. Sandy and the Prince of Wales (now Duke of Windsor) had been stalking and as we approached we saw them standing outside Sandy's cottage at Luibeg. The Prince came out to meet us (we both knew him well) and Sandy told me afterwards that they had been spying us through their stalking glasses and that the Prince had told him that Major Hay and he had been through the early part of the 1914–1918 war in France together and that it was strange that Major Hay, the tallest man in the army, should have been wounded in the foot. That day they had been stalking on the high ground of Ben MacDhui and their stalk was spoiled by a tourist who gave the deer his wind. The Prince said 'Shall I fire a shot a few hundred yards from him, Sandy, just to let him know there are stalkers on the hill?' 'Na, na, Your Royal Highness' replied Sandy 'it would maybe get into the *Daily —*', mentioning a newspaper of socialistic leanings.

Shortly after the end of the 1914–1918 war, Sandy found what he supposed to have been a bomb on the hillside behind his cottage. He took the object home and that summer when the Prince of Wales was out stalking showed him the 'bomb'. The Prince sent it to the Air Ministry, where it was recognised as a flare and later found to have been dropped by a Zeppelin in 1916.

HY-44

Seton Gordon had followed up this incident.

On May 2 1916 Zeppelin L20 left Germany under the command of Captain-Lieutenant Stabert on a raiding voyage to Britain. The great aircraft crossed the coast of Scotland at Lunan Bay, turned inland past Montrose, and then set a course that brought her over the Forest of Mar. Above the small village of Inverey the menacing roar of her engines was heard by the stalkers and their wives. A tell-tale light in the skylight window of one cottage attracted the airship. She circled overhead in the darkness and the people of the house, momentarily expecting a bomb to fall in their midst, were quick to darken that window! But the Zeppelin passed on in peace, and sailed high above Ben Mac Dhui to the valley of the Spey, thence across the Monadh Liath range and the Caledonian Canal beyond. She re-crossed the North Sea and, driven by a storm against high land on the Norwegian coast on the morning of May 3, sank in the deep water of a fjord.

CHS-25

INSHORE FISHING

When we saw the first solan of 1943 (March 23) Alasdair and I were setting small lines for codlings and flounders. The day, after months of wild weather, was calm and sunny. Setting a small line involves considerable labour. Lug-worms have to be dug in the sand at low tide, and in the Isle of Skye sandy shores are few and far between. After the worms have been dug several hundred hooks have to be baited; the boat must then be launched over a rough shingly shore and the line set about a quarter of a mile off, preferably on a rising tide. The line may be lifted an hour after it has been set: I think a two-hour interval is best. If the line is left down too long dogfish, crabs and molluscs eat the fish off the hooks.

A strong, gusty wind, which brought with it the faint scent of burning heather, had suddenly sprung up from the east, buffeting the shags as they fought their way home to their roosting island. To lift the line under these conditions was no easy task, for the wind threatened to sweep the boat off its course as it was rowed slowly above the line, one of us rowing, the other lifting the hooks. From the darkening waters of the sea flounders and codlings gradually emerged and were hauled over the side until a fair-sized collection of fish lay at the bottom of the boat. It was a stiff row to the shore and in the swell a landing was not too easy.

March is the season for setting the great or long lines. These are set a mile or more off-shore, for cod, ling, hake, roker (a skate-like fish) and skate. Inside the three-mile limit (an imaginary line drawn three miles from land) no trawler is permitted to work. Even in peacetime it was difficult to keep trawlers from the prohibited area: in wartime they trawl where they like. It may be said that under these abnormal conditions it is their right to gather as much of the sea harvest as possible but it is not generally realised that the deep-sea fish which enter the West Highland lochs and inshore waters in early spring come there for the purpose of spawning. Trawlers dragging their trawls backwards and forwards over the spawning beds destroy millions upon millions of ova and must seriously affect the future supply of fish. The local long-line fishermen are now afraid to set their lines, for they have learnt by experience that these are trawled up and destroyed during the hours of darkness—and under war conditions it is almost impossible to buy new lines or even second-hand ones.

HY-44

Cliffs of Hermaness on Unst, Shetland.

THE MAIL-BOAT

To the dwellers in the Hebridean Isles of Coll and Tiree, the one link between them and civilisation is the small but sturdy steamer which, summer and winter, regularly brings their mails, and indeed, most of the necessaries of life.

Manned by a sturdy crew of Gaelic-speaking Highlanders, and in charge of a skipper who is one of the finest navigators of his time, the mail-boat succeeds in making her call at the narrow and rock-girt loch at Arinagour, in Coll, and at the surf-ridden Gott Bay, in Tiree, when no other vessel would attempt a landing.

I have many a time crossed over to the islands from Mull where he was then Board in the mail-boat but one which remains most vividly on the memory was a wild morning of early December. The previous day was dull and quiet, with mist hanging low on all the hills, and with the barometer extraordinarily low—it stood at 28.4 inches—and still falling. It was after dark when I started on my way to Tobermory, that little seaport at the northern entrance to the Sound of Mull, from which the steamer was wont to start out before daybreak. There was as yet no wind, but across the northern sky the aurora played incessantly. From the northwestern horizon, where the sky was free from storm clouds, pale shafts of greenish light shot up, remained for a few seconds, then vanished, to reappear elsewhere. As far as the zenith the glow extended, and flickering shafts of light, as though from sheet-lightning, lit up the sky. The dark waters of that narrow sea-way, the Sound of Mull, lay almost unruffled, with the flashing lights of the Grey Islands at Salen and Craignure showing up brightly.

An hour or two after midnight the quietness was suddenly broken by a raging gale from the south, which tore up through the Sound of Mull with the speed of an express train, and heaped up the tide before it, so that it was by far the highest of the year and flooded many of the low-lying haughs. At the hour of the sailing the gale was at the height of its strength and the darkness was so impenetrable what with mist and driving squalls of rain that the captain decided to await daybreak at his moorings.

So shortly after eight of the morning the boat put out from the sheltered anchorage of Tobermory and set course for Kilchoan on Ardnamurchan, the first port of call. We had steamed perhaps a mile when a patch of open sky, green, and fringed with wild storm clouds, appeared to the west, followed a minute or two later by a terrific squall of rain and hail, which flattened the turbulent sea as though oil had been cast on it. And with the deluge there came, as is customary on the western coast, a shifting of the wind from south to west—a wind which, while bringing, with it the full force of the Atlantic swell, was more favourable to the chance of making a landing at the islands whither the ship was bound.

As we came in sight of Kilchoan we could see the ferry-boat put to sea in the teeth of the gale and laboriously move forward, foot by foot, propelled by such powerful thrusts that the strong oars bent almost to breaking point. But just as it appeared possible that the ferry would in time be able to fight her way out to the steamer the wind increased to hurricane force, with blinding hail and rain, so that one feared the small craft might founder—it was now quite hidden from view by the squall—and the mail-boat headed to sea for her life and set her course for the distant Isle of Tiree. And the wildness of this passage I shall not easily forget.

Constantly swept by heavy seas—even on the bridge we were every moment drenched with spray—the plucky boat forged ahead surely and steadily. At times the sky would show patches of watery greenish blue, and even a feeble sun would occasionally light up the rocky outline of the Isle of Coll. But with the momentary ceasing of the rain the sea ran even higher and, to add to the force of the gale, a strong, spring tide was running dead against the storm. As we passed by Loch nan Ceall, Ben More stood out for a moment, clad in unrelieved white and with driving mists swirling past its cone-shaped summit. Past the group of the Treshnish Isles, with the outlying members of the islands bearing the full strength of the Atlantic rollers, we should have been well in sight of our destination but the mist was so thick that no land could be made out. Even the skipper—who knows these rock-strewn waters as very few can do—seemed not without anxiety.

After a while the mist lifted a little and before us lay the turbulent waters of the creek known as Gott Bay, with its dangerous sunken rocks through which we must thread our way to the pier. Once into the bay the wind blew to us from the land and, as even a strong wind from this quarter is favourable to a landing, I expected to be able to be put ashore, the gale notwithstanding. But I had not realised the power of the wind.

Though our arrival had been watched by a small crowd in the shelter of the pier, and although the skipper brought his ship to within thirty yards and less of the pier itself, the gale was such that no one on the shore could stand on the exposed portion of the pier to throw out a rope, and we were obliged to steam out to sea once more, our object unaccomplished.

We now set our course for the Isle of Coll, and for this run we had a fair wind and sea, so that in spite of some very heavy rolling, I think we must have covered the distance in record time. Loch an Eatharna in Coll gives rather more shelter than the landing place on Tiree and so it was possible to put ashore the mails and a few half-fainting passengers who moaned piteously and incessantly. I think that on this occasion the unfortunate passengers for Kilchoan were deserving of more than a little sympathy. They had joined the boat at Tobermory expecting to be set down at their journey's end after half an hour's sail through comparatively land-locked waters. As it was they perforce endured at least eight hours of wildest Atlantic storm and ultimately were set ashore at Kilchoan late in the afternoon in a state of collapse. As the captain observed, "They have indeed had their ninepence worth." – the fare from Tobermory to Kilchoan.

Other memories are of still and frosty days of winter, days of setting out from the Island of Mull and looking back on to the snow-capped hills bathed in the rosy light of the dawn. Save for the slight heave of the Atlantic, the waters were glassy calm on these days. As we neared Loch an Eatharna in Coll one clear morning of mid-winter that I remember, the sun rose red and big from behind the summit of Ben More and flooded the island before us in its rays. One saw far afield these clear mornings, and the sea was wrapped in quietness and mystery those early hours before the coming of the sun.

During the Great War the mail-boat was taken away to do her share in the fighting. I often thought of her breasting, the short, steep waves of the North Sea with, maybe, a bleak and desolate shore in view, and dodging here and there through mine-strewn waters, where in the end she met her doom. And I think she must often have wished to feel the heave of the Atlantic and to see the sun rise from behind Ben More, or sink of a summer night behind the rocks of lonely Barra Head.

LHG-20

THOSE SORT OF SITUATIONS

I chuckled to myself when an acquaintance rang me up one day to tell me that he had seen three eagles perched on telegraph poles and that the royal birds had not troubled to fly away when his car had passed. I had not the heart to disillusion him and tell him they were the less noble buzzard. It is rarely a safe thing to say that a bird *never* does this or that—I remember Lord Grey of Fallodon saying that the only thing it was really safe to say was that the cock bird *never* laid the eggs—but I am fairly sure that the eagle does not perch on telegraph posts lining a main road and am quite sure that *three* eagles would not have been seen perched thus. This recollection of Lord Grey's remark recalls to my mind the occasion of a joint lecture which Lord Grey and I gave to the English-Speaking Union in Edinburgh. Upwards of forty slides, from photographs which I had taken, were shown of his waterfowl at Fallodon. There were three of us on the platform. Lord Linlithgow (later Viceroy of India), Lord Grey and myself. Because of his blindness Lord Grey could not see the slides and as he described each I had to point out the features of interest. He had memorised the order in which the slides came, and he told me that he would be 'done' if the operator got the order wrong.

I once showed slides and a film in the state drawing room of No. 10 Downing Street in aid of a charity. Ramsay MacDonald, who was Prime Minister at the time, presided, coming straight from the House of Commons, and made a very kind and friendly speech. Three guineas were charged for seats, and the room was well filled. Those days seem indeed remote at the present time.

Increasing deafness now makes it difficult for me to hear chairman's remarks (a greater loss is that unaided I can hear no bird song) and thus arose an embarrassing incident when lecturing to a church society. It had been arranged that a piper should play a tune after the chairman's remarks. But unknown to me the chairman, his address ended, called on a member of the audience to engage in prayer. Before he could comply, in all innocence I rose to my feet, and in a loud voice called for a tune. I noticed that there was a certain embarrassment visible but it was not until afterwards that I knew what I had done for the piper at once rose and played of his best. I told the story later to Lord Lang, then Archbishop of Canterbury, and he said with a chuckle, 'Did the piper win?'

An even better story was told me by a friend, of a Highland concert at which the chairman proclaimed that the proceedings were to be opened by music played by a certain piper. Now the skill of this piper was not rated too highly locally and he had scarcely walked on to the platform when one of the audience yelled at the top of his voice 'Sit doon, ye ————'. At once the chairman was on his feet and called out in stern and disapproving tones, 'Who called the piper a ————?' Came the answer instantly, in the broadest Scots, 'Fa caa'd the ———— a *piper?*

HY-44

A visit to a seal colony on Shillay.

DARA AND DILEAS

Until two winters ago I used to bathe in the sea before breakfast all the year round. There is a natural bathing pool with about fifteen feet of water at high tide below our house and of a frosty winter's morning it was sometimes Dara and sometimes I who took that first icy plunge. Those were cold swims in the half-light when all the earth to the tide mark was frozen iron-hard and when there was ice even on the rock pools where the sea anemones were torpid from the cold, but the splendour of the rising sun upon the snow-clad hills of the Outer Hebrides on our return journey was an ample reward. Sometimes in rough winter weather one had to time to a nicety one's plunge so as to be able to climb out during a momentary lessening in the fury of the waves. Dara, I have discovered, watches the far-out oncoming waves just as carefully as I do and if she sees a distant wave of unusual size she cannot be induced to enter the water.

Writing of Dara makes me remember her predecessor, Dileas (pronounced *Jeelus*, Gaelic for *Faithful*), a collie from the Isle of Mull, black and white, lightly built and swift of foot. She was our constant, most devoted companion for many years, a remarkable dog in many ways. Dara is a philosopher, and her appetite never fails, Dileas had a more sad nature, and the sight of a suitcase being packed used to cause her grave disquiet until she realised that she was to accompany us. She knew by name each member of the family, and when told to go to any particular one did so without hesitation. Like Dara she loved the water, was an accomplished swimmer and liked retrieving a stick. Dara, when she has brought the stick to land, soon drops it but Dileas used to carry the stick for miles; on one occasion she carried a small fir branch through the Lairig Ghru all the way from Mar to Rothiemurchus. I remember that on one occasion she greatly impressed Ralph Armstrong, for many years head stalker at Langwell. My wife and I were out on the hill with Ralph. When we were eating our lunch he was sitting a little way from us, out of our sight. He had in his game bag a couple of oranges which we wished to eat. We wrote our wants on a piece of paper, and told Dileas to go and find Ralph. He read the paper which had been put inside her collar and brought us what we had asked for. I find that most people think our two collies remarkable in their intelligence, but of this I am doubtful. (The average dog owner does not develop a dog's intelligence). A dog can be a great friend and companion—almost one's greatest friend and companion in some respects.

At last our beloved Dileas fell sick of a mortal illness. Each morning she, like Dara, was accustomed to accompany me to the sea for a swim. That morning she came with me a short distance, very, very sorrowful, then turned back. She was more than sorrowful; she was in despair, for she knew that she was shortly going out on that long journey which would separate her from those she loved. She had sat in hides with us as we watched the golden eagle; she had listened to the love song of the greenshank and had seen the ptarmigan rise from the high corries of the Cairngorms. She had accompanied us in the track of the hill blizzard and beneath the hot summer sun and had heard the thunder roll between Braeriach and Sgoran Dubh. Her life had been bound closely to our lives and now she knew she was going, to an unknown land, far from us both. Her look of sadness and despair remains with me after more than twelve years.

That day I had to be from home, but my wife remained with Dileas. In the afternoon I knew there was sadness in my home, and knowing this I was ready for the news I received when I returned. That night we wrapped our beloved Dileas in her faded tartan rug, which had been her bed for many years, and when we had dug her grave we laid her to rest in it and built a cairn of stones over her body. I write 'over her body' advisedly, for I am sure that dogs, like human beings, are not extinguished by the great experience called Death, but go on to the world yonder which holds the spirit forms of trees and flowers, rivers, lakes and seas, birds and animals, and all those beings that we see in their material form on this earth. And so perhaps we shall some day find Dileas again.

HY-44

ON GARDENS

The more closely you examine gardens the more mysterious their purpose becomes. At one level they are simply outdoor extensions of the house: places of personal territory that you can decorate as you please and in which you can enjoy – as you do central heating and armchairs indoors – sun, air and privacy. Yet they are also plainly seen as pockets of condensed countryside. Gardens are above all places where things are *grown*. You would not feel comfortable calling the surroundings of a house that were utterly devoid of plants a garden. But the word is grown, not grow. The owner feels he is in control over the unruliness of natural growth. He decides which living organisms shall be encouraged and which weeded out. And the patterns in which the chosen few are arranged are ones you would never find in the open country-side. Grass is grown in flat, shaven terraces, edges and borders cut square, flowers arranged in geometrical patterns and shrubs pruned back until they resemble household brushes. Tidiness is the virtue most commonly sought after, sometimes with such enthusiasm that the fact that plants are living things seems almost incidental.

Yet suggest to most gardeners that they might achieve the order they are after more effectively, and with considerably less backache, if they replaced every living plant with a plastic replica, and they will be outraged. The yen to be not simply a dictator but a partner in a plant's growth, to be rewarded for hard and skilful husbandry, to experience a little of the unpredictables and seasonal changes of the natural work is, I think, lurking behind the clipped hedges of the fussiest gardener. I am sure that much of the excessive tidying in gardens is more a result of social convention than deep-seated need. Rampant weeds in the vegetable patch or an unkempt shrubbery are, to some eyes, as sure signs of un-neighbourliness as peeling paint. Two friends of mine who moved to a semi in a New Town in the North and allowed their front hedge to grow luxuriantly were visited during the night by the community vigilantes; who pruned back the offending bushes until they were the standard height for the street.

Convention decrees that the best lawns are those with the closest-cut and most uniform grass. Any other plants are black marks – despite the burnish of colour they give to the turf throughout the year, from the rash of speedwell blue in the spring to the rough purples of self-heal in the autumn.

I have counted over twenty different species of wild flower on my lawn, many of them just those plants through which, in children's games, we have our first physical intimacy with nature: dandelion seed-heads for telling the time; daisies for chaplets; buttercups to shine under the chin; couch grass to wind into sister's hair as a Chinese Torture; ratstail plantains for guns; Lady's slipper and clovers to suck for nectar.

These flowers are part of children's lives precisely because they are weeds, abundant and resilient plants that grow comfortingly and accessibly close to us. If we drive them out of their domestic refuges into ghettoes in the deep countryside they will be driven out of what remains of our folk-lore as well. Lady's slipper – birdsfoot trefoil in the books – has over seventy different local names, including boxing gloves, butter-and-eggs, cuckoo's stockings, Devil's claws, fell bloom, grandmother's toenails, ground honeysuckle, kitty-two-shoes, milk maidens, pattens-and-clogs, rosy mom, Tom Thumb. It is an astonishing profusion of names for such a lowly plant, a record of fancies, superstitions, deep-felt beliefs and the sharp eyes and vividly functional vocabularies of our rural forebears. So the shoe-shaped, orange and egg-yolk yellow flowers became footwear, soft and fragrant enough for Our Lady – or for a cuckoo! Later in the year the flowers transmute into pods, four or five black, bird-like claws – the Devil's fingers.

in The Book of the Highlands
(Inverness Board of Advertising, 1930s)

AUTUMN

The autumn of 1939 brought to the Western Isles a succession of golden days, when summer seemed to return from the south and cheer the isles before their plunge into winter storms.

It was on one of the most beautiful of those mornings that I climbed Helaval Mór, *MacLeod's Great Table*, that green-sloped hill which rises to a height of 1600 feet. Helaval, like most Hebridean hills, retains its Norse name; it may be translated *Flagstone Hill,* and received its name because of its curiously level summit, verdant and symmetrical and the grazing place of many sheep.

Beneath Helaval Mór Dunvegan Castle stands at the very edge of the tide, on the shore of the sea loch that bears its name. The old trees beside that still older castle were in the glory of their autumn foliage: their yellow leaves, warmed by the sun, did not stir in the quiet air and Rory More's Waterfall was so shrunken that its song was scarcely heard. Near that fall blackberries glistened in the sun, and the last of the heather was purple.

In a narrow glen on the slopes of MacLeod's Table a flock of redwings were feeding on the rowan berries that hung thickly on the trees. When disturbed those Scandinavian immigrants rose almost vertically into the blue sky, swung round, then settled once more farther down the glen. Ravens patrolled the upper slopes, and a gannet, no larger than a snow-white speck, fished above Loch Bracadale, where King Haco's war galleys rested on their northward passage after the Battle of Largs in 1263. On the south horizon rose the long range of the Cuillin, clouds falling at times to their narrow summits where storms in winter hold wild revelry.

From that table-like summit of Helaval Mór I looked to the Outer Hebrides across the blue Minch on which toy-like steamers sailed. Far beyond those isles, across North Uist, was Boreray of St. Kilda with its attendant rock stack, rising with the faintness of extreme distance. Far to the west the lighthouse upon Barra Head, 60 miles away, was plain in the field of a telescope. On the ocean horizon, silvered beneath the track of the sun, were tiny ships. The hills of Tiree climbed from that ocean, and the long line of rocky Coll stood out against the sky. Here and there showers drifted south on the Black Wind and at the heart of one of those showers the sun had kindled mystic fires of rainbow colours. Magnificent *cumulus* clouds, noble and massive, drifted with white depths that seemed substantial and enduring as the hills themselves. At sunset those clouds were rosy, but as the sun left them this warm light passed swiftly to palest grey, cold and soft.

Low above the slopes of MacLeod's Great Table hung the young moon, and as the last of the afterglow was leaving the western sky the Merry Dancers sprang to life. Sudden shafts of white light stabbed the heavens, or felt their way stealthily upwards from the horizon to near the zenith. Mars, large and red, burned above the darkening spires of the Black Cuillin, as the peat smoke from crofters' houses beside the sea loch rose blue and aromatic into the air and the stillness and peace of an autumn night descended upon the Isle of Skye.

When I reached home I heard from the wireless that the first enemy air raid upon the shores of Britain had that afternoon taken place over Rosyth in the Firth of Forth.

ISNB-41

A Hebridean croft.

SETON GORDON'S 1945 DIARY

Seton Gordon's day to day pocket diaries are in the National Library of Scotland and make interesting perusal. They were seldom kept regularly yet give a good idea of his travels and doings. I've copied a selection from the year 1945 to illustrate his range of interests. The war is noted on one occasion, its ending not at all. At the start income is noted for 1944: "Lit. £207-5-0, Lec. £34-5-0, but then a Portree- Edinburgh return journey cost £2-11-5 and a journey from Skye to Edinburgh to Larbert to Whitehaven to Pitlochry to Stirling to Skye cost £6-11-0.

January 9: Fine view of male peregrine ..., 22: Rooks turned back by peregrine, 24: Tobogganing, Sue & C, 25: Snowbunting at bird table, 27: 50 Italian prisoners working on the road, February 12: To Gargunnock ... good and attentive audience, 19: First lark in song, 28: Stamp, Feb: £1-9-11., March 13: Cambridge. Piped at Latham Road, 14: To Oxford. Gave lecture ..., 18: To Holkham. Christopher Columbus' letter, 20: Flew to Haynford. German planes over and bombs dropped, 25: Knole. Grand trees and a great house, 27: St James Park. 50 year old pelican, 29: Lunch with Granville Poole and Charles at the Ritz. Saw about deaf aids, April 9: Invershin, 11: Rain. 1 salmon, 12lbs. Angus told of angler who hooked a frog and a wild duck, 14: Returned. Got goods to Achnashellach where had a walk with Dara. [Invershin travel, tips etc came to £2-15-2], 24: Pair of swallows passing. May 5: New eyrie watch, 9: Could just see the eggs, 14: To Inverbroom, 18: Sgurr na Clach Geala. Fine day, 19: Martin's Island. Saw the old cross there, 22: To Crathie. "Road blocked by snow" on the Lecht but open. Fear Bealachbuie eagle robbed and old tree almost destroyed by fire, 25: Carr Bridge. Played a piobairsachd to Callerwood, 30: Mowed lawn, June 1: Stoat killed rabbit in midstream. Sparrow impudently took food from the stuffed bill of a starling, 5: 30 terns nests, Fladday, 9: Bagshot. Bridie's wedding, 14: Liathach ... wind gusts lifting the waterfalls and blowing them back uphill ..., 16: Eagle attacking wildcat in snow, the two rolling over, the wildcat getting clear and escaping. (MacDonald), 19: Ben Wyvis. One hen ptarmigan with young. Many swifts, 20: Achiltibuie, 30: Found new eyrie ... saw where eagle roosts. Bladder campion in flower. Heavy rain, p.m., July 3: Teampuil Oran .... graves of unbaptised children and murderers, 4: To Port Ellen but made a bad landing and the pilot accelerated and returned to Tiree, 5: Loch a' Phuill. No phalarope. Arctic tern colony on small islet, 9: Gigha. Tigh Mor and the Brownie's Chair. Eclipse, 12: Got the *Loch Nevis* to Port Ellen. Flew to Tiree … calm … without swell even on Dubh Hirteach. [These flights etc part of his wartime work], 13: Left Scaranish in the *Dunadd…* Elgol 5.30. Sailed thro' Sound of Rum then called at Soay and Portnalong. Dara walked to Carbost, 19: John saw wee corncrakes. [Long blank, a Glenfinnan tour expenses noted – and haircut, 2/-.] Aug 28: Ben A'an. Azalea in full flower. Pair of eagles! Buzzard at Linn, also goosander. Sept 6: Donald, Angus, Murdo and I did a big day at the oats, 19: finished cutting corn, Oct 1: Finished putting up oats into small stacks, 6: Finished harvest. 4 stacks, 12: Garbh Choire snowbeds, smaller, dirty but larger than 3 years ago. Hard frost, 13: Crathie. Heard Brown pipe, 14: A summer day. Tea at Baile na Coille. The two princesses there …, 15: Morven. A grand view of an eagle – thought he was a plane!!, 16: Lecture, Aberdeen, 17: Dundee, 18: Monadh Liath, 19: Meall Fourvounie, 20: Ben Nevis, 22: Tayinloan, 30: Spean Bridge, Nov 5: Very fine butterfly at Uig. Fiscavaig and Tallisker. Splendid roses and begonias in the garden, 20: The Garbh Choire. Pocket of snow *empty*. Other, small snowbed 17½x12 feet and about 2½ feet deep, Dec 1: Cotton grass in second flower. Meall na Suireanach, 11: Blair, 12: Lecture. Newbattle Abbey, 13: Lecture, Usher Hall, 15: Lecture, Glasgow. A very good audience, 17: Newcastle for Seabirds lecture and on to Alnmouth, 20: Lairig Ghru entirely without snow.

As usual, expenses are noted. December stamps, including Christmas, £1-17-3, Edinburgh-Newcastle fare was 25/9, tea 1/6 and the porter at Alnmouth (wife's family home) 2/-.

TOWARDS HOME

It was night when we finished our fishing. We hauled in the last copper-coloured pollack and hoisted our small brown sail. More than five miles distant, our landing-place at Duntuilm was hidden by the darkness. The hills of Skye rose black against the horizon, but there was no darkness upon the sea where we sailed, but rather the twilight which in fine weather remains on the ocean from dusk to dawn. Through this mysterious twilight we steered, the water lapping softly against our bows and the lights of passing ships showing golden as setting planets around us. In the eastern sky Trodday light was green; the lighthouse upon Scalpay threw its powerful golden flashes across the sleeping Minch.

Suddenly a bright, glowing light appeared on the north-east horizon… The waning moon climbed from the sea. About her orange disk was a warm glowing nimbus. Minutes passed and at last she had risen clear of the waters, already casting a pathway of subdued light upon the ocean. The evening breeze dropped to a light air. The sail hung idly. We took to the oars. At each stroke pale fires were kindled in the sea. Globules of glowing light drifted away astern as the phosphorescent plankton we had disturbed signalled with tiny lamps to the stars. Thus in our passage across the Minch we were cheered by the lights of the land, of the heavens, and of the ocean herself.

IOW-33

BLESSING, BLESSINGS

During one wild [South Uist] October day I chanced to pass by a small thatched cottage and, calling in to shelter awhile, found the house tenanted by a middle-aged woman and her mother. The old lady was well over ninety years of age, and shivered as she sat close up to the small fire of peat, for the day was a cold one. She had no word of English, but spoke continuously in Gaelic as she rocked herself on her chair. When younger she had done much weaving and she showed me with pride a kilt of MacDonald tartan she had woven for one of her sons. She had that indefinable quality of refinement so characteristic of the best type of West Highlander and one could imagine she would have been at home in the most exalted circumstances as in the most lowly.

The following summer, when the sun shone warm upon the machair, and the loch near her house, with its ruined castle, lay bathed in the mystic light of the west, I again visited the wee dwelling. The old lady was abed and failing fast. She crooned to herself as she lay upon the bed, and her voice was more feeble. Yet she spoke much, and seemed glad that my wife and I had come again to visit her. Especially glad, I remember, was she to greet our small daughter, whom she saw for the first time. At our parting she seemed to realize that we should not meet again, for she was greatly affected—holding our hands and speaking words of blessing and farewell. And even as we left the room and gained the doorway her words followed us: "Beannachd, beannachd" (Blessings, blessings) were the two last words we heard, and I shall always remember them, and the simple dignity with which they were spoken. This old lady had lived out all her long life without ever leaving her native island.

HM-23

327

St Kilda, from Soay looking to Hirta and the Cone of Conachair.

EPILOGUE

SGEIR NAM MAOL
(A NORTHERN OUTPOST OF SKYE)

The sound of waves, unceasingly hurling themselves against a dark rock, far from land. Faintly pencilled the hills of Sutherland in thin blue haze.

The mellow September light upon the sea.

A small boat swaying at anchor.

A huge bull grey seal regarding it solemn-eyed from the green depths. A brown seal lying upon dark sea-wrack where clustered turnstones twitter.

Clisham of Harris rising sentinel over the Minch.

The sky quiet, dappled.

Sparkling in sunlight come the waves.

Solans, strong-winged and determined, passing low above the water for St Kilda, invisible beyond Harris.

A single fulmar flying, owl-like, east.

The sheer rock-face of MacDonald's Table black against the noontide sun. On the west horizon Beinn Mhor and Hecia of South Uist.

Eaval of North Uist rising like some stack from the blue sea. A vital breeze from Lochlann stirring the Minch.

The Shiant Isles dappled with sun and shade.

Rocks, with barnacles thick upon them, showing grey beneath the tide.

The flood streaming north-east. Eagerly the waves roll in; eagerly they pass.

COS-29

Seton Gordon's
Cairngorms

An Anthology

Compiled by Hamish Brown

Seton Gordon was a pioneering naturalist, photographer and writer – an ecologist before the word was coined. He was a prolific author with 27 books to his name, the first appearing when he was just eighteen. He wrote with a revelational wonder and freshness, crafting descriptions that could only be written by someone intimately at home in the hills with their fauna and flora, geology and landscape, Gaelic culture, history and folklore.

Seton Gordon lived to a great age but the Cairngorms were his first love, the place he returned to many times throughout his life and his writing. In this companion volume to *Seton Gordon's Scotland* Hamish Brown has gathered an engaging selection from Seton Gordon's extensive writings about these hills, much of which comes from books other than the well-known *The Cairngorms Hills of Scotland* (1925).

Seton Gordon's Cairngorms encapsulates the beauty and majesty of these hills – with descriptions of hill days throughout the seasons – now much changed – and intimate descriptions of wildlife. Hamish Brown has garnered a collection of gems enhanced by archive photographs to create the essential distillation of *Seton Gordon's Cairngorms*.

As the great authority on Gordon's work Hamish Brown points out that for the first three decades of the twentieth century Gordon was the only full-time practising naturalist in Britain. This at a time when attitudes to Britain's wildlife, and in particular birds of prey, ranged from the callous to the brutal. As the writer Jim Crumley … notes, Gordon stood apart as someone who looked at eagles 'through camera and telescope rather than the barrel of a shotgun'.

—*from the Afterword by James Macdonald Lockhart*

This compilation will benefit many new readers and visitors and instil the desire to admire, wonder and respect, in turn encouraging a new generation prepared to use lungs and limbs, and ultimately be guardians of the Cairngorms.

—*from the Foreword by Dick Balharry*

ISBN 978-1904445-88-3   240 × 170 mm   256pp   liberally illustrated with original b/w photos   hardback   £25
December 2009

To order contact:
Whittles Publishing • Dunbeath Mains Cottages • Dunbeath • KW6 6EY • UK
Tel: +44 (0)1593-731 333 • Fax: +44(0)1593-731 400
e-mail: info@whittlespublishing.com   www.whittlespublishing.com